HINDI TEACHER
FOR ENGLISH SPEAKING PEOPLE,

New Enlarged Edition

*Novel scientific way of **making 'your own'** Hindi sentences.*

PRIMARY TO INTERMEDIATE HINDĪ

Prof. Ratnakar Narale
Sunita Narale

Ratnakar
PUSTAK BHARATI
BOOKS-INDIA

Author :

Dr. Ratnakar Narale

B.Sc. (Nagpur Univ.), M.Sc. (Pune Univ.), Ph.D. (IIT), Ph.D. (Kalidas Sanskrit Univ.);
Prof Hindi, Ryerson University, Toronto.
web : www.books-india.com * email : books.india.books@gmail.com

Sunita Narale,
B.A., Punjab Univ.

Book Title :

Hindi Teacher for English Speaking People, New Enlarged Edition.

This methodical book is based on extensive **R&D**, Effective Techniques and Improved Ways beneficial to the Readers to give them proper reture for their investment of Time and Money. The book begins with simple primary steps and moves forward with **authentic examples** coupled with **Progressive Exercises** suitable to each context to bring home the topic being discussed. The Vocabulary and Illustrations are selected carefully to offer a window to the topics, as used in Real Life Situations. You will not find such contemplative work in any Hindi learning book.

Fonts used in the Book :

Ratnakar-H for Hindī typing
Ratnakar-T for Transliteration Typing

Published by :
PUSTAK BHARATI (Books-India)
Division of PC Plus Ltd.,
www.books-india.com
email : books.india.books@gmail.com

FOR :
Sanskrit Hindi Research Institute, Toronto

ISBN 978-1-897416-60-0

ISBN 978-1-897416-60-0
90000
9 781897 416600

Dedicated to

Our Loving Grandchildren
Samay, Sahas, Saanjh and Saaya Narale

HINDI
TEACHER
FOR
HINDU
CHILDREN
Prof. Ratnakar Narale
Sunita Narale
Ratnakar
Pustak-Bharati
Books-India

Learn Hindi
Through English Medium
IN 20 EASY STEPS
Hindi Level I
Ratnakar Narale

SANSKRIT
PRIMER
Primary to Intermediate
Prof. Ratnakar Narale
Ratnakar
Pustak-Bharati
Books-India

SANSKRIT TEACHER,
All-in-One
With transliteration
For All Levels
ALL IN ONE A-Z
Prof. Ratnakar Narale
Ratnakar
Pustak-Bharati
Books-India
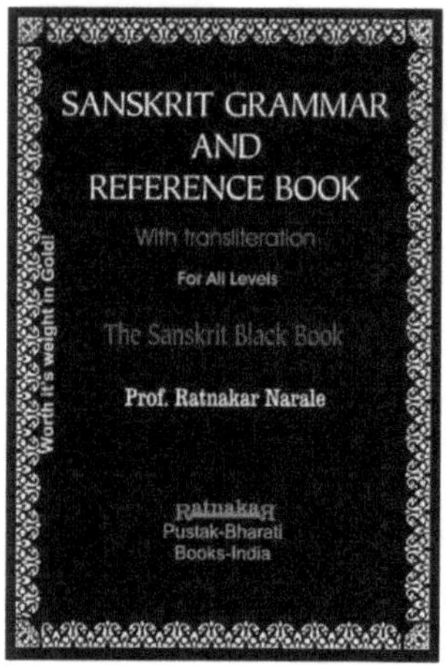
SANSKRIT GRAMMAR
AND
REFERENCE BOOK
With transliteration
For All Levels
The Sanskrit Black Book
Prof. Ratnakar Narale
Worth it's weight in Gold!
Ratnakar
Pustak-Bharati
Books-India

TAMIL
TEACHER
With Transliteration & Devanagari
Primary to Intermediate
Self-Tutor
Prof. Ratnakar Narale
Ratnakar
Pustak-Bharati
Books-India

URDU
TEACHER
With Transliteration & Devanagari
Primary to Intermediate
Self-Tutor
Prof. Ratnakar Narale
Ratnakar
Pustak-Bharati
Books-India

Learn Sanskrit
Through English Medium
Without Transliteration
Ratnakar Narale
SANSKRIT HINDI RESEARCH INSTITUTE

Learn Bengali
Through English / Hindi
With Transliteration & Devanagari
Ratnakar Narale
Self-Tutor

Learn Marathi
Through English / Hindi
With Transliteration & Devanagari
Ratnakar Narale
Self-Tutor

Learn Punjabi
Through English / Hindi
With Transliteration & Devanagari
Ratnakar Narale
Self-Tutor

Learn Gujrati
Through English / Hindi
With Transliteration & Devanagari
Ratnakar Narale
Self-Tutor

GITA AS SHE IS
In Krishna's Own Words
Volume II
Ratnakar

Gita ka Shabdakosh
Grammatical Dictionary
of the Gita
गीता का शब्दकोश
और अनुक्रमणी
New Edition
Prof. Ratnakar Narale
Ratnakar
Pustak-Bharati
Books-India
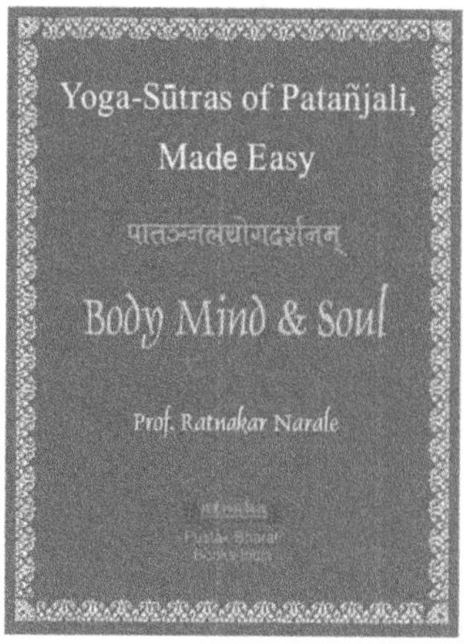
Yoga-Sūtras of Patañjali,
Made Easy
Body Mind & Soul
Prof. Ratnakar Narale

मेरे भजन
MERE BHAJAN
With English Transliteration and Meaning
VOLUME 1
Ratnakar Narale

FOREWORD

Hindi is one of the world's main languages, with over 650 million speakers in India, and millions more on every continent. There are many primers that teach children who can already speak Hindi—how to read and write their language. As the title *Hindi Shikshak for English Speaking People* suggests, Dr. Ratnakar Narale has written this book with a different audience in mind: English speakers of all ages who want to learn Hindi from scratch. This audience includes many kinds of people: the inhabitants of non-Hindi-speaking parts of India; Canadians, Americans, and West Indians whose ancestors came from India, but whose first language is English; and many others who have no personal connection to India, but who are interested in Hindi for business purposes, scholarly reasons, or the pleasure of studying a new language.

Hindi Shikshak for English Speaking People is logically arranged. It begins by giving students a thorough grounding in the Devanagari script. The characters are taught according to their shape rather than in the usual alphabetical order. This novel method helps learners to keep straight different characters that resemble one another. Directions are given on both the pronunciation and the formation of each character, and there is plenty of opportunity to practise reading and writing them. At first, Hindi words are transcribed into the Roman alphabet. As the student learns more and more, however, the transliteration becomes redundant, and it is dispensed with. By the time the learner finishes the first part of the book, he or she will have mastered the vowels, consonants, and conjunct characters of Devanagari. Along the way, the exercises provide a basic vocabulary of several dozen words.

Then comes a section teaching the Hindi numerals, followed by the core of the book, a thorough exposition of Hindi grammar laid out in a systematic order. At each stage, Dr. Narale reminds readers of the principles of English grammar before introducing the corresponding Hindi forms. Along the way, hundreds of new words are introduced, and the frequent exercises let the student learn to speak and write Hindi sentences almost without knowing them. *Hindi Shikshak for English Speaking People* closes with exercises in correcting faulty sentences, reading dialogues, telling the time, and writing letters. There are also useful lists of proverbs, synonyms and antonyms, and so on. A section on words that resemble each other and hence are easily confused is especially helpful.

Dr. Narale has been careful to draw most of the examples in his book from words and concepts that are familiar to Westerners. This emphasizes that Hindi is a world language, and not merely an Indian one. At the same time, *Hindi Shikshak for English Speaking People* does not shirk the task of introducing some aspects of the culture in which the Hindi language developed. For example, one reading exercise not only provides practice in Devanagari, 'The Hindi World' discusses the Hindi-speaking people of India, Trinidad, Guyana, Suriname and Fiji.

Hindi Shikshak for English Speaking People may be used either as a classroom text under the guidance of a teacher, or by students who are studying Hindi on their own. It represents hundreds of hours of careful thought and hard effort by Dr. Ratnakar Narale, who is to be felicitated for his work. I heartily commend this book to any person who already knows English and wishes to learn Hindi.

—JOHN McLEOD*

---

*Dr. John McLeod is Associate Professor of History at the University of Louisville, Kentucky, USA. He has a Ph.D. in Indian history from the University of Toronto, and is a former Postdoctoral Fellow of the Shastri Indo-Canadian Institute in New Delhi. He has written two books and numerous articles on the history of India. His research on the Royal Families of India was recognised, when he was appointed Honorary Rajvanshi Genealogist of the Rajvara Heritage Institution at Rajkumar College, Rajkot, by His Highness the Maharaja Sriraj of Dharangadhara, the President of the College.

INDEX

BOOK 1

	Ratnakar's Nine Noble Truths	x
Lesson 1	The Hindī Alphabet	1
Lesson 2	Common Hindī Consonants	2
Lesson 3	Speaking Hindī Characters	3
Lesson 4	Reading and Writing Hindī Consonants	5
Lesson 5	Reading and Writing Hindī Vowels	13
Lesson 6	Reading and Writing Hindī Vowel Signs	14
Lesson 7	Reading and Writing Hindī Compound Consonants	17
Lesson 8	Reading and Writing Special Characters	20
	Ratnakar's Children Songs (शिशु गीत)	22
Lesson 9	Introduction to *Sandhi*	32
Lesson 10	Introduction to Hindī Numerals	33
Lesson 11	Making your own Hindī sentences	36
Lesson 12	The Pictorial Hindī Dictionary	43
Lesson 13	Using Action Words	57
Lesson 14	Making Sentences for Completed Actions	77
	Brain Surgery of the Hindī Grammar	90
	X-Ray Vision through the Hindī Syntax	92
Lesson 15	Relational Suffixes	95
Lesson 16	Adjectives and Adverbs	122
Lesson 17	Conjunctions and Expressions	126
Lesson 18	General Knowledge	130
Lesson 19	General Dialogues	132
Lesson 20	HINGLISH for English Speaking People	147
Summary of Tenses		151

RATNAKAR'S NINE NOBLE TRUTHS :

First three Noble Truths :	(singular to plural)	38
Fourth Noble Truth :	(potential mood)	73
Fifth Noble Truth :	(*kyā*)	73
Sixth Noble Truth :	(perfect tense)	78
Seventh Noble Truth :	(the suffixes)	81
Eighth Noble Truth :	(attaching suffixes)	95
Ninth Noble Truth :	(changes in pronouns)	98

BOOK 2 : HINDI ADVANCED

Lesson 1	Hindī Word Processing	35
Lesson 2	Review of Volume I, Tenses and Cases	36
Lesson 3	Degree of Comparison	42
Lesson 4	Adverbs	44
Lesson 5	Number Conversion	45
Lesson 6	Gender Conversion	46
Lesson 7	Particles of Expression	47

hī **ही (47),** ***bhī*** **भी (47),** ***kar*** **कर (49),** ***vālā*** **वाला (49),** ***lagā*** **लगा (51),**
chāhe **चाहे (52),** ***sakā*** **सका (52),** ***paḍā*** **पड़ा (52),** ***gayā*** **गया (52),**
ḍālā **ड़ाला (53),** ***huā*** **हुआ (53),** ***bhar*** **भर (54),** ***sā*** **सा (55),** ***tak*** **तक (55),**
to bhī **तो भी (55),** ***apne āp*** **अपने आप (58),** ***ke pās*** **के पास (58),**
ke sāth **के साथ (58),** ***ke liye*** **के लिये (59),** ***ke pahale*** **के पहले (59),**
ke bād **के बाद (60),** ***ke pār*** **के पार (60),** ***ke āge*** **के आगे (61),**
ke sāmane **के सामने (61),** ***ke pīchhe*** **के पीछे (61),** ***ke pahā̃*** **के यहाँ (61),**
kī tarah **की तरह (62),** ***kī taraf*** **की तरफ (62),** ***te hue*** **ते हुए (62),**
nā chāhatā **ना चाहता (63),** ***nā chāhiye*** **ना चाहिये (63),** ***ne dījiye*** **ने दीजिये (64),**
ne lāyak **ने लायक (64),** ***fir*** **फिर (65),** ***fir se*** **फिर से (65)** ***nā*** **ना (66)**

Lesson 8	Hindi Proofreading	68
Lesson 9	Role Plays	73
Lesson 10	Golden Rules of Life	77
Lesson 11	Letter Writing	78
Lesson 12	Idioms and Proverbs	81
Lesson 13	Synonyms	83
Lesson 14	Words with Many Meanings	87
Lesson 15	Resembling Words	88
Lesson 16	Antonyms	91
Lesson 17	One word for Many Words	92
Lesson 18	Prepositions	93
Lesson 19	हिंदी के महान साहित्यकार (The Great Hindī Writers)	96
Lesson 20	मेरे भजन (My Devotional Songs)	122
Lesson 21	Bollywood	126
Lesson 22	Hindī Learner's English-Hindi *Transliterated* Dictionary	137

INTRODUCTION

Many children and adults who come from West Indies, Guyana, Suriname, Fiji, Pakistan, America, UK, Canada, Africa and Europe do want to learn Hindī. There are many people in India, more so in English Schools and in non-Hindī speaking States, who want to learn Hindī through English medium.

While learning Hindī, one must understand the grammatical aspects such as tenses, cases, gender, person, number etc. step-by-step and only then one can learn Hindī properly. Rather than learning pre-made pet sentences, one should understand the basics and learn to make his/her own sentences. Without this, one may speak like हम जाता है *(ham jātā hai),* हम करेगा *(ham karegā)* and मैंने करा *mane̐ karā.* Having understood the grammar, one may still use some English vocabulary and speak like चाय का कप लीजिए *(chāya kā* cup *lījiye)* or यह मेरी कार है *(yah merī* car *hai) ...* but it is quite alright for English speaking people. In fact in India it is a fashion to speak the 'Hinglish' language.

While this book is a 'Teach Yourself' manual, it also is a good tool for the teachers who teach Hindī to English speaking people. It starts with 'How to Write' the Hindī Alphabet and pronounce each character. It is unique in this book, but interesting to note that for teaching the alphabet, the characters are grouped according to their shapes, and not with their usual alphabetical order. It is seen that, with this method it is easy to recognize, relate, differentiate and remember the characters without a mix up.

In this book, the examples and exercises have been given based ONLY on what is learnt in previous steps and pages. The book is filled with virtually thousands of examples, and each dialogue is designed with the view of its practical value for the targetted people.

Hindī language being originated from Sanskrit language, introduction to that language becomes automatic while learning Hindī. In order to bring this important point to the readres' notice, the Sanskrit words that apprear in the Hindī writings in this book, are identified with a dotted underline.

I hope that you will follow this material step-by-step and page-by-page. In order to help new students, English transliteration of Hindī terms is provided. However, it is hoped that, at certain stage, you will skip the transliteration and will be comfortable reading the Hindī text. Follow the book with this technique and your success in learning Hindī will be assured.

RATNAKAR'S NINE NOBLE TRUTHS

THE FIRST NOBLE TRUTH : If a Masculine word ends in ā (आ), the ā (आ) changes to *e* (ए) in plural. e.g. singular m∘ Boy लड़का *laḍkā* → plural m∘ Boys लड़के *laḍke.* If a Feminine word ends in ā (आ), *ẽ* (एँ) is added in plural. f∘ language भाषा *bhāshā* → plural भाषाएँ *bhāshāẽ* ... Page 38

THE SECOND NOBLE TRUTH : If a Feminine word ends in a consonant or in *ā* (आ), then *ẽ* (एँ) is added in plural. e.g. singular f∘ Book किताब *kitāb* → plural f∘ Books किताबें *kitābẽ;* f∘ Language भाषा *bhāṣā* → plural f∘ Languages भाषाएँ *bhāṣāẽ;* ... Page 38

THE THIRD NOBLE TRUTH : If a Feminine word ends in ī (ई), the ī (ई) changes to iyā̃ (इयाँ) in plural. e.g. singular f∘ Girl लड़की *laḍkī* → plural f∘ Girls लड़कियाँ *laḍkiyā̃* ... Page 38

THE FOURTH NOBLE TRUTH : (Potential Mood) A Verb in Potential Mood needs only a suffix indicating 'Person' (i.e. 1st, 2nd or 3rd; singular or plural). That is, it does not need any tense suffix (ह, थ, ग), mode suffix (त, रह, चुक) or gender suffix (आ, ए, ई, ईं). ... Page 73

THE FIFTH NOBLE TRUTH : '*kyā*' (क्या) : When '*kyā*' (क्या) comes at the beginning or at the end of a sentence, *kyā* (क्या) indicates question mark (?). But, when *kyā* (क्या) comes anywhere in the sentence, then this *kyā* (क्या) = "What" .. Page 73

THE SIXTH NOBLE TRUTH : (Perfect tense)

If an action is completed on a transitive verb, suffix *ne* (ने) is attached to the subject. ... Page 78

THE SEVENTH NOBLE TRUTH : The 16 SUFFIXES : (1) Present tense = 'h' (ह); **(2)** Past tense = 'th' (थ); **(3)** Future tense = 'g' (ग); **(4)** Habitual 'do' mode = 't' (त); **(5)** Continuous (imperfect) '-ing' mode = 'rah' (रह); **(6)** Already 'done' mode = 'chuk' (चुक); **(7)** Masculine singular= 'ā ' (आ); Masculine plural = 'e' (ए); **(8)** Feminine singular = 'ī ' (ई); Feminine plural = 'iyā̃' (इयाँ); **(9)** First person singular (I) = 'ū̃ ' (ऊँ); **(10)** Third person singular (he, she) = 'ai' (ऐ); **(11)** Any Third person plural (we, you, they) = 'aĩ ' (एँ) ; **(12)** Any Perfect action = 'ā ' (आ); **(13)** Transitive Perfect action = 'ne' (ने); **(14)** am = 'hū̃ ' (हूँ); **(15)** is, has, have = 'hai' (है); **(16)** was, had = 'thā ' (था). ... Page 81

THE EIGHTH NOBLE TRUTH : (attaching Case suffixes) (i) When ANY SUFFIX (*ko* को, *se* से, *mẽ* में, *par* पर or any other suffix) comes after a MASCULINE SINGULAR noun ending in *ā* (आ), this *ā* (आ) is changed to *e* (ए). (ii) When ANY SUFFIX comes after ANY PLURAL NOUN, particle *õ* (ओं) must be added to that noun, before attaching the suffix. ... Page 95

THE NINTH NOBLE TRUTH (change in pronouns) : I = *maĩ* मैं। He, she, that = *vah* वह। It, this = *yah* यह। They, those = *ve* वे। These = *ye* ये। When any suffix is attached to these pronouns : (i) *maĩ* मैं changes to → *muz* मुझ। (ii) *vah* वह changes to → *us* उस। (iii) *yah* यह changes to → *is* इस। (iv) *ve* वे changes to → *un* उन। and (v) *ye* ये changes to → *in* इन। ... Page 96

विद्या देवी वंदना

राग : खमाज

(रत्नाकर कृत)

स्थायी : जै जै स्वरदा माता । देवी स्मरण तेरा भाता।
चरणन तुमरे मंगल । दरशन तुमरे सुंदर । चाहे सब ध्याता।
ॐ जै सरस्वती माता।।

अंतरा : जो आवे गुण पाने। ध्यान लगाने का। देवी ज्ञान बढ़ाने का।
तेरे दर वर पावे। झोली भर कर जावे। ध्येय सफल उसका।
ॐ जै सरस्वती माता।।

जो आवे सुर पाने। गान बजाने का। देवी तान सजाने का।
संगित नृत्य सिखाने। नाट्य कला को दिखाने। मार्ग सरल उसका।
ॐ जै सरस्वती माता।।

जो प्यासा है कला का। चित्राकारी का। देवी शिल्पाकारी का।
चौंसठ सारी कलाएँ। विद्या अष्ट लीलाएँ। साध्य सकल उसका।
ॐ जै सरस्वती माता।।

जो कवि गायक लेखक। वाङ्मय विरचेता। देवी सरगम रचयेता।
साहित्य साधन पावे। बुद्धि का धन आवे। हेतु सबल उसका।
ॐ जै सरस्वती माता।।

शुभ्र वसन नथ माला। काजल तिल काला। देवी हाथ कमल नीला।
केयुर कंठी छल्ला। गजरा कुंदन ड़ाला। मुकुट है नग वाला।
ॐ जै सरस्वती माता।।

नारद किन्नर शंकर। तुमरे गुण गाते। देवी तुमरे ऋण ध्याते।
भगत जो शरण में आता। भजन ये तुमरे गाता। मोक्ष अटल उसका।
ॐ जै सरस्वती माता।।

(इस भजन के हारमोनियम के सुरों के लिये, कृपया इस पुस्तक के लेखक को लिखें)

LEVEL-1 HINDI TEACHING AND HOMEWORK GUIDE
TRIED AND TESTED 20-STEP SYLLABUS COURSE OUTLINE

Name of the self learner or Student in the class: --

Name of the Instructor : --- --------

NOTE : A step may take between 0.5 Hour to 3.5 hours, depending on the number of students in the class, their age and their locale.

Step 1 :

(1) Introduction to the Hindī Language, a general discussion and importance,

(2) Introduction to Hindī Phonetics and the Chart of Hindī Alphabet

(3) Chart of Hindī Alphabet (Lesson 2 and the Chart on Back Cover)

(4) Knowing the English Transliteration ā, ī, ū, ṭ, ṭh, ḍ, ḍh, ṇ, ś, ṣ and ṛ (Lesson 3)

(5) Read, write and speak alphabets व, ब, क; प, ष, फ (v, b, k; p, ṣ, ph) (Lessons 4.1-2)

(6) Read, write and speak consonants त, न, ग, म, भ, ण (t, n, g, m, bh, ṇ) (Lesson 4.3)

(7) LEARNING TO MAKE AND SPEAK YOUR OWN SENTENCES (Lessons 11.1-2, Table 1)

(8) Read, write and speak the words formed with letters we learned so far.

Step 2 :

(1) Review of the 1st Step; practicing to speak what we learned in the 1st step (for 15 min◦).

(2) Introduction to Hindī Numerals (Lesson 10.1)

(3) Read, write and say consonants च, ज, ञ, ल; घ, ध, छ (ch, j, ñ, l; gh, dh, chh) (Lessons 4.4-5)

(4) Read, write and speak the words formed with letters we learned so far.

(5) Read, write, say letters र, स, ख, श and य, थ; क्ष, ज्ञ (r, s, kh, ś; y, th, kṣ, gya) (Lessons 4.6-7)

(6) Making your own and speaking simple sentences for past actions (lesson 11.3, Table 2)

(7) Review of what we just learned (Summary Table 3)

Step 3 :

(1) Review what we learned so far; practicing to speak what we learned in 2 steps (for 15 min◦).

(2) Read, write and say say consonants ट, ठ, ढ, द, ड, ङ, झ, ह (ṭ, ṭh, ḍh, d, ḍ, ṅ, jh, h) (Lesson 4.8)

(3) Read, write and say consonants क्ष, त्र, ज्ञ, अं, अः (*kṣa, tra, gya; ṁ, ḥ*) (Lessons 4.9-10)

(4) Read, write and speak the words formed with letters we learned so far.

(5) Read write, say अ, आ, इ, ई, उ, ऊ, ऋ, ए, ऐ, ओ, औ a, ā, i, ī, u, ū, ṛ, e, ai, o, au (Lessons 5.1-2)

(6) Read, write and say the words formed with above given vowels and consonants.

(7) Study simple Hindī action words (Tables 5A-5B)

Step 4 :

(1) Review of what we learned so far; practicing to speak what we learned so far (for 15 min◦).

(2) Study the Hindī vowel signs for आ, इ, ई, उ, ए, ऐ, ओ, औ, अं, अँ, अः (Lesson 6.1)

(3) Read Hindī Characters with vowel signs (Lessons 6.2-3)

(4) Counting to twenty and 10, 20, 30, 40, 50, 60, 70, 80, 90, 100 (Lessons 10.2)

(5) Special Compound Characters (Lesson 7.2 and 8.1)

(6) Review of simple actions (Table 3).

Step 5 :

(1) Study Hindī Vocabulary through the Pictorial Dictionary (Table 4)

(3) Speaking the Simple Present events in Hindī, with 'I am a ---' (I am a boy, I am a girl etc)

(4) Speaking the Present events in Hindī, using simple action words (I eat, I drink etc)

(5) Making and speaking your own sentences for present actions (Lesson 13, Tables 5 and 6)

(6) Review of what we learned so far. practicing to speak what we learned in 5 steps (for 15 min◦).

FIRST QUARTER TEST

Step 6 :

(1) English-Hindī Syntax (First four lines of x-ray vision, Lesson 14)

(2) Speaking Present Continuous (imperfect) events in Hindī (I am eating, I am drinking etc) (Table 7)

(3) Speaking Past Continuous (imperfect) events in Hindī (I was eating, I was drinking etc) (Table 8)

(4) Use of 'already' completed actions ('*khā chukā, pī chukā*' I have eaten etc) (Tables 9-10)

(5) Review of what we learned so far; practicing to speak what we learned so far (for 15 min◦).

Step 7 :

(1) Hindī Vocabulary (Pictorial Dictionary, Table 4); Study of Lesson 7.2

(2) Using pronouns I, we, you, he, she, it, they - with present and past actions we learned. (Table 11)

(3) Use of Hindī vocabulary with the Pronouns, Present and Past actions we learned. (Exercises 17-21)

(4) Review of what we learned so far; practicing to speak what we learned so far (for 15 min◦).

SECOND QUARTER TEST

Step 8 :

(1) Review of what we learned in Table 12. practicing to speak what we learned so far (for 15 min◦).

(2) Speaking past habitual actions (Table 12 and Exercise 22)

(3) Speaking simple sentences for Future events (I will eat, I will drink etc.) (Lesson 13.2, Table 13)

(4) Introduction to Lesson 11.6 and Tables 15-17.

Step 9 :

(1) Speaking sentences for 'perfect' actions with ने (I went, I came; I ate, I drank etc) (Lesson 14)

Step 10 :

(1) Use of 'to, with, by, from' : को, and से (राम को, घर से etc.) (Lessons 15.1-2)

(2) Use of postpositions 'in, on, at' : में, and पर (घर में, घर पर etc.) (Lesson 15.3, Tables 19-22)

(3) Use of 'for, with, near, has' के लिये, के साथ, के पास (राम-के लिये, के साथ, के पास) (Lesson 15.5)

(4) Review of what we learned so far (Tables 15, 16, 17 and 18). Speak what we learned (15 min◦)

Step 11 :

(1) Use of 'for' : के लिये, चाहिये (राम के लिये, राम को चाहिये etc.) (Lesson 15.4)

(2) Use of 'of' : का, की (राम का, राम की etc.) (Lesson 15.6)

(3) Review of what we learned so far, review of Tables 18 and 18A, Speaking Hindī (15 min◦)

Step 12 :

(1) Use of को, से, में, पर, का, की with I, you, we, he, she, it, they (आपको, आपका etc.) (Table 23-24)

(2) Review of what we learned so far; practicing to speak what we learned so far (for 15 min◦).

Step 13 :

(1) Asking Question hs: what, should I, may I? (आपका नाम क्या है ? etc.) (Lesson 19)

(2) Saying Subjunctive actions : I should, I may etc. (आप आएं, आप करें etc.) (Lesson 13.2, Table 13)

(3) Saying actions with requests : do you? does he etc. (आइये, खाइये, जाइये etc.) (Lesson 15.6)

(4) Study the similarity between pronouns (Lesson 15, Table 25);

(5) Review of what we learned so far; practicing to speak what we learned so far (for 15 min◦).

Step 14 :

(1) Use of Adjectives : hot, good, red etc. (गरम, अच्छा, लाल etc.) (Lesson 16.1)

(2) Use of Adverbs : very, less etc. (बहुत, कम etc) (Lesson 16.2)

(3) Use of Conjunctions : and, or, but, if etc. (और, या, मगर, यदि etc.) (Lesson 17.1)

(4) Review of what we learned so far; practicing to speak what we learned so far (for 15 min∘).

THIRD QUARTER TEST

Step 15 :

(1) Speaking of actions with phrase ‘having done’ -कर (Lesson 17.2)

(2) Intensive use of verb applications, with all we learned so far. (Lessons Table 26, Lesson15.9)

(3) Use of चाहिये (I want, I should go etc.) आपको चाय चाहिये क्या? मुझे घर जाना चाहिये (Lesson 15.6)

(4) Review of what we learned so far. (Table 18); Speaking what we learned so far (for 15 min∘).

Step 16 :

(1) General Conversation (Lesson 16.1); practicing to speak what we learned so far (for 15 min∘).

(2) Reading Hindī Story Books. पंचतंत्र, अमर चित्रकथा etc. शिशुगीत-1 (Lesson 8.2)

Step 17 :

(1) Speaking complex sentences (Lesson 16); Speaking what we learned so far (for 15 min∘).

(2) Speaking paragraphs (Teacher gives suitable simple English and Hindī paragraphs to translate)

(3) Story Reading (own stories), शिशुगीत-2 (Lesson 19)

Step 18 :

(1) Short Story telling (stories from story books); Speaking what we learned so far (for 15 min∘).

(2) Telling How to make tea, how to play hockey, how go to New York, how to shovel snow, how to cut grass, how to drive a car, how to build a house, how to write a letter etc.

Step 19 :

(1) General Knowledge in Hindī : Names of the days, time, relations etc. (Lesson 18)

(2) Stories from Panchatantra, Mahabharata etc; Speaking what we learned so far (for 15 min∘).

Step 20 :

(1) Review of what we learned; practicing to speak what we learned so far (for 15 min∘).

(2) Preparation for the Final Test. Discussion on any last minute questions the students may have.

FOURTH QUARTER, FINAL TEST

MODEL FORMAT FOR THE **FIRST** QUARTERLY TEST

QUESTION 1 : Read and Write the Following Hindī words five times.

1. भारत --
2. नमस्ते --
3. हिंदुस्थान --
4. मंदिर --
5. भगवान् --

QUESTION 2 : Say it in Hindī.

1. I am a student. ------------------------------------ 2. My name is xxxxxx. ---------------------------
3. We drink milk . ----------------------------------- 4. They are going. -------------------------------
5. You are speaking Hindī. ------------------------ 6. He is writing. ---------------------------------

QUESTION 3 : Say it in Hindī.

1. She was here. -- 2. I was there. ---------------------------------------
3. Anita is driving a red car. --
4. They run 10 km. -- 5. You can go now. ---------------------------------

QUESTION 4 : Write the names of the verbs (action words) in Hindī :

1. cry --------- 2. write --------- 3. give -------- 4. come -------- 5. Say -------- 6. sleep ---------
7. do -------- 8. become ------ 9. be able ------ 10. want ------- 11. walk ------ 12. drive --------
13. laugh --------- 14. hear --------- 15. see ------- 16. cook -------- 17. run --------- 18. sing ---------

QUESTION 5 : Say it in Hindī.

1. Now I can drive. ------------------------------------- 2. I want hot coffee. ------------------------------------
3. He can sing Hind songs. ---------------------------- 4. She can make Samosas. -----------------------------
5. You can go to India. ------------------------------------6. They want money. -----------------------------------
7. Tomorrow is my birthday. ------------------------- 8. I want two apples. ------------------------------------
9. He was watching a Hindī Movie. -------------------------- ---
10. The tea is very hot. --------------------------------- 11. They want money. ---------------------------------
12. You can go to India. -------------------------------- 13. Rām is not here. -------------------------------------
14. Say the following numbers in Hindī : 5, 3, 100, 10, 4, 2, 7, 20, 9

MODEL FORMAT FOR THE **SECOND** QUARTERLY TEST

QUESTION 1 : Write the order of Hindī SYNTAX for the words of a sentence :

1. Adjective, verb, object, subject, tense suffixes, adverb (e.g. She was singing a Hindī song loudly. वह हिंदी गाना जोरसे गा रही थी।).

QUESTION 2 : Write the Hindī names of following things :

1. boy --------- 2. girl --------- 3. dog -------- 4. cat -------- 5. letter --------- 6. tea ---------
7. ear --------- 8. nose -------- 9. hand ---------- 10. leg ---------- 11. egg --------- 12. tail ---------
13. mango --------- 14. apple -------- 15. banana ------ 16. plate --------- 17. car --------- 18. knife ---------
19. fan ----------- 20. book -------- 21. ball --------- 22. chair --------- 23. key --------- 24. window -----

QUESTION 3 : Say in Hindī :

1. I was driving a black car. ---
2. They were drinking hot tea slowly. --
3. She has already gone home. ---
4. He already knows it. --
5. I used to live in Boston. ---

QUESTION 4 : Say in Hindī :

1. What is your name? ---
2. Where do you live. ---
3. How are you? I am alright. --

QUESTION 5 : Say in Hindī :

1. I sleep at 10.00 O' Clock. ---
2. You used to read Gita. --
3. They used to drink black tea. ---

QUESTION 6 : Say in Hindī :

1. Rādhā should go to school. --
2. Sītā will come to New York. --
3. Please do not sit here. --

MODEL FORMAT FOR THE <u>THIRD</u> QUARTERLY TEST

QUESTION 1 : Write the Hindī suffixes used for saying following expressions :

1. to --------- 2. by ---------------- 3. from ---------- 4. for ----------------- 5. in --------------------
6. on -------- 7. near ------------- 8. together with ------------------------ 9. of ---------------------

QUESTION 2 : Say in Hindī :

1. What should I say? --
2. What will Tony eat? ---
3. When does Ramesh play? --
4. What was happening yeaterday? ---
5. What will happen tomorrow? --
6. Who is she? ---
7. Where is the dog? ---

QUESTION 3 : Find the Intransitive and Transitive actions and say them in Hindī :

1. to laugh ------------------ 2. to cook ------------------- 3. to walk ------------------- 4. to drive -----------
5. to see ------------------- 6. to hear -------------------- 7. to write ------------------ 8. to tell --------------

QUESTION 4 : Say in Hindī :

1. This book is for Mīnā. --
2. Davis will come tomorrow at 5 O' Clock. ---
3. The milk is in the cup. ---
4. The cat is near the dog. ---

QUESTION 5 : Say in Hindī :

1. Please come with me. ---
2. This is Tony's car. ---
3. Please stop near the tree. --
4. Keep the book on the table. --
5. Keshav ran 10 km. --
6. Lisā ate two Samosas and one Roṭī. ---
7. Belā brought three books. ---

MODEL FORMAT FOR THE <u>FOURTH</u> QUARTERLY TEST

QUESTION 1 : Say in Hindī :

1. I gave you ten Rupees. --
2. They sat on the chairs. --
3. I opened the doorfor the teacher. ---
4. There is no gas in the car. --
5. Please give me two pencils. ---

QUESTION 2 : Say in Hindī :

1. to her ------------------	2. to them -------------------	3. for her -------------------	4. to us -------------
5. near him -----------------	6. from you ------------------	7. by train ------------------	8. from you --------
9. for us ----------------	10. by them ------------------	11. in him ------------------	12. of our ----------

QUESTION 3 : Tell in Hindī :

1. How to make tea?
2. You are travelling by bus and you meet an old friend. Give him-her the directions to come to your home from his-her home by a car.
3. You are in India, someone asked you how to play the game of ice-hockey? Or, you are in Canada and someone asked you how to play the game of Kabaddi?
4. You want to order food in an Indian restaurant, say ten sentences to ask about the restaurant and to order the food.
5. Tell your friend about a car accident that happened to you or to someone else.

QUESTION 4 : Tell in Hindī :

1. What will you do in the holidays?
2. What will happen on your birthday?
3. Tell about you in ten sentences.
4. Tell about your friend ten sentences.
5. Tell about yor car ten sentences.
6. Tell on short story.
7. Read a paragraph from a story book
8. Copy and write a paragraph from a story book in Hindī.
9. From the paragraph you wrote in item no. 8, write as many sentences as you remember.

HINDI
TEACHER
FOR
HINDU
CHILDREN
Prof. Ratnakar Narale
Sunita Narale
Ratnakar
Pustak-Bharati
Books-India

LESSON 1

पहला पाठ

THE HINDI ALPHABET

Hindī Vowels :

अ	आ	इ	ई	उ	ऊ	ऋ	ए	ऐ	ओ	औ	अं	अ:
a	ā	i	ī	u	ū	ṛ	e	ai	o	au	ṁ	ḥ

Hindī Consonants :

क्	ख्	ग्	घ्	ङ्
k	kh	g	gh	ṅ
च्	छ्	ज्	झ्	ञ्
ch	chh	j	jh, z	ñ
ट्	ठ्	ड्	ढ्	ण्
ṭ	ṭh	ḍ	ḍh	ṇ
त्	थ्	द्	ध्	न्
t	th	d	dh	n
प्	फ्	ब्	भ्	म्
p	ph, f	b	bh	m

य्	र्	ल्	व्
y	r	l	v, w
श्	ष्	स्	ह्
ś, sh	ṣ, ṣh	s	h

LESSON 2

दूसरा पाठ

COMMON HINDI CONSONANTS

(Refer to the colourful chart on the Back Cover of this book, for more details)

The Class Consonants :

क	ख	ग	घ	ङ
ka	kha	ga	gha	ṅa (nga)
च	छ	ज	झ	ञ
cha	Chha	ja	jha, za	ña
ट	ठ	ड	ढ	ण
ṭa	ṭha	ḍa	ḍha	ṇa
त	थ	द	ध	न
ta	tha	da	dha	na
प	फ	ब	भ	म
pa	pha, fa	ba	bha	ma

The non-Class Consonants :

य	र	ल	व
ya	ra	la	va, wa
श	ष	स	ह
śa, sha	ṣa, sḥa	sa	ha

Special Compound Characterss :

क्ष	त्र	ज्ञ
kṣa	tra	gya, jña (*gya* is popular in Hindī, Sanskrit pronounciation is *jña*)

LESSON 3

SPEAKING THE HINDI CHARACTERS

Alphabet	Hindī	Sounds like, as in		
a	(अ)	a	in	particular
ā	(आ)	a	in	pāpā
i	(इ)	I	in	pin
ī	(ई)	ee	in	peel
u	(उ)	u	in	pull, put
ū	(ऊ)	oo	in	pool
ṛ	(ऋ)	ri	in	print
e	(ए)	e, ay	in	pen, pay
ai	(ऐ)	i, ai	in	Spine,Saigaon
o	(ओ)	o	in	pole
au	(औ)	ow, au	in	powder, sauna
k	(क्)	k	in	pink
kh	(ख्)	kh	in	Khyber
g	(ग्)	g	in	peg
gh	(घ्)	gh	in	ghost
ṅ	(ङ्)	n	in	packing
ch	(च्)	ch	in	chop
chh	(छ्)	chh		witch-hunt
j	(ज्)	j	in	jump
jh, z	(झ्)	dgeh	in	hedgehop
ñ	(ञ्)	n	in	punch

Alphabet	Hindī	Sounds like, as in		
ṭ	(ट्)	t	in	pet
ṭh	(ठ्)	th	in	hot-house
ḍ	(ड्)	d	in	pod
ḍh	(ढ्)	dh	in	adhere
ṇ	(ण्)	n	in	pant
t	(त्)	t	in	Istanbul
th	(थ्)	th	in	panther
d	(द्)	th	in	other
dh	(ध्)	dh	in	Buddha
n	(न्)	n	in	pen
p	(प्)	p	in	pup
ph,f	(फ्)	ph, f	in	photo-frame
b	(ब्)	b	in	pub
bh	(भ्)	bh	in	abhore
m	(म्)	m	in	map
y	(य्)	y	in	yes, yelp
r	(र्)	r	in	rip
l	(ल्, ल्)	l	in	lip
v,w	(व्)	v, w	in	Volkswagon
ś, sh	(श्)	sh	in	shop
ṣ	(ष्)	sh	in	push
s	(स्)	s	in	soap
h	(ह्)	h	in	hop

CHARACTERS WRITING GUIDE

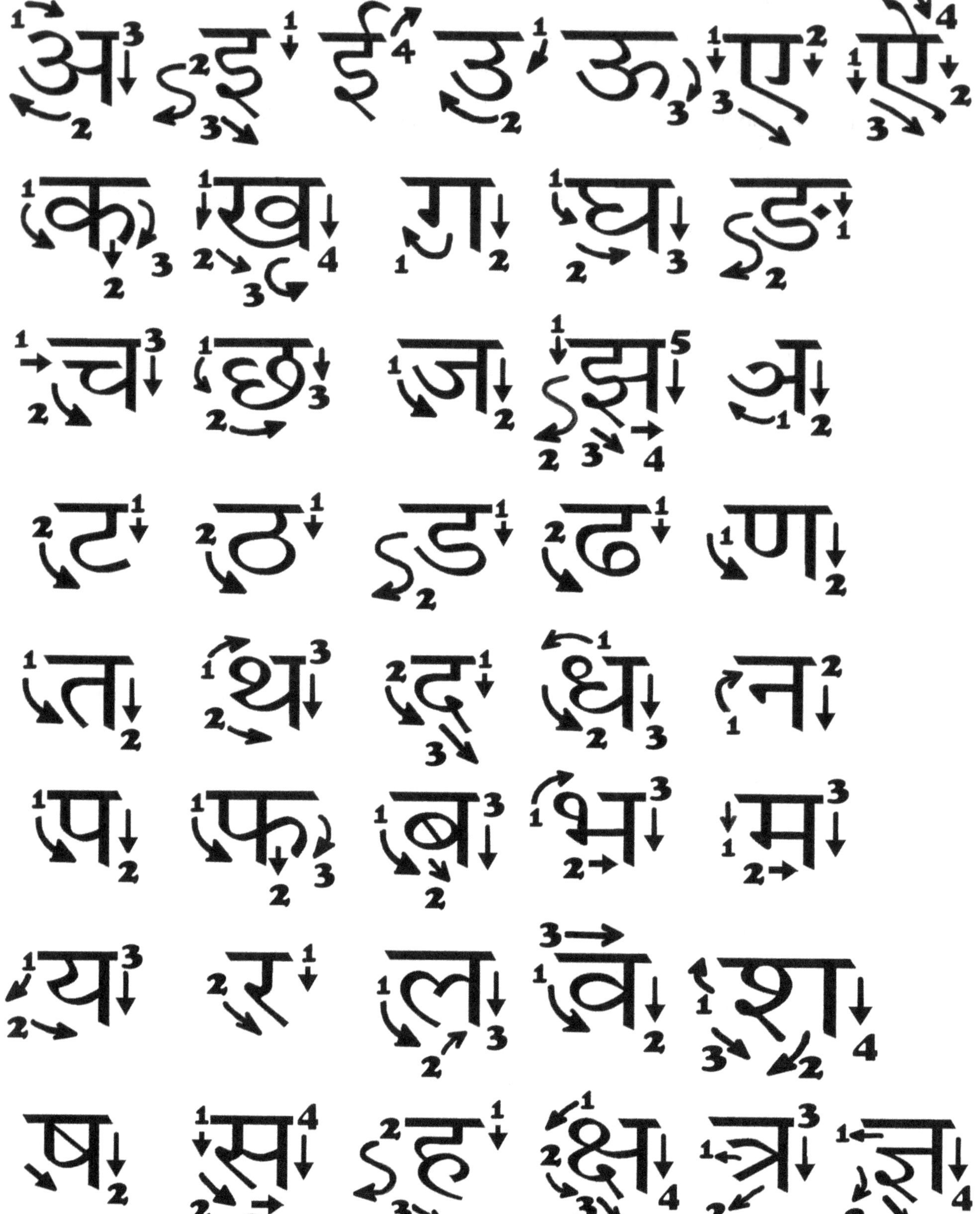

LESSON 4

चौथा पाठ

READING AND WRITING SIMPLE HINDI CONSONANTS

(4.1) **व va, ब ba, क ka** (Shown with Yellow Colour on the Back Cover)

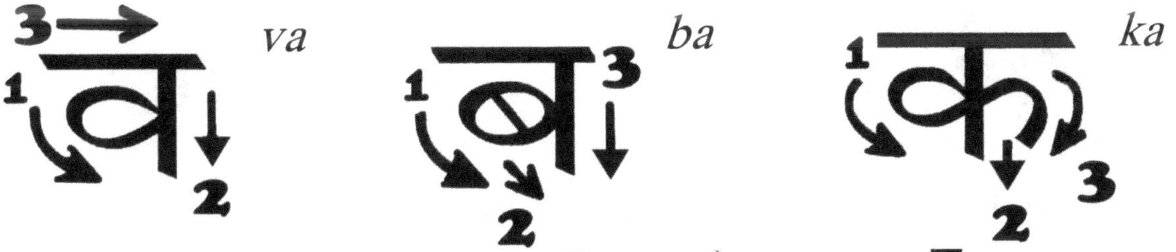

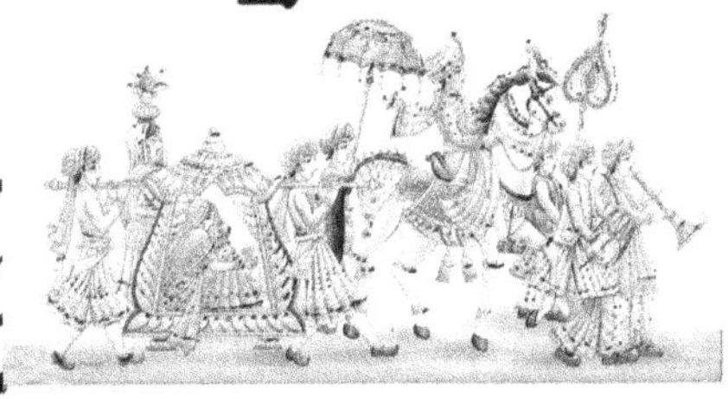

vimān (airplane) *barāt* (wedding procession) *kelā* (banana)

EXERCISE 1 : (Only on what we learned so far) Read and Write the following in Hindī :

1. ka ba ka 2. ba va ka 3. va ba ka 4. kaba, baka

5. कब, बक 6. कक, वब 7. वब, वक 8. कक, बव 9. क, ब, व,

10. कक, कब, कव 11. बब, बक, वव 12. कबव, कवब, वबक, बकव

HINDI WORD PROCESSING : *For typing practice in Hindi, please install the Ratnakar-H font on your PC and type the items 5 to 12 and compare them as shown in the book.* ***Do the same for all Exercises given in this book.*** (if you have any problem with the Hindi font, please write to the author)

ANSWERS AND VOCABULARY: *1. क ब क 2. ब व क 3. व ब क 4. कब (when?), बक (a crane or duck) 5. kab (when), bak (a crane or duck) 6. kaka, vaba 7. vaba, vaka 8. kaka, bava 9. k, ba, va 10. kaka, kaba (when), kava 11. baba, baka (crane or duck), vava 12. kabava, kavaba, vabaka, bakava.*

** In Hindī, if a word ends in a simple consonant, this ending consonant is said with less stress. e.g. *kaba* is actually said as if it was *'kab,' baka* as *'bak'* and so on.

PLEASE NOTICE : THE (i) CLOSE SIMILARITY AMONG THE CHARACTERS OF THE व, ब, क GROUP GIVEN ABOVE. Also notice, (ii) CLOSE SIMILARITY BETWEEN THE CHARACTERS OF व, ब क GROUP AND THE CHARACTERS OF THE प, ष, फ GROUP, GIVEN BELOW. YOU MAY DO SAME FOR ALL SHAPE GROUPS. SEE BACK COVER FOR COLOUR CODING OF THE CHARACTER SHAPE GROUPS.

(4.2) प pa, ष ṣa, फ pha (Shown with Light Green Colour on the Back Cover)

pa

ṣa

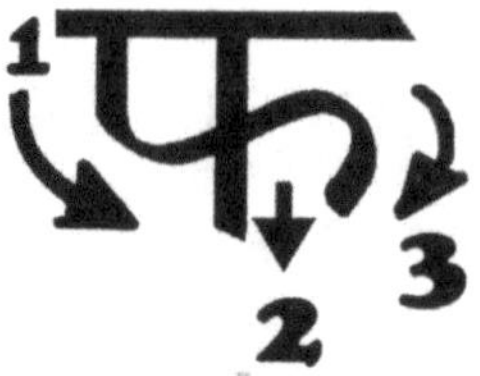
pha, fa

peḍ (plant)

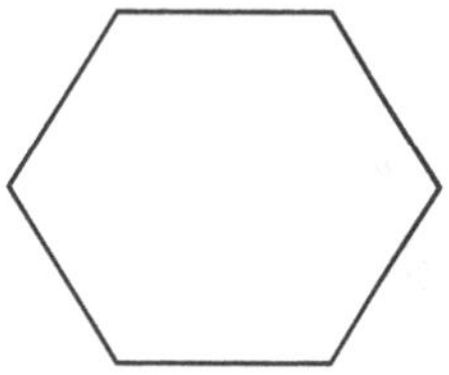
ṣaṭakoṇa (hexagon)

faṭfaṭī (m. bike)

EXERCISE 2 : (only on what we learned so far, the 'cumulative learning')

Read and Write the following in Hindī :

1. kapa, ka 2. paṣa, kaṣa 3. pha, ba, ka, ṣa, pa, pava 4. bakabaka, kaba

5. पव, पफ 6. कप, कब 7. कष, पष, कफ 8. वफ, वब, पफब

ANSWERS and VOCABULARY : *1. कप, क 2. पष, कष 3. फ, ब, क, ष, प, पव 4. बकबक (chatter), कब (when?) 5. pava, papha 6. kap (cup), kab (when?) 7. kaṣa, paṣa, kaph (cough) 8. vapha, vaba, paphaba.*

(4.3) त ta, न na, ग ga, म ma, भ bha, ण ṇa (Shown with White Colour on the Back Cover)

ta

na

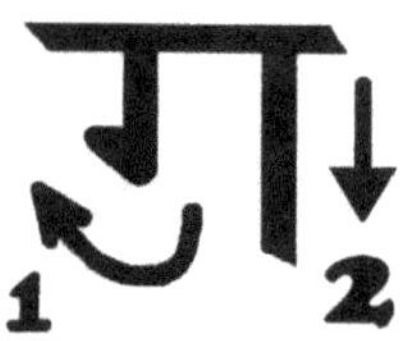
ga

tablā (Drum)

nāg (cobra)

gāy (cow)

ma

bha

ṇa

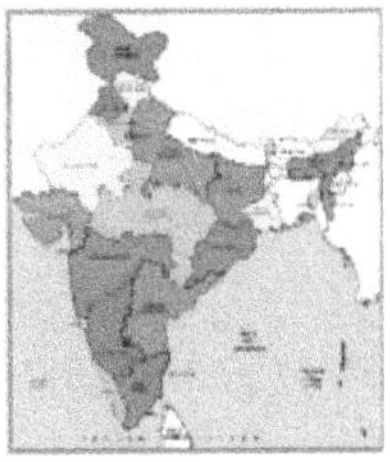

mā̐-bāp (māmā-pāpā) *bhārat* (India) *bāṇa* (arrow)

EXERCISE 3 : (only on what we learned so far, the 'cumulative learning') Read and Write the following in Hindī

1. क, ब, व, ब 2. कक, कब, कव 3. बब, बक 4. वव, वक, वब 5. कबव, कवब 6. वबक, बकव 7. म, न, त 8. तत, तन 9. कक, वब 10. गबन, भव, मगन, वतन, वन, वमन, कम, नभ, नव, नमन, तब, बम, मनन 11. ष, प, फ, म, भ, न, त, वतन, भगत, गमन, मनन, पवन।

ANSWERS AND VOCABULARY : *1. ka, ba, va, ba 2. kaka, kaba (when?), kava 3. baba, baka 4. vava, vaka, vaba 5. kabava, kavaba 6. vabaka, bakava 7. ma, na, ta 8. tata, tan (body) 9. kaka, vaba 10. gaban (embezzlement), bhava, magan (engrosses), vatan (motherland), van (forest), vaman (vomit), kam (less), nabh (sky), nav (new), naman (salute), tab (then), bam (bomb), manan (meditation) 11. Ṣha, pa, pha , ma, bha, na, ta, vatan (motherland), bhagat (devotee), gaman (going), manan (contemplation), pavan (wind).*

(4.4) च cha, ज ja, ञ ña, ल la **(Shown with Light Orange Colour on the Back Cover)**

cha

ja

ña

la

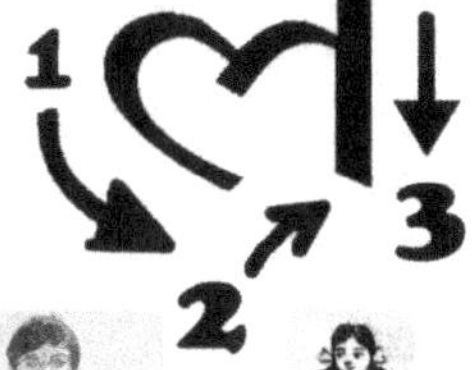

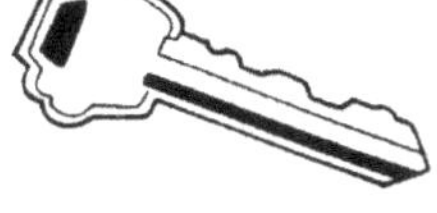

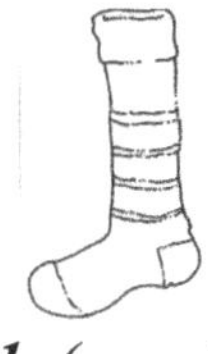

chābī (key) *jurāb* (sock) *laḍkā/laḍki* (boy/girl)

NOTE : Character ñ (ञ) is rarely used in Hindī. It is mostly used in Sanskrit language.

EXERCISE 4 : (only on what we learned so far) Read and Write the following in Hindī :

1. कप, चमचम 2. तन, मन, गगन 3. भगत, पतन, मनन 4. भव, गण, गणक 5. नल, लगन 6. पलक, बन, पग, गम 7. जल, चल, मल 8. कण, कल, पल 9. मत, तम

ANSWERS AND VOCABULARY : *1. kap (cup), chamcham (a sweet) 2. tan (body), man (mind), gagan (sky) 3. bhagat (devotee), patan (downfall), manan (contemplation) 4. bhav (world), gaṇ (class), gaṇak (computer) 5. nal (water tap), lagan (devotion) 6. palak (wink), ban (forest), pag (step), gam (sorrow) 7. jal (water), chal (let us go), mal (dirt) 8. kaṇ (particle), kal (tomorrow, yesterday), pal (moment) 9. mat (do not), tam (darkness).*

(4.5) घ gha, ध dha, छ chha (Shown with Light Blue Colour on the Back Cover)

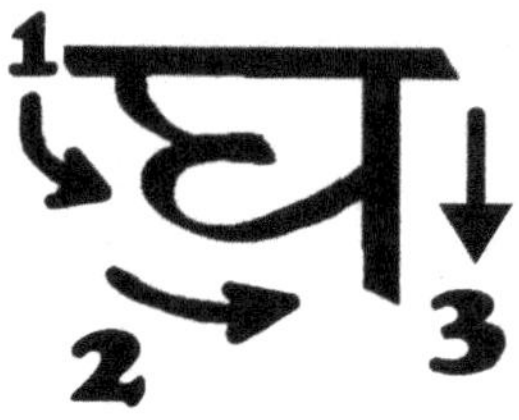

gha

dha

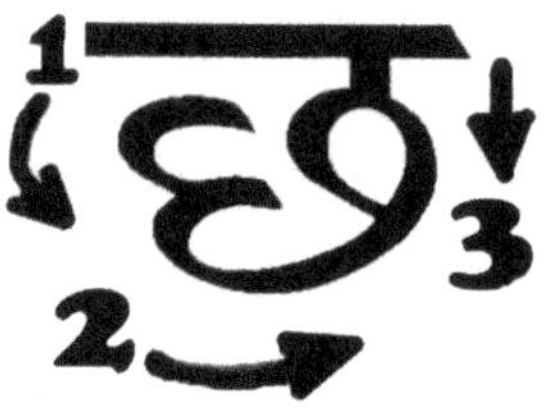

chha

ghar (house)

dhan (wealth)

chhatr (Umbrella)

EXERCISE 5, on what is covered up to 4.6 : Read and Write the following characters.

1. ज, च, ञ 2. ल, ज, च 3. क, ल 4. गणक, जलज 5. च, ज, ल, 6. र, स, ख, श 7. रस, शर, रख, सच 8. सन, फल 9. कमल, सरल

10. शतक, फरक, परख, भरत, चमन, शकल 11. लगन, वजन, सब, सच 12. बम, बरफ, चपल 13. मगज, जल, खल, नर, पर, सम 14. चमक, चल, चख 15. जज, छल, जग, घर 16. धन, कब, वध, शक, मगज

***ANSWERS AND VOCABULARY**: 1. ja, ca, ña 2. la, ja, cha 3. ka, la 4. gaṇak (counter), jalaj (aquatic) 5. cha, ja, la 6. ra, sa, kha, śa 7. ras (juice), shar (arrow), rakh (keep), sach (true) 8. san (year), fal (fruit) 9. kamal (lotus), saral (easy) 10. śatak (century), farak (difference), parakh (assay), bharat (Bharat), chaman (garden), śakal (face) 11. lagan (devotion), vajan (weight), sab (all), sach (truth) 12. bam (bomb), baraf (ice), chapal (quick) 13. magaj (brain), jal (water), khal (enemy), nar (man), par (other), sam (equal) 14. chamak (shine), chal (let us go), chakha (taste) 15. jaj (judge), chhal (deception), jag (world), ghar (house) 16. dhan (wealth), kab (when?), vadh (murder), śak (doubt), magaj (brain).*

(NOTE : The words like *śakal, baraf, farak* are their distorted but common forms, actually the proper forms are *śakl, barf, fark,* with compound characters which are covered in lesson 7).

(4.6) र ra, स sa, ख kha, श śa (Shown with Grey Colour on the Back Cover)

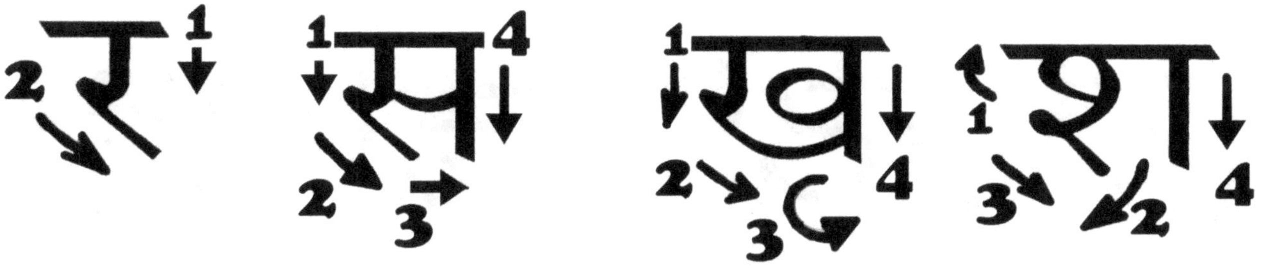

ra *sa* *kha* *śa*

rupayā (Rupee) *sīḍī* (CD) *khat* (letter) *shādī* (marriage)

(4.7) य ya, थ tha (Shown with Greenish Yellow Colour on the Back Cover)

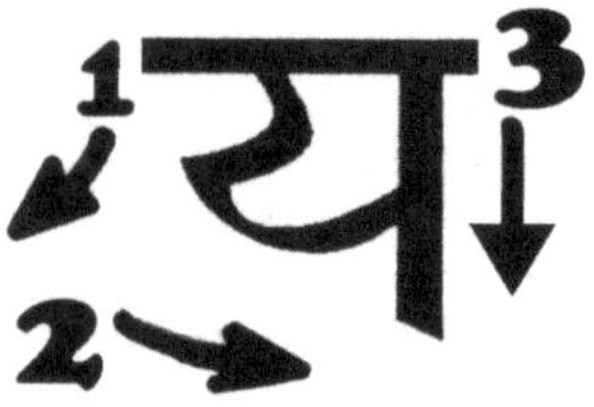

y a

yagya (ceremonial fire)

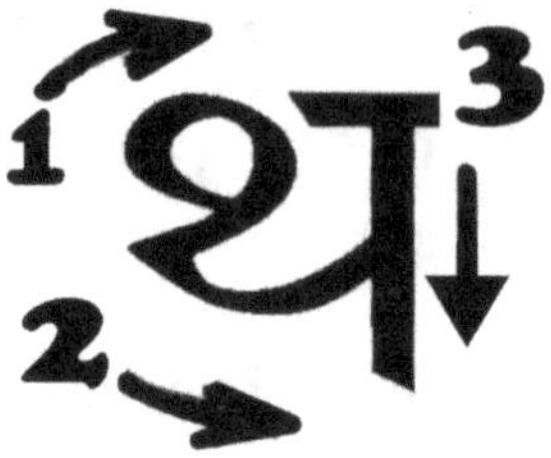

tha

thālī (plate)

EXERCISE 6 : (only on what we learned so far) Read and Write the following in Hindī :

1. घर, मत, रथ, धन 2. घन, फल, कल, वश, कर, सम, नरम 3. सब, जय
4. भय, शयन, चलन, रण, फसल, सरल 5. धर, जल

ANSWERS AND VOCABULARY : *1. ghar (house), mat (do not), rath (chariot), dhan (wealth) 2. ghan (dense), fal (fruit), kal (yesterday, tomorrow), vash (in control), kar (do), sam (same), naram (soft) 3. sab (all), jay (victory) 4. bhay (fear), śayan (sleep), chalan (behaviour), raṇ (battlefield), fasal (crop), saral (straight) 5. dhar (hold), jal (water)*

(4.8) ṭa ट, ṭha ठ, ḍha ढ, da द, ḍa ड, ṅa ङ, jha झ, ha ह

(Shown with Red Colour on the Back Cover)

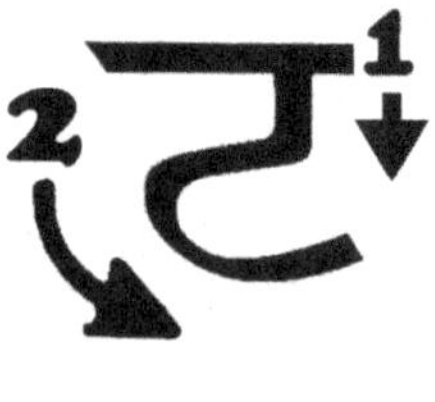

ṭa

ṭamāṭar (tomato)

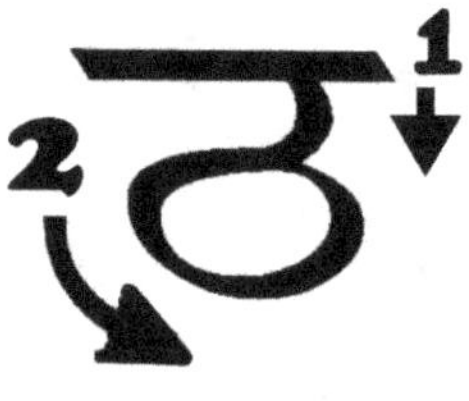

ṭha

ṭhappā (stamp)

ḍha

ḍhaknā (lid)

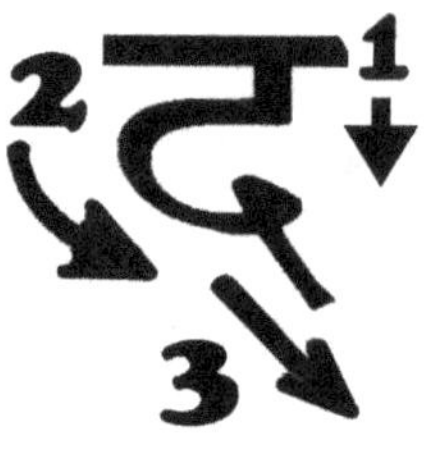

da

dil (heart)

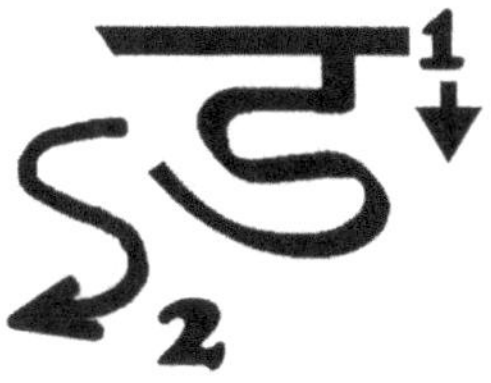

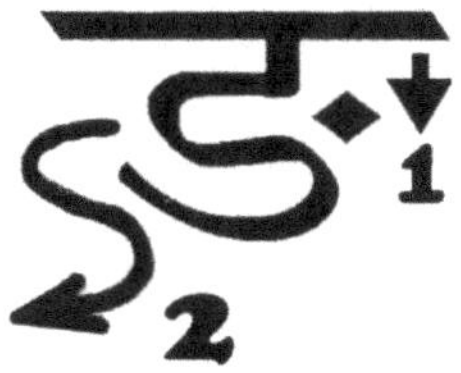

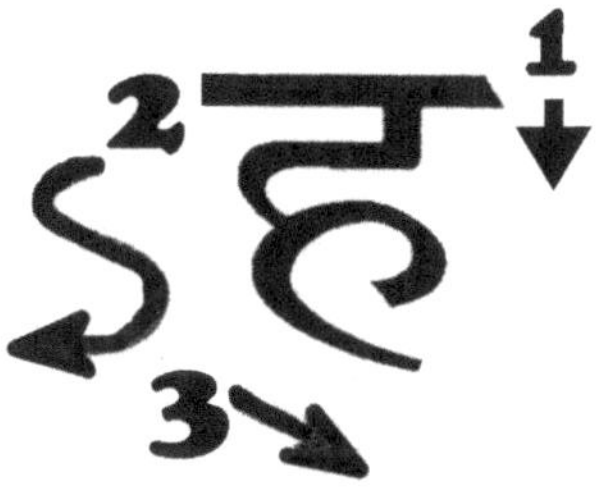

ḍa *ṅa* *jha* *ha*

ḍor (rope) *jhāḍū* (broom) *hāthī* (elephant)

EXERCISE 7 : (only on what we learned so far, the 'cumulative learning')

Read and Write the following in Hindī :

1. ट, ठ, ढ, ढ़, द 2. ड, ड़, ङ, झ 3. झ, ह, झ 4. दल, टब, ढल, बन 5. डबल, डर 6. दहन, कदम 7. बदन, बदल, मठ 8. हठ, मत 9. कम, तट, बरगद 10. सब, हम, गम

ANSWERS AND VOCABULARY *: 1. ṭa, ṭha, ḍha, ḍha, da 2. ḍa, ḍa, ṅa, jha 3. jha, ha, jha 4. dal (group), ṭab (tub), ḍhal (pass away), ban (forest) 5. ḍabal (double), ḍar (fear) 6. dahan (noun. burning), kadam (step) 7. badan (body), badal (change) maṭh (ashram, abode) 8. haṭh (stubborn-ness), mat (noun. vote; adverb. don't) 9. kam (less), taṭ (rampart), baragad (Banyan tree) 10. sab (all), ham (we), gam (sorrow)*

(4.9) The Compound Consonants : क्ष kṣa, त्र tra, ज्ञ gya (jña) (Shown with Pink Colour on the Back Cover)

kṣa

tra

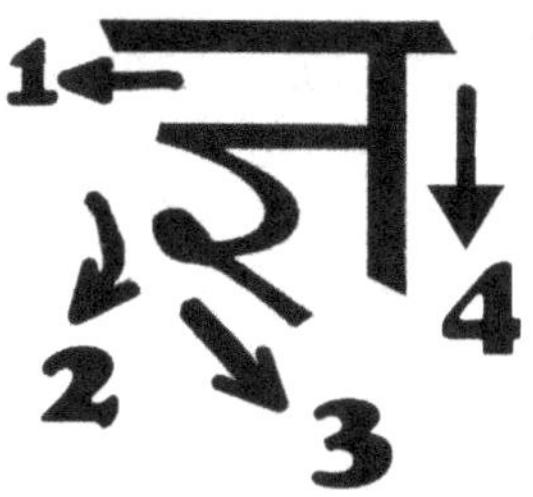

jña

NOTE : क्ष, त्र and ज्ञ *(kṣa, tra, and jña)* are compound characters, they are not alphabet.

(4.9) Anuswāra, Chandrabindī and the Visarga - अं ṁ, अँ ṁ, अः ḥ

अं   अँ   अः

aṁ   *a̐*   *aḥ*

EXERCISE 8 : Read and Write the following Hindī words :

1. अं (*aṁ*) अः (*aḥ*) 2. कंबल (*kambal* blanket) बंदर (*bandar* monkey) वंश (*vaṁsh* linage) पंकज (*pañkaj* lotus) 3. अंग (*aṅg* body) नंबर (*nambar* number) अनंत (*anant* endless) कंठ (*kaṇṭh* throat) 4. मंतर (*mantar* a spell) दंड (*daṇd* stick) रंग (*raṅg* colour) 5. संग (*saṅg* union) संशय (*saṁśay* doubt) हंस (*haṁsa* swan) लंच (*lañch* lunch) 6. अंतर (*antar* distance) स्वतः (*svataḥ* oneself) 7. चंदन (*chandan* sandlewood) कंप (*kamp* tremor) पतंग (*pataṅg* kite) खंदक (*khandak* moat) खंजर (*khañjar* dagger) मंजन (*mañjan* dentifrice) कंगन (*kaṅgan* bracelet) सः (*saḥ* he) 8. गंधक (*gandhak* sulphur) ठंढक (*ṭhanḍhak* cold) डंठल (*ḍaṇṭhal* stem) ढंग (*ḍhaṅg* mode) तरंग (*taraṅg* wave) शंख (*śaṅkh* conch) संचय (*sañchay* accumulation) छः (*chaḥ* six) 9. अंब (*amb* mother) जंगल (*jaṅgal* jungle) मंच (*mañch* dias) अंबर (*ambar* sky) लंदन (*landan* London) 10. बंपर (*bampar* bumper) अंदर (*andar* inside) छंद (*chand* meter) बंद (*band* closed) वंदन (*vandan* salute) मंद (*mand* slow) संघ (*sangh* group)

ँ

a̐   ड़ *ḍa*   ढ़ *ḍha*

(A) CHARACTERS WITH CHANDRABINDI : कहाँ (*kahā̐* where), काँपना (*kā̐panā* to tremble), खाँसना (*khā̐sanā* to cough), गाँव (*gā̐v* village), चाँद (*chā̐nd* moon), छाँव (*chā̐v* shadow), जहाँ (*jahā̐* where), कहाँ (*kahā̐* where?), यहाँ (*yahā̐* here), वहाँ (*vahā̐* there), दाँत (*dā̐t* tooth), पाँच (*pā̐ch* five), बाँह (*bā̐ha* forearm), भाँजा (*bhā̐ñjā* nephew), माँ (*mā̐* mother), हँसना (*ha̐sanā* to laugh),

(B) THE FLAPS : उड़ना (*uḍanā* to fly), कीड़ा (*kīḍā* worm), खड़ा (*khaḍā* standing), पीड़ा (*pīḍā* pain), लड़ना (*laḍanā* to fight), सड़ना (*saḍanā* to rot),

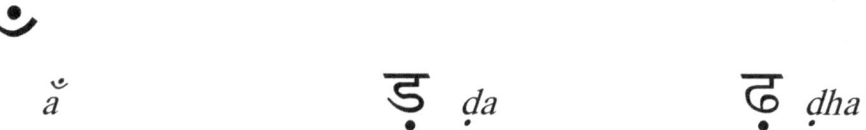

LESSON 5
पाँचवाँ पाठ
LEARNING THE HINDI VOWELS

(5.1) अ a, आ ā, ओ o, औ au   इ i, ई ī

अ a   आ ā   ओ o   औ au   इ i   ई ī

EXERCISE 9 : (only on what we learned so far) Read and then Write the following in Hindī:
1. आ, ओ, औ, आप 2. आ, अ, औ, आन 3. ओ, औ, ओट 4. अब, आँख, अक्षर 5. ओर, और, औंधा 6. ओझल, ओम, अज्ञ 7. अघ, औरस, आम, आस, आह, आज, औरत, अंबर, अजः, अंशः, ओघः 8. इ, ई, ईख 9. कई, नई, इधर 10. अंक, ईंधन, अंदाज, चौराह।

ANSWERS AND VOCABULARY: *1. ā, o, au, āp 2. ā, a, au, ān (swear) 3. o, au, oṭ (shelter) 4. ab (now), ā̃kh (eye), akṣhar (alphabet) 5. or (towards), aur (and), aundha (face down) 6. ojhal (disappear), om (Om), Ajña (ignorant) 7. agha (sin), auras (legitimate), ām (mango), ās (longing), āh (sorrow), āj (today), aurat (woman), ambar (sky), ajḥ (unborn), am̃shaḥ (fraction), oghaḥ (flow), 8. i, ī, īkh (sugarcane), 9. kaī (many), naī (new) idhar (on this side) 10. aṅk (number), indhan (fuel), andāj (estimate), chaurāh (intersection).*

(5.2) उ u, ऊ ū, ऋ ṛ; ए e, ऐ ai					(रु ru, रू rū)	
उ	ऊ	ऋ	ए	ऐ	रु	रू
u	ū	ṛ	e	ai	ru	rū

EXERCISE 10 : (only on what we learned so far) Read and Write the following in Hindī :
1. उ, ऊ, ऋ 2. उधर, उछल 3. उमर, ऊपर 4. उगम, ऊन 5. ऊँट, उठ 6. उतर, इधर 7. ए, ऐ, ऋ 8. गए, नए 9. उछल, उभर 10. एक, ऐनक, अतः। 11. रूप, तरु।

ANSWERS AND VOCABULARY: 1. u, ū, ṛ 2. udhar (on that side), uchhal (jump) 3. umar (age), ūpar (above) 4. ugam (source), ūn (wool) 5. ū̃ṭ (camel), uṭh (get up) 6. utar (get down), idhar (here), 7. e, at, ṛ 8. gae (gone), nae (new) 9. uchhal (bounce), ubhar (grow) 10. ek (one), ainak (spectacles), ataḥ (therefore). 11. rūp (form), taru (tree).

LESSON 6
छठा पाठ

6.1 WRITING HINDI VOWEL SIGNS

Vowels	अ	आ	इ	ई	उ	ऊ	ऋ	ए	ऐ	ओ	औ
Signs		ा	ि	ी	ु	ू	ृ	े	ै	ो	ौ
Sound	a	ā	i	ī	u	ū	ṛ	e	ai	o	au
		aa		ee		oo	ri	é			

ा	ि	ी	ु	ू	ृ	े	ै	ो	ौ
ā	i	ī	u	ū	ṛ	é	ai	o	au
पा	पि	पी	पु	पू	पृ	पे	पै	पो	पौ
pā, paa	pi	pī, pee	pu	pū, poo	pṛ	pé	pai	po	pau

EXERCISE 11 : Read and write the Hindī words :
जितना, जीतना, मृत, चिंता, जूता, कुछ, वैसा, औंधा, दिया, दीया, बेकारी, सूखा, सुखी, भेद, मैं, भिक्षा, ज्ञानी, सुंदरता, कोका कोला, महानता, सुख दुःख, चूहा, ज्ञानयोग, भारतीय, अमरीकन, पौराणिक।

ANSWERS AND VOCABULARY : jitnā (as much), jītnā (to win), mrit (dead), chintā (worry), jūtā (shoe), kuchh (some), vaisā (like that), aundhā (face down), diyā (gave), dīyā (lamp), bekārī (unemployment), sUkhā (dry), sukhi (happy), bhed (difference), maĩ (I), bhikshā (alms), jñānī (knowledgable), sundartā (beauty), kokā kolā (coke), mahānatā (greatness), sukh duḥkh (happyness and sorrow), chūhā (mouse), jñānayoga (yoga of knowledge), bhāratiya (Indian), amarikan (American), paurāṇik (ancient).

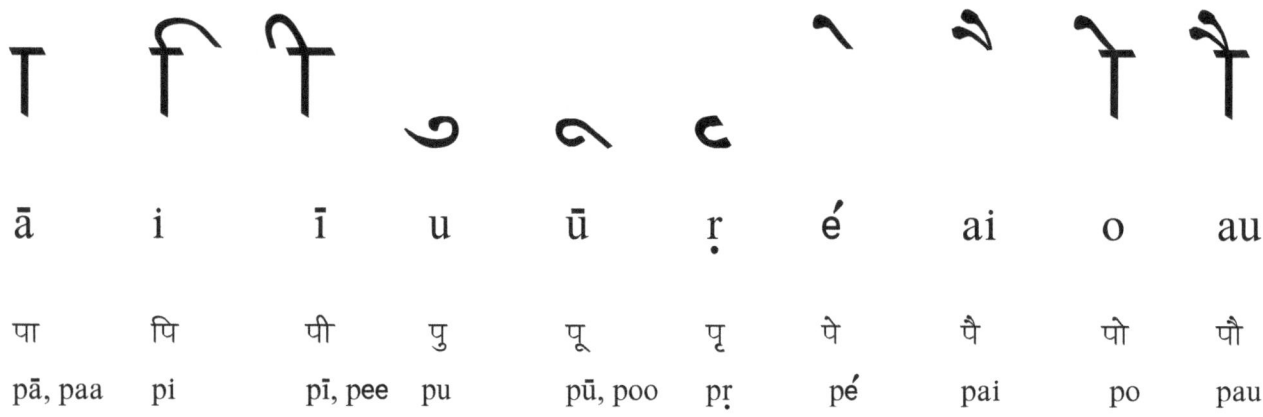

6.2 CHART OF ALPHABET WITH VOWEL SIGNS

अ	आ	इ	ई	उ	ऊ	ऋ	ए	ऐ	ओ	औ	अं	अः
	ा	ि	ी	ु	ू	ृ	े	ै	ो	ौ	ं	:
	(क्= ा)	(क्+ ि)	(क्+ ी)	(क्+ ु)	(क्+ ू)	(क्+ ृ)	(क्+ े)	(क्+ ै)	(क्+ ो)	(क्+ ौ)	(क्+ ं)	(क्+ :)
क	का	कि	की	कु	कू	कृ	के	कै	को	कौ	कं	कः
ख	खा	खि	खी	खु	खू	खृ	खे	खै	खो	खौ	खं	खः
ग	गा	गि	गी	गु	गू	गृ	गे	गै	गो	गौ	गं	गः
घ	घा	घि	घी	घु	घू	घृ	घे	घै	घो	घौ	घं	घः
ङ	ङा	ङि	ङी	ङु	ङू	–	ङे	ङै	ङो	ङौ	ङं	ङः
च	चा	चि	ची	चु	चू	चृ	चे	चै	चो	चौ	चं	चः
छ	छा	छि	छी	छु	छू	छृ	छे	छै	छो	छौ	छं	छः
ज	जा	जि	जी	जु	जू	जृ	जे	जै	जो	जौ	जं	जः
झ	झा	झि	झी	झु	झू	झृ	झे	झै	झो	झौ	झं	झः
ञ	ञा	ञि	ञी	ञु	ञू	–	ञे	ञै	ञो	ञौ	ञं	ञः
ट	टा	टि	टी	टु	टू	टृ	टे	टै	टो	टौ	टं	टः
ठ	ठा	ठि	ठी	ठु	ठू	ठृ	ठे	ठै	ठो	ठौ	ठं	ठः
ड	डा	डि	डी	डु	डू	डृ	डे	डै	डो	डौ	डं	डः
ढ	ढा	ढि	ढी	ढु	ढू	ढृ	ढे	ढै	ढो	ढौ	ढं	ढः
ण	णा	णि	णी	णु	णू	णृ	णे	णै	णो	णौ	णं	णः
त	ता	ति	ती	तु	तू	तृ	ते	तै	तो	तौ	तं	तः
थ	था	थि	थी	थु	थू	थृ	थे	थै	थो	थौ	थं	थः
द	दा	दि	दी	दु	दू	दृ	दे	दै	दो	दौ	दं	दः
ध	धा	धि	धी	धु	धू	धृ	धे	धै	धो	धौ	धं	धः
न	ना	नि	नी	नु	नू	नृ	ने	नै	नो	नौ	नं	नः
प	पा	पि	पी	पु	पू	पृ	पे	पै	पो	पौ	पं	पः
फ	फा	फि	फी	फु	फू	फृ	फे	फै	फो	फौ	फं	फः
ब	बा	बि	बी	बु	बू	बृ	बे	बै	बो	बौ	बं	बः
भ	भा	भि	भी	भु	भू	भृ	भे	भै	भो	भौ	भं	भः
म	मा	मि	मी	मु	मू	मृ	मे	मै	मो	मौ	मं	मः
य	या	यि	यी	यु	यू	यृ	ये	यै	यो	यौ	यं	यः
र	रा	रि	री	रु	रू	ऋ	रे	रै	रो	रौ	रं	रः
ल	ला	लि	ली	लु	लू	लृ	ले	लै	लो	लौ	लं	लः
व	वा	वि	वी	वु	वू	वृ	वे	वै	वो	वौ	वं	वः
श	शा	शि	शी	शु	शू	शृ	शे	शै	शो	शौ	शं	शः
ष	षा	षि	षी	षु	षू	षृ	षे	षै	षो	षौ	षं	षः
स	सा	सि	सी	सु	सू	सृ	से	सै	सो	सौ	सं	सः
ह	हा	हि	ही	हु	हू	हृ	हे	है	हो	हौ	हं	हः

EXERCISE 12 : What we learned so far, the 'cumulative learning'

6.3 A PRELIMINARY VOCABULARY OF KEY HINDI WORDS

READ the Hindī words and WRITE them. Understand and remember as many as possible.

मैं (*maĩ*; I), हूँ (*hũ*; am), हम (*ham*; we),
आप (*āp*; you), तुम (*tum*; you), वह (*vah*; he-she),
वो (*vo*; he, she), वे (*ve*; they), हमें (*hamẽ*; to us),
आपको (*āp ko*; to you), उसको (*us ko*; to him-her), उनको (*un ko*; to them),
मैंने (*maĩ ne*; I), आपने (*āp ne*; you), तूने (*tū ne*; you),
तुमने (*tum ne*; you), उसने (*us ne*; he, she), मुझे (*mujhe*; to me),
आपसे (*āp se*; from you), मुझसे (*mujh se*; from me), तुझसे (*tujh se*; from you)
तुमसे (*tum se*; from you), उससे (*us se*; from him-her), उनसे (*un se*; from them),
मेरे पास (*mere pās*; with me), मेरे लिये (*mere liye*; for me), आपके लिये (*āpke liye*; for you),
हमारे लिये (*hamāre liye*; for us), उनके लिये (*unke liye*; for them), मेरा (*merā*; my m∘),
मेरी (*merī*; my f∘), मेरे (*mere*; my plural∘), हमारा (*hamārā*; our m∘),
हमारी (*hamārī*; our f∘), हमारे (*hamāre*; our pl∘), आपका (*āp kā*; your),
आपकी (*āp kī*; your), उसका (*his, her*), मुझमें (*mujh mẽ*; in me),
तुझमें (*tujh mẽ*; in you), आपमें (*āp mẽ*; in you), उसमें (*us mẽ*; in him, her),
उनमें (*un mẽ*; in them), मुझ पर (*mujh par*; on me), तुम पर (*tum par*; on you),
तुझ पर (*tujh par*; on you), आप पर (*āp par*; on you), उस पर (*us par*; on him, her),
उन पर (*un par*; on them), मैं हूँ (*maĩ hũ*; I am), तुम हो (*tum ho*; you are),
आप हैं (*āp haĩ*; you are). हूँ (*hũ*; am), है (*hai*; is, has, Sg∘ have),
हैं (*haĩ*; are, Pl∘ have), था (*thā*; was, had, used to), क्या (*kyā*; what),
कैसा, कैसी, कैसे (m∘ *kaisā*, f∘ *kaisī*, plural∘ *kaise*; how), ठीक (*ṭhīk*; ok, alright),
नाम (*nām*; name), लड़का (*laḍkā*; Boy), लड़की (*laḍkī*; Girl),
कुत्ता (*kuttā*; Dog), बिल्ली (*billī*; Cat), घर (*ghar*; House, home),
चाय (*chāy*; Tea). पी (*pī*; to Drink). गरम (*garam*; Hot).

LESSON 7
सातवाँ पाठ

7.1 COMPOUNDING THE CONSONANTS

(Compare the following chart with the one given on page 1)

Hindī Half-Characters :

क्‍ (क्)	ख्‍ (ख्)	ग्‍ (ग्)	घ्‍ (घ्)	ङ्
k	kh	g	gh	ṅ
च्‍ (च्)	छ्	ज्‍ (ज्)	झ्‍ (झ्)	ञ्‍ (ञ्)
ch	chh	j	jh, z	ñ
ट्	ठ्	ड्	ढ्	ण्‍ (ण्)
ṭ	ṭh	ḍ	ḍh	ṇ
त्‍ (त्)	थ्‍ (थ्)	द्	ध्‍ (ध्)	न्‍ (न्)
t	th	d	dh	n
प्‍ (प्)	फ्‍ (फ्)	ब्‍ (ब्)	भ्‍ (भ्)	म्‍ (म्)
p	ph, f	b	bh	m

य्‍ (य्)	र्	ल्‍ (ल्)	व्‍ (व्)
y	r	l	v,w
श्‍ (श्)	ष्‍ (ष्)	स्‍ (स्)	ह्
ś, sha	ṣ, ṣh	s	h

7.2 USE OF THE HALF CHARACTERS TO MAKE HINDI COMPOUND LETTERS AND WORDS

*Character k (क्, क) : पक्का (k + k *pakkā* strong), क्लेष (k + l *kleṣa* distress), क्या (k + y *kyā* what?), वक्त (k + t *vakta* time) रुक्मिणी (k + m *rukmiṇī* Rukmiṇī)

*Character kh (ख्, ख) : ख्याल (kh + y *khyāl* thought) ख्वाब (kh + w *khwāb* dream)

*Character g (ग्, ग) : ग्लास (g + l *glās* glass), दुग्ध (g + dh *dugdha* milk), अग्नि (g + n *agni* fire), भाग्य (g + y *bhāgya* fortune), ग्वाला (g + w *gwālā* milkman)

*Character gh (घ्, घ) : विघ्न विघ्न विघ्न (gh + n *vighna* obstacle), लघ्वाशी लघ्वाशी (gh + v *laghvāshī* moderate eater)

*Character ch (च्, च) : बच्चा (ch + ch *bachchā* kid), अच्युत (ch + y *achyut* Krishṇa, Viṣṇu), अच्छा (ch + chh *achchhā* good)

*Character j (ज्, ज) : राज्य (j + y *rājya* kingdom), सज्ज (j + j *sajja* ready), उज्ज्वल (j + j + v *ujjaval* bright), ज्वाला (j + w *jwālā* flame)

*Character ṭ (ट्) : मिट्टी, मिट्टी (ṭ + ṭ *miṭṭī* soil) मुट्ठी (ṭ + ṭh *muṭṭhī* fist)

*Character ḍ (ड्) : हड्डी हड्डी (ḍ + ḍ *haḍḍī* bone)

*Character ṇ (ण्, ण) : कण्ठ (ṇ + ṭh *kaṇṭha* throat), कण्टक (ṇ + ṭh *kaṇṭak* thorn), षण्मास (ṇ + m *ṣaṇmās* six months), अण्डा (ṇ + ḍ *aṇḍā* egg)

*Character t (त्, त) : सत्कार (t + k *satkār* honour), रत्नाकर (t + n *ratnākar* Ratnakar), आत्मा (t + m *ātmā* soul), त्याग (t + y *tyāg* sacrifice), त्रास (t + r *trās* trouble), त्वरा (t + v *tvarā* rush), सत्त्व, सत्त्व, सत्त्व (t + t + v *sattava* truth)

*Character th (थ्, थ) : तथ्य (th + y *tathya* reality)

*Character dh (ध्, ध) : ध्वज (dh + v *dhvaj* flag), दध्म (dh + m *dadhma* to blow), मध्य (dh + y *madhya* centre), ध्वनि (dh + v *dhvani* soundon)

*Character n (न्, न) : आनन्द (n + d *ānand* joy), अन्न (n + n *anna* food), जन्म (n + m *janma* birth), धन्यवाद (n + y *dhanyavād* thanks), इन्तजार (n + t *intajār* wait), अन्धेरा (n + dh *andherā* darkness)

*Character p (प्, ‌) : समाप्ति (p + t *samāpti* end), प्यार (p + y *pyār* love), स्वप्न (p + n *svapna* dream), प्लव (p + l *plava* floating)

*Character ph, f (फ्, ‌) : फ्लावर (f + l *flāwar* flower), हफ्ता (f + t *haftā* week)

*Character b (ब्, ‌) : धब्बा (b + b *dhabbā* spot), ब्लू (b + l *blū* blue), शब्द (b + d *shabda* sound), ब्याह (b + y *byāha* wedding), सब्जी (b + j *sabjī* vegetable)

*Character bh (भ्, ‌) : अभ्यास (bh + y *abhyās* study),

*Character m (म्, ‌) : सम्पदा (m + p *sampadā* wealth), सम्यक् (m + y *samyak* proper), सम्मान (m + m *sammāna* honour), मुम्बई (m + b *mumbaī* Bombay), अम्ल (m + l *amla* sour), साम्य (m + y*sāmya* similarity)

*Character y (य्, ‌) : शय्या (y + y *shayyā* bed)

*Character r (र्) : तर्क (r + k *tarka* philosophy), वर्ग (r + g *varga* class), अर्चना (r + ch *archnā* worship), कर्ज (r + j *karja* laon), वर्ण (r + ṇ *varṇa* colour, letter, class), नर्तकी (r + t *nartakī* dancer), व्यर्थ (r + th *vyartha* unnecessary), दर्द (r + d *dard* pain), वर्धन (r + dh *vardhan* growth), सर्प (r + p *sarpa* snake), दर्भ (r + bh *darbha* grass), कर्म (r + m *karma* work, deed), कार्य (r + y *kārya* duty)

Compounds with (र) : क्रिया (k + ra *kriyā* action), ग्रीवा (g + ra *grīvā* neck), वज्र (j + ra *vajra* thunderboalt), राष्ट्र (ṣ + ṭ + ra *rāṣṭra* nation), त्रिशूल (t + ra *triśūl* trident), भद्र (d + ra *bhadra* gentle), प्रकाश (p + ra *prakāsh* light), ब्रह्मा (b + ra *Brahmā* creator), व्रत (v + ra *vrat* austerity), श्रीमती (ś + ra *śrīmatī* madam)

*Character l (ल्, ‌) : वल्क (l + k *valka* bark), जुल्फ (l + f *julfa* haired), गुल्म (l + m *gulma* bush, a cluster of plants), कल्याण (l + y *kalyāṇ* benefit)

LESSON 8
आठवाँ पाठ

8.1 SPECIAL COMPOUND CHARACTERS

(1) Character d (द्) forms following commonly used SEVEN compound letters :

(i). d + ga = dga writen as :	द् + ग = द्‌ग = द्ग	भगवद्गीता	*bhagavadgītā*
(ii) d + da = dda written as :	द् + द = द्‌द = द्द	उद्देश	*uddesha* (aim)
(iii) d + dha = ddha written as	द् + ध = द्‌ध = द्ध	बुद्ध	*buddha*
(v) d + bha = dbha written as :	द् + भ = द्‌भ = द्भ	श्रीमद्भगवद्गीता	*shrīmatbhagavadgītā*
(v) d + ya = dya written as :	द् + य् = द्‌य = द्य	विद्या	*vidyā* (knowledge)
(vi) d + ma = dma written as :	द् + म् = द्‌म = द्म	पद्म	*padma* (lotus)
(vii) d + va = dva written as :	द् + व् = द्‌व = द्व	द्वार	*dvār* (gate)

(2) Characters *ra* and *r* (र, र्) form following TWO types of compounds :

(A) WHEN FULL CONSONANT *ra* (र) comes after a half consonant character, it is written as a slant line attached to that (half) consonant. (Note : Even though that half consonant apprars to be written as a full consonant, it is actually a half consonant) :

(i) k (half) + ra (full) = kra	(क् + र = क्‌र = क्र)	चक्र	*chakra* (wheel)
(ii) g + ra = gra	(ग् + र = ग्‌र = ग्र)	अग्र	*agra* (tip)
(iii) t + ra = tra	(त् + र = त्‌र = त्र)	पवित्र	*pavitra* (holy)
(iv) d + ra = dra	(द् + र = द्र)	द्रव	*drava* (liquid)
(v) sh + ra =shra	(श् + र = श्र)	श्री	*shrī* (lofty)
(vi) ṭ or ḍ+ ra= tra, ḍra	(ट् + र = ट्र)	राष्ट्र	*rāṣṭra* (nation)
(vii) s + ra = sra	(स् + र = स्‌र = स्र)	सहस्र	*sahasra* (thousand)
s + t + ra = stra	(स् +त् + र = स्‌त्‌र =स्त्र)	स्त्री	*strī* (woman)

(B) WHEN THE <u>HALF CONSONANT</u> *r* (र्) comes <u>before</u> any full consonant character, the *r* (र्) is written as (᳚) over that full consonant.

(viii) r + k (᳚) र् + क = र्क। अर्क (*arka* extract), स्वर्ग (*svarga* heaven),

<u>AGAIN REMEMBER</u> :

(i) The slant line character (्) represents the full र (*ra*), it does not represent half र् (r)

e.g. प्र = प् + र प्रकाश

(ii) The curved line character (᳚) represents half र् (*r*), it does not represent full र (*ra*)

e.g. र्प = र् + प सर्प

(3) Character ह् forms following three types of very common compound letters :

(i) h + ma = hma (ह् + म = ह्म) ब्रह्मा (*brahmā* the Creator)

(ii) h + ya = hya (ह् + य = ह्य) बाह्य (*bahya* outer)

(iii) h + ṛ = hṛ (ह् + ऋ = हृ) हृदय (*hṛday* heart)

THE SPECIAL LETTER *kta*

क्त (क्‌त)

(4) Character k : character k + ta = kta. *kta* can be written as क् + त = क्‌त। but there is a special character for this combo which is written as क् + त = क्‌त = क्त

e.g. रक्त (*rakta* blood), भक्ति भक्‌ति (*bhakti* devotion), वक्ता वक्‌ता (*vaktā* speaker), मुक्त मुक्‌त (*mukta* free), आसक्ति, आसक्‌ति (*āsakti* attachment), पंक्ति पंक्‌ति (*paṅkti* line) ...etc

COMPOUNDING DEVANAGARI CONSONANTS

+	क	ख	ग	घ	च	छ	ज	झ	ट	ठ	ड	ढ	ण	त	थ	द
क्	क्क	क्ख	क्ग	क्घ	क्च	क्छ	क्ज	क्झ	क्ट	क्ठ	क्ड	क्ढ	ल्ण	क्त	क्थ	क्द
ख्	ख्क	ख्ख	ख्ग	ख्घ	ख्च	ख्छ	ख्ज	ख्झ	ख्ट	ख्ठ	ख्ड	डढ	ख्ण	ख्त	ख्थ	ख्द
ग्	ग्क	ग्ख	ग्ग	ग्घ	ग्च	ग्छ	ग्ज	ग्झ	ग्ट	ग्ठ	ग्ड	ग्ढ	ग्ण	ग्त	ग्थ	ग्द
घ्	घ्क	घ्ख	घ्ग	घ्घ	घ्च	घ्छ	घ्ज	घ्झ	घ्ट	घ्ठ	घ्ड	घ्ढ	घ्ण	घ्त	घ्थ	घ्द
ङ्	ङ्क	ङ्ख	ङ्ग	ङ्घ	ङ्च	ङ्छ	ङ्ज	ङ्झ	ङ्ट	ङ्ठ	ङ्ड	ङ्ढ	ङ्ण	ङ्त	ङ्थ	ङ्द
च्	च्क	च्ख	च्ग	च्घ	च्च	च्छ	च्ज	च्झ	च्ट	च्ठ	च्ड	च्ढ	च्ण	च्त	च्थ	च्द
छ्	छ्क	छ्ख	छ्ग	छ्घ	छ्च	छ्छ	छ्ज	छ्झ	छ्ट	छ्ठ	छ्ड	छ्ढ	छ्ण	छ्त	छ्थ	छ्द
ज्	ज्क	ज्ख	ज्ग	ज्घ	ज्च	ज्छ	ज्ज	ज्झ	ज्ट	ज्ठ	ज्ड	ज्ढ	ज्ण	ज्त	ज्थ	ज्द
झ्	झ्क	झ्ख	झ्ग	झ्घ	झ्च	झ्छ	झ्ज	झ्झ	झ्ट	झ्ठ	झ्ड	झ्ढ	झ्ण	झ्त	झ्थ	झ्द
ञ्	ञ्क	ञ्ख	ञ्ग	ञ्घ	ञ्च	ञ्छ	ञ्ज	ञ्झ	ञ्ट	ञ्ठ	ञ्ड	ञ्ढ	ञ्ण	ञ्त	ञ्थ	ञ्द
ट्	ट्क	ट्ख	ट्ग	ट्घ	ट्च	ट्छ	ट्ज	ट्झ	ट्ट	ट्ठ	ट्ड	ट्ढ	ट्ण	ट्त	ट्थ	ट्द
ठ्	ठ्क	ठ्ख	ठ्ग	ठ्घ	ठ्च	ठ्छ	ठ्ज	ठ्झ	ठ्ट	ठ्ठ	ठ्ड	ठ्ढ	ठ्ण	ठ्त	ठ्थ	ठ्द
ड्	ड्क	ड्ख	ड्ग	ड्घ	ड्च	ड्छ	ड्ज	ड्झ	ड्ट	ड्ठ	ड्ड	ड्ढ	ड्ण	ड्त	ड्थ	ड्द
ढ्	ढ्क	ढ्ख	ढ्ग	ढ्घ	ढ्च	ढ्छ	ढ्ज	ढ्झ	ढ्ट	ढ्ठ	ढ्ड	ढ्ढ	ढ्ण	ढ्त	ढ्थ	ढ्द
ण्	ण्क	ण्ख	ण्ग	ण्घ	ण्च	ण्छ	ण्ज	ण्झ	ण्ट	ण्ठ	ण्ड	ण्ढ	ण्ण	ण्त	ण्थ	ण्द
त्	त्क	त्ख	द्ग	द्घ	च्च	छ्छ	ज्ज	झ्झ	द्ट	द्ठ	द्ड	द्ढ	द्ण	त्त	त्थ	द्द
थ्	थ्क	थ्ख	ध्ग	ध्घ	थ्च	थ्छ	थ्ज	थ्झ	थ्ट	थ्ठ	थ्ड	थ्ढ	थ्ण	थ्त	थ्थ	ध्द
द्	द्क	द्ख	द्ग	द्घ	च्च	छ्छ	ज्ज	झ्झ	द्ट	द्ठ	द्ड	द्ढ	द्ण	त्त	त्थ	द्द
ध्	ध्क	ध्ख	ध्ग	ध्घ	ध्च	ध्छ	ध्ज	ध्झ	ध्ट	ध्ठ	ध्ड	ध्ढ	ध्ण	ध्त	ध्थ	ध्द
न्	न्क	न्ख	न्ग	न्घ	ञ्च	ञ्छ	ञ्ज	ञ्झ	ण्ट	ण्ठ	ण्ड	ण्ढ	ण्ण	न्त	न्थ	न्द
प्	प्क	प्ख	प्ग	प्घ	प्च	प्छ	प्ज	प्झ	प्ट	प्ठ	प्ड	प्ढ	प्ण	प्त	प्थ	प्द
फ्	फ्क	फ्ख	फ्ग	फ्घ	फ्च	फ्छ	फ्ज	फ्झ	फ्ट	फ्ठ	फ्ड	फ्ढ	फ्ण	फ्त	फ्थ	फ्द
ब्	ब्क	ब्ख	ब्ग	ब्घ	ब्च	ब्छ	ब्ज	ब्झ	ब्ट	ब्ठ	ब्ड	ब्ढ	ब्ण	ब्त	ब्थ	ब्द
भ्	भ्क	भ्ख	भ्ग	भ्घ	भ्च	भ्छ	भ्ज	भ्झ	भ्ट	भ्ठ	भ्ड	भ्ढ	भ्ण	भ्त	भ्थ	भ्द
म्	ङ्क	ङ्ख	ङ्ग	ङ्घ	ङ्च	ङ्छ	ङ्ज	ङ्झ	म्ट	म्ठ	म्ड	म्ढ	म्ण	म्त	म्थ	म्द
य्	य्क	य्ख	य्ग	य्घ	य्च	य्छ	य्ज	य्झ	य्ट	य्ठ	य्ड	य्ढ	य्ण	य्त	य्थ	य्द
र्	र्क	र्ख	र्ग	र्घ	र्च	र्छ	र्ज	र्झ	र्ट	र्ठ	र्ड	र्ढ	र्ण	र्त	र्थ	र्द
ल्	ल्क	ल्ख	ल्ग	ल्घ	ल्च	ल्छ	ल्ज	ल्झ	ल्ट	ल्ठ	ल्ड	ल्ढ	ल्ण	ल्त	ल्थ	ल्द
व्	व्क	व्ख	व्ग	व्घ	व्च	व्छ	व्ज	व्झ	व्ट	व्ठ	व्ड	व्ढ	व्ण	व्त	व्थ	व्द
श्	श्क	श्ख	श्ग	श्घ	श्च	श्छ	श्ज	श्झ	श्ट	श्ठ	श्ड	श्ढ	श्ण	श्त	श्थ	श्द
ष्	ष्क	ष्ख	ष्ग	ष्घ	ष्च	ष्छ	ष्ज	ष्झ	ष्ट	ष्ठ	ष्ड	ष्ढ	ष्ण	ष्त	ष्थ	ष्द
स्	स्क	स्ख	स्ग	स्घ	स्च	स्छ	स्ज	स्झ	स्ट	स्ठ	स्ड	स्ढ	स्ण	स्त	स्थ	स्द
ह्	ह्क	ह्ख	ह्ग	ह्घ	ह्च	ह्छ	ह्ज	ह्झ	ह्ट	ह्ठ	ह्ड	ह्ढ	ह्ण	ह्त	ह्थ	ह्द

+	ध	न	प	फ	ब	भ	म	य	र	ल	व	श	ष	स	ह
क्	क्ध	क्न	ग्प	ग्फ	ग्ब	ग्भ	क्म	क्य	क्र	क्ल	क्व	क्श	क्ष	क्स	ख
ख्	ख्ध	ख्न	ख्प	ख्फ	ख्ब	ख्भ	ख्म	ख्य	ख्र	ख्ल	ख्व	ख्श	ख्ष	ख्स	ख्ख
ग्	ग्ध	ग्न	ग्प	ग्फ	ग्ब	ग्भ	ग्म	ग्य	ग्र	ग्ल	ग्व	ग्श	ग्ष	ग्स	घ
घ्	घ्ध	घ्न	घ्प	घ्फ	घ्ब	घ्भ	घ्म	घ्य	घ्र	घ्ल	घ्व	घ्श	घ्ष	घ्स	घ्ह
ङ्	ङ्ध	ङ्न	ङ्प	ङ्फ	ङ्ब	ङ्भ	ङ्म	ङ्य	ङ्र	ङ्ल	ङ्व	ङ्श	ङ्क्ष	ङ्स	ङ्ह
च्	च्ध	च्न	ज्प	ज्फ	च्ब	च्भ	च्म	च्य	च्र	च्ल	च्व	च्श	च्ष	च्त	छ
छ्	छ्ध	छ्न	छ्प	छ्फ	छ्ब	छ्भ	छ्म	छ्य	छ्र	छ्ल	छ्व	छ्श	छ्ष	छ्स	छ्छ
ज्	ज्ध	ज्न	ज्प	ज्फ	ज्ब	ज्भ	ज्म	ज्य	ज्र	ज्ल	ज्व	ज्श	ज्ष	ज्स	ज्झ
झ्	झ्ध	झ्न	झ्प	झ्फ	झ्ब	झ्भ	झ्म	झ्य	झ्र	झ्ल	झ्व	झ्श	झ्ष	झ्स	झ्झ
ञ्	ञ्ध	ञ्न	ञ्प	ञ्फ	ञ्ब	ञ्भ	ञ्म	ञ्य	ञ्र	ञ्ल	ञ्व	ञ्श	ञ्ष	ञ्स	ञ्ह
ट्	ट्ध	ट्ण	ट्प	ट्फ	ट्ब	ट्भ	ट्म	ट्य	ट्र	ट्ल	ट्व	ट्श	ट्ष	ट्स	ठ
ठ्	ठ्ध	ठ्ण	ठ्प	ठ्फ	ठ्ब	ठ्भ	ठ्म	ठ्य	ठ्र	ठ्ल	ठ्व	ठ्श	ठ्ष	ठ्स	ठ्ह
ड्	ड्ध	ड्ण	ड्प	ड्फ	ड्ब	ड्भ	ड्म	ड्य	ड्र	ड्ल	ड्व	ड्श	ड्ष	ड्स	ढ
ढ्	ढ्ध	ढ्ण	ढ्प	ढ्फ	ढ्ब	ढ्भ	ढ्म	ढ्य	ढ्र	ढ्ल	ढ्व	ढ्श	ढ्ष	ढ्स	ढ्ह
ण्	ण्ध	ण्ण	ण्प	ण्फ	ण्बा	ण्भ	ण्म	ण्य	ण्र	ण्ल	ण्व	ण्श	ण्ष	ण्स	ण्ह
त्	द्ध	त्न	त्प	त्फ	द्ब	द्भ	त्म	त्य	त्र	त्ल	त्व	त्श	त्ष	त्स	थ
थ्	थ्ध	थ्न	ध्प	ध्फ	थ्ब	थ्भ	थ्म	थ्य	थ्र	थ्ल	थ्व	थ्श	थ्ष	थ्स	थ्थ
द्	द्ध	द्न	द्प	द्फ	द्ब	द्भ	द्ज	द्झ	द्र	द्ल	द्व	द्श	द्ष	द्स	ध्ह
ध्	ध्ध	ध्न	ध्प	ध्फ	ध्ब	ध्भ	ध्म	ध्य	ध्र	ध्ल	ध्व	ध्श	ध्ष	ध्स	ध्ध
न्	न्ध	न्न	न्प	न्फ	न्ब	न्भ	न्म	न्य	न्र	न्ल	न्व	ञ्श	ञ्ष	न्स	न्ह
प्	प्ध	प्न	प्प	प्फ	प्ब	प्भ	प्म	प्य	प्र	प्ल	प्व	प्श	प्ष	प्स	प्ह
फ्	फ्फ	फ्न	फ्प	फ्फ	फ्ब	फ्भ	फ्म	फ्य	फ्र	फ्ल	फ्ब	फ्श	फ्ष	फ्स	फ्ह
ब्	ब्ध	ब्न	ब्प	ब्फ	ब्ब	ब्भ	ब्म	ब्य	ब्र	ब्ल	ब्व	ब्श	ब्ष	ब्स	भ
भ्	भ्ध	भ्न	भ्प	भ्फ	भ्ब	भ्भ	भ्म	भ्य	भ्र	भ्ल	भ्ब	भ्श	भ्ष	भ्स	भ्ह
म्	म्ध	म्न	म्प	म्फ	म्ब	म्भ	म्म	म्य	म्र	म्ल	म्व	म्श	म्ष	म्स	म्ह
य्	य्ध	य्न	य्प	य्फ	य्ब	य्भ	य्म	य्य	य्र	य्ल	य्व	य्श	य्ष	य्स	य्ह
र्	र्ध	र्न	र्प	र्फ	र्ब	र्भ	र्म	र्य	र्र	र्ल	र्व	र्श	र्ष	र्स	र्ह
ल्	ल्ध	ल्न	ल्प	ल्फ	ल्ब	ल्भ	ल्म	ल्य	ल्र	ल्ल	ल्व	ल्श	ल्ष	ल्स	ल्ह
व्	व्ध	व्न	व्प	व्फ	व्ब	व्भ	व्म	व्य	व्र	व्ल	व्व	व्श	व्ष	व्स	व्ह
श्	श्ध	श्न	श्प	श्फ	श्ब	श्भ	श्म	श्य	श्र	श्ल	श्व	श्श	श्ष	श्स	श्ह
ष्	ष्क	ष्ख	ष्प	ष्फ	ष्ब	ष्भ	ष्म	ष्य	ष्र	ष्ल	ष्व	ष्श	ष्ष	ष्स	ष्थ
स्	स्ध	स्न	स्प	स्फ	स्ब	स्भ	स्म	स्य	स्त्र	स्ल	स्व	स्श	स्ष	स्स	स्ह
ह्	ह्ध	ह्न	ह्प	ह्फ	ह्ब	ह्भ	ह्म	ह्य	ह्र	ह्ल	ह्व	ह्श	ह्ष	ह्स	ह्ह

8.2 RATNAKAR'S CHILDREN SONGS

रत्नाकर के शिशु गीत

EXERCISE 13 : Read the following Hindi Childrens' songs :

1	**गुलाब**	**Gulāb**	**Rose flower**
	लाल गुलाबी सुंदर फूल । डाली के काँटे देते शूल । पत्तों पर हो चाहे धूल । फिर भी लगता सबसे 'कूल' ।।	Lāl gulābī sundar phool, Ḍālī ke kā̃ṭe dete shūl, Pattõ par ho chāhe dhūl, Fir bhī lagatā sab se "Cool."	*A beautiful pink-red rose flower, even if there are thorns on the branch and dust on the leaves, it still is the "Coolest" of all flowersl.*
2	**लड़का**	**Laḍkā**	**Boy**
	सात साल का मैं हूँ बाल । बाल काले गोरे गाल । माँ का प्यारा मैं हूँ लाल । नाम मेरा राधे गोपाल ।।	Sāt sāl kā maĩ hū̃ bāl, Bāl kāle, gore gāl, Mā̃ kā pyārā maĩ hū̃ lāl, Nām merā Radhe-Gopāl.	*I am a seven years old boy. My hair are black and cheeks are fair. I am my mother's dear lad. My name is Radhe-Gopal.*
3	**लड़की**	**Laḍkī**	**Girl**
	सात साल की मैं बाला । नाम मेरा मोती माला । हार गले में हीरों वाला । चमकीला है मैंने डाला ।।	Sāt sāl kī maĩ bālā, Nām merā Moti-Mālā, Hār gale mẽ hīrõ wālā, Chamkīlā hai maĩne ḍālā.	*I am a seven year old girl. My name is Moti-mala. I am wearing a shiny diamond necklace.*
4	**रेल गाड़ी**	**Tail-gāḍī**	**Train**
	छुक छुक चलती गाड़ी रेल । टन्टन् टन्टन् बज गयी बेल। देखो देखो आयी मेल । आना जाना उसका खेल ।।	Chhuk chhuk chaltī gāḍī rel, Ṭan ṭan ṭan ṭan baj gayī bel, Dekho dekho āyī mel, Aanā jānā uskā khel.	*The train goes, "chhook chhook!" The bell rings tan-tan tan-tan. Look! the train has come. Coming and going is its every day game.*
5	**घर**	**Ghar**	**House**
	छोटा सा है मेरा घर । फिर भी लगता है सुंदर । साफ और सुथरा है अंदर । एक दिन ऊपर था बंदर ।।	Chhotā sā hai merā ghar, Fir bhī lagtā hai sundar, Sāf aur suthrā hai andar, Ek din ūpar thā bandar.	*My house is small. Still it looks nice. It is clean and tidy inside. One day a monkey was sitting ovet it.*

6	**बरफ**	**Baraf**	**Ice, snow**
	बाहर है जब गिरती बरफ । सफेद सफेद चारों तरफ ।। बाहर है जब गिरती बरफ । ठंढा ठंढा चारों तरफ ।।	Bāhar hai jab girtī baraf, Safed safed chāro̐ taraf, Bāhar hai jab girtī baraf, Ṭhaṇḍā ṭhaṇḍā chāro̐ taraf.	*When it snows outside, it is white everywhere. When it snows outside, it is cold everywhere.*
7	**टेलीफून**	**Telephūn**	**Telephone**
	टन् टन् घंटी टेलीफोन । हलो! बोल रहा है कौन? ।। मैं हूँ मिस्टर डेवीड जौन । धीमी धीमी मेरी टोन ।।	Ṭan ṭan ghaṇṭī ṭelīphone, Hello! Bol rahā hai kaun? Mai̐ hū̐ Mister David John, Dhīmī dhīmī merī ṭon.	*Telephone bell is ringing, tan tan. Heool! Who is speaking? I am mister Devid John. My tone is slow.*
8	**मेपल लीफ़**	**Mepal līf**	**Maple Leaf**
	कैनेडा का मेपल लीफ । सारे पत्तों में है चीफ ।। जग में उसकी है तारीफ । रंग लाल से सब वाकिफ ।।	Canaḍā kā Maple leaf, Sāre patto̐ me̐ hai chief, Jag me̐ uskī hai tārīf, Raṅg lāl se sab wākif.	*Canada's Maple-leaf, is the cheif of all leaves. The whole world knows it by its red colour, and they love it.*
9	**सिगरेट**	**Sigreṭ**	**Cigarette**
	सिगरेट पीना मना है । कानून ऐसा बना है ।। क्योंकि धोखा घना है । कैंसर का ये तना है ।।	Sigreṭ pīnā manā hai, Kānūn aisā banā hai, Kyo̐ ki dhokhā ghanā hai, Cancer kā ye tanā hai.	*Smoking is prohibited. It is the rule. Because this weed is dangerous and it causes cancer.*
10	**गाना**	**Gānā**	**Song**
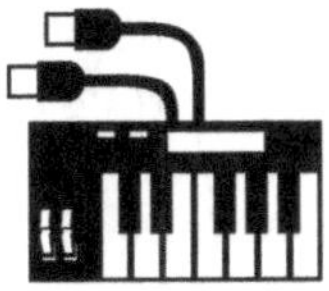	आओ मिलकर गाएँ गाना । सबने गाना जो है जाना ।। मीठा सुर है सबको भाना । उसका आनंद सबने पाना ।।	Aao mil kar gāe̐ gānā, Sab ne gānā jo hai jānā, Mīṭhā sur hai sab kao bhānā, Uskā ānand sab ne pānā.	*Come! Let's sing a song, the one that everyone knows. Everyone will love a sweet voice, they will enjoy it.*
11	**कार**	**Kār**	**Car**
	लाल रंग की मेरी कार । पेट्रोल पीती बारंबार ।। दीये दो हैं, चक्के चार । फिरती लेकर सबका भार ।।	Lāl rang kī merī kār, Petrol pītī bārambār, Dīye do hai̐, chakke chār, Firtī le kar sab kā bhār.	*My car is of red colour. It guzzles gas again and again. It has two lamps and four wheels. It runs around carrying everyone.*

12	**मुर्गी, मुर्गा**	**Murgī, Murgā**	**Hen, Rooster**
	कुकडूँ कुकडूँ मुर्गी बोले । तब सवेरे आँखे खोले ।। अंडे पनीर भटूरे छोले । खाकर मन मामू का डोले ।।	Kukdū̐ kukdū̐ murgā bole, Tab savere ā̐khe khole, aṇḍe panīr bhaṭure chhole, Khā kar māmū kā man ḍole.	*When the rooster crows kaaka-doole-doo! then my uncle opens his eyes in the morning. Eating eggs, chees,chhole and bhature,he becomes happy.*
13	**मोर**	**Mor**	**Peacock**
	किहूँऽ किहूँऽ करके शोर । घूम घूम कर नाचे मोर ।। पंख पसारे जिसकी ओर । उसके चित्त का है ये चोर ।।	Kīhū̐ kīhū̐ kar ke shor, ghūm ghūm kar nāche mor, Paṅkha pasāre jiskī or, Us ke chitt kā hai ye chor.	*The peacock makes keehoo keehoo noise and dances turning round and round. He steals people's heart by spreading his wings towards them.*
14	**तोता**	**Totā**	**Parrot**
	मिट्ठू मियाँ तोता हूँ । हरे रंग का होता हूँ ।। डाल डाल पर जाता हूँ । मीठे फल मैं खाता हूँ ।।	Miṭṭhū Miyā totā hū̐, Hare raṅg kā hotā hū̐, Ḍāl ḍal par jātā hū̐, Mīṭhe fal mai̐ khātā hū̐.	*I am a parrot. My name is Mitthu-Miya. I am of green colour. I go from branch to branch and eat the sweet fruits.*
15	**आम**	**Aam**	**Mango**
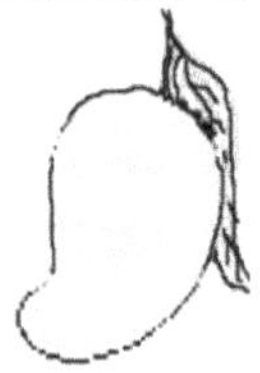	फलों का राजा आम है । भारत उसका धाम है ।। जग में उसका नाम है । ललचाना उसका काम है ।।	Falo̐ kā rājā ām hai. Bhārat us kā dhām hai, Jag me̐ us kā nām hai, Lalchānā us kā kām hai.	*Mango is the king of the fruits. India is its abode. Mango is well known in the whole world. Everyone likes it.*
16	**कुत्ता**	**Kuttā**	**Dog**
	कुत्ते से है डरता चोर । भों भों भों भों करता शोर ।। दाँतों में है उसके जोर । काटके हड्डी ड़ाले तोर ।।	Kutte se hai ḍartā chor, Bho̐ bho̐ bho̐ bho̐ kartā shor, Dā̐to̐ me̐ hai us ke zor, Kāṭke haḍḍī ḍāle toḍ.	*Thief is afraid of a dog. The dog barks bho bho bho bho! His teeth are strong. He can crack your bone with one bite.*

17	**बिल्ली**	**Billī**	**Cat**
	काले रंग की मेरी बिल्ली । उसको अच्छी लगती दिल्ली ।। मोटी मोटी आँखों वाली । बड़े प्यार से मैंने पाली ।।	Kāle rang kī merī billī, Us ko achhī lagtī Dillī, Moṭī moṭī ā̃khō̃ wālī, Baḍe pyār se maĩ ne pālī.	*My cat is black. It loves living in Dehli. It has big eyes. I raised it with great love.*
18	**घोड़ा**	**Ghoḍā**	**Horse**
	भूरे रंग का देखो घोड़ा । भागे ज्यादा, बैठे थोड़ा ।। टप टप करता जब ये दौड़ा । सीना उसका होता चौड़ा ।।	Bhūre rang kā dekho ghoḍā, Bhāge jyādā, baiṭhe thoḍā, Ṭap ṭap kartā jab ye dauḍā, Sīnā uskā hotā chauḍā.	*Look at the gray coloured horse. It runs more and sits less. When he gallops tap tap, his chest grows big with pride.*
19	**शेर**	**Sher**	**Tiger, Lion**
	भागो भागो आया शेर । कोई भी ना करना देर ।। मोटे मोटे उसके पैर । उनके आगे किसकी खैर? ।।	Bhāgo! bhāgo! āyā sher, Koī bhī nā karnā der, Moṭe moṭe uske pair, Un ke āge kis kī khair?	*Run! run! a tiger came. Don't anyone be slow. He has strong paws. No body is safe from him.*
20	**हाथी**	**Hāthī**	**Elephent**
	सबसे भारी होता हाथी । राजाओं का ये है साथी ।। लम्बे लम्बे उसके दाँत । काम में लाए जैसे हाथ ।।	Sab se bhārī hotā hāthī, Rājāō̃ kā ye hai sāthī, Lambe lambe uske dā̃t, Kām mẽ lāye jaise hāth.	*Elephant is the biggest and heaviest of all animals. He is a friend of the kings. He has long teeth, which he uses like his hands.*
21	**गाय**	**Gāy**	**Cow**
	'गाय हमारी माता है' । इसका जो नर ज्ञाता है ।। पुण्य बहुत वह पाता है । और स्वर्ग में जाता है ।।	Gāy hamārī mātā hai, Is kā jo nar gyātā hai, Puṇya bahut vah pātā hai, Aur swarg mẽ jātā hai.	*Cow is our mother. He who knows this, burns his sins and goes to heaven.*

22	**माँ**	**Mā̃**	**Mother**
	सबसे प्यारी होती माँ । सबसे न्यारी होती माँ ।। कोई कहता उसको 'अम्मा' । कोई 'मम्मी' कोई 'मामा' ।।	Sab se pyārī hotī mā̃, Sab se nyārī hotī mā̃, Koī kahatā us ko ammā, Koī mummy, koī māmā.	*Mother is most dear of all. Mother is different from all. Some call her Amma, some call Mummy and some call her Mama*
23	**माउस**	**Māus**	**Mouse**
	कम्प्यूटर का माउस है । इसके विना न हाउस है ।। बिजली पर ये चलता है । माउस-पैड पर पलता है ।।	Computer kā mouse hai, Us ke binā na Hāus hai, Bijlī par ye chaltā hai, Mouse Pad par ye paltā hai.	*This is a computer mouse. Now-a days, there is no house without it. It runs on electricity and lives on a mouse-pad.*
24	**चोर**	**Chor**	**Thief**
	देखो देखो आया चोर । पकड़ो पकड़ो मच गया शोर ।। छुपा हुआ है उधर की ओर । बांधें उसको लाओ डोर ।।	Dekho dekho āyā chor, Pakḍo pakḍo mach gayā shor, Chhupā huā hai udhar kī or, Bāndhẽ us ko, lāo ḍor.	*Oh! Look, there is a thief. Everyone is shouting, "catch him," "catch him." He is hiding on that side. Bring a rope and let's tie him up.*
25	**मिरची**	**Mirchī**	**Chilli**
	ये मिरची हरी है । तीखेपन से भरी है । फिर भी सबको प्यारी है । अजीब सी तरकारी है ।।	Ye mirchī harī hai. Tīkhe-pan se bharī hai, Fir bhī sab ko pyārī hai, Ajīb sī tarkārī hai.	*This chilli is green. It is very hot. Even though it is very hot, people love it. My goodness! it is a strange vegetable.*
26	**किताब**	**Kitāb**	**Book**
	बच्चों रखना ध्यान है । किताब देती ज्ञान है ।। ज्ञान से मिलता मान है । जिसमें सच्ची शान है ।	Bachchõ rakhnā dhyān hai, Kitāb detī gyān hai, Gyān se miltā mān hai, Jis me scchchī shān hai.	*Children! remember, the book gives you knowledge. The knowledge gives you respect. With respect comes honour.*

27	**जन्म दिन**	**Janma-din**	**Birthday**
	जनम दिन फिर आया है । हर कोई तोहफा लाया है ।। 'हैपी बर्थ डे' भी गाया है । सब कुछ मन को भाया है ।।	Janam din fir āyā hai, Har koī tohfā lāyā hai, "Happy Birthday" bhī gāyā hai, Sab kuchh man ko bhāyā hai.	*Birthday has come again. Everyone brought a gift. They sang "Happy Birth Day to You." Everything pleased my mind.*
28	**चिठ्ठी**	**Chiṭhṭhī**	**Letter**
	राम की चिठ्ठी आयी है । खुश खबरी ये लायी है ।। लिखा है कल सगाई है । सुंदर मिली लुगाई है ।।	Rām kī chiṭṭhī āyī hai, Khush khabrī ye lāyī hai, Likhā hai kal sagāī hai, Sundar milī lugāī hai.	*Ram's letter has come. It has brought a good news. It says tomorrow is his wedding. He got a beautiful bride.*
29	**ताला**	**MTālā**	**Lock**
	ये जो दिखता काला है । गोल आकार का ताला है ।। बिना चाबी से खुला है । क्योंकि नंबर वाला है ।।	Ye jo dikhtā kālā hai, Gol ākār kā tālā hai, Binā chābī se khulā hai, Kyo̐ kī number wālā hai.	*The thing in black colour in this picture is a lock. It is round in shape. It opens without a key, because it is a number lock.*
30	**सूरज**	**Sūraj**	**Sun**
	सूरज दिन का तारा है । तेज किरण की धारा है ।। चमकाता जग सारा है । जीवन दाता न्यारा है ।।	Sūraj din kā tārā hai, Tez kiraṇ kī dhārā hai, Chamkātā jag sārā hai, Jīvan dātā nyārā hai.	*The Sun is the star of the day-time. It's light is a flow of bright powerful rays. It shines the whole world. It is a unique life giver.*
31	**वर्षा, बारिश**	**Varshā, bārish**	**Rain**
	वर्षा नभ से गिरती है । नदियों में जल भरती है ।। हरी रंगाती धरती है । जीवन सुखमय करती है ।।	Varṣhā nabh se girtī hai, Nadiyao̐ me̐ jal bhartī hai, Harī raṅgātī dhartī hai, Jīvan sukh-may kartī hai.	*Rain falls from the sky. It fills up the rivers. It paints the earth green with vegetation, and fills life with happiness.*

32	**चाँद**	**Chā̐nd**	**Moon**
	चाँद रात में आता है । समय सुहाना लाता है ।। सबका दिल बहलाता है । सबके मन को भाता है ।।	Chānd gagan me̐ ātā hai, Samay suhānā lātā hai, Sab kā dil bahalātā hai, Sab ke man ko bhātā hai.	*Moon shines at night. It brings a pleasent time. It amuses everyone's mind. Everyone likes it.*
33	**बच्चा**	**Bachachā**	**Baby**
	मुन्ना राजा सोया है । सारी रात ये रोया है ।। कंबल में लिपटा होया है । अब सपनों में खोया है ।।	Munnā rājā soyā hai, Sārī rāt ye royā hai, Kambal me̐ lipṭā hoyā hai, Ab sapno̐ me̐ khoyā hai.	*The baby is sleeping. He cried all night. Now he is wrapped up in a blanket and he is lost in his sweet dreams.*
34	**परछाई**	**Parachhāī**	**Shadow**
	उंगलियाँ यूं लगाई हैं । तसवीर फिर बनाई है ।। ये केवल परछाई है । सबके मन को भाई है ।।	Ungliyā̐ yū̐ lagāī hai̐, Tasvīr fir banāī hai, Ye keval parchhāī hai, Sab ke man ko bhāī hai.	*Fingers are arranged in such a fashion, that they formed a figure on the wall. It is only a shadow, but it pleased everyone.*
35	**जादू**	**Jadū**	**Magic**
	देखो हाथ सफाई है । ये जादू का भाई है ।। कला ये जिसने पाई है । उसने जनता बहलाई है ।।	Dekho hāth safāī hai, Ye jādū kā bhāī hai, Kalā ye jisne pāyī hai, Usne janatā bahalāyī hai.	*See this hand tric. It is a younger brother of a magic. One who has learned this art, he has entertained people.*
36	**आलू**	**Aalū**	**Potato**
	सब्जियों मे आलू है । जैसा बिहारी लालू है ।। गोभी मटर में डालूं मैं । रोटी लेकर खालूं मैं ।।	Sabziyo̐ me̐ ālū hai, Jaisā Bihārī Lālū hai, Gobhī maṭar me̐ ḍālū̐ mai̐, Roṭī le kar khālū̐ mai̐.	*Potato in the vegetables, is like the Lalu of the Bihar. I may put potato in cauliflower curry and eat it with my roti.*

37	**मछली**	**Machalī**	**Fish**
	मछली लाल पीली है । धारें उस पर नीली हैं ।। गोल आँखें काली है । जल में रहने वाली है ।।	Machhalī lāl pīlī hai, Dhare̐ us par nīlī hai̐, Gol ā̐khe̐ kālī hai̐, Jal me̐ rahane wālī hai.	*This fish is red and yellow. It has blue stripes over it. It's eyes are round and black. The fish lives in water.*
38	**आँख**	**ā̐nkh**	**Eye**
	आंखे हमको देकर दृष्टि । दिखलाती हैं सारी सृष्टि ।। जल हिम फूलों की वृष्टि । देखो देती मन को तुष्टि ।।	Aā̐nkhe̐ ham ko detī driṣhṭi, Dikhalātī hai sārī sriṣhṭi, Jal, him, fūlo̐ kī vriṣhṭi, Dekho man ko detī tuṣhṭi.	*Eyes give us vision, They show us the whole universe. They show us the showers of rain, snow and flowers, And give happiness to our mind.*
39	**तितली**	**Titlī**	**Butterfly**
	फूल पर बैठी तितली है । टांगे उसकी पतली हैं ।। रंग बिरंगों वाली है । आंखे उसकी काली हैं ।।	Fūl par baiṭhī titlī hai, Ṭā̐nge̐ us kī patlī hai̐, Rang birango̐ wālī hai, Aā̐nkhe̐ uskī kālī hai̐.	*Butterfly is sitting on a flower. It has skiny legs. It is colourful. It's eyes are bleck.*
40	**पैसा**	**Paisā**	**Money**
	पैसा जिसके पास है । हवा में उसका वास है ।। क्योंकि उसको भास है । कि दुनिया उसकी दास है ।।	Paisā jis ke pās hai, Gagan me̐ us kā vās hai, Kyo̐ ki us ko bhās hai, Ki duniyā us kī dās hai.	*One who has money, he lives in the heaven. Because, he carries a notion that, the whole world is at his feet.*
41	**मंदिर**	**Mandir**	**Temple**
	बहुत पुराना मंदर है । शिव की मूर्ति अंदर है । भगत गा रहे सुंदर हैं । गायत्री का मंतर है ।।	Bahut purāna mandar hai, Mūrti Shiva kī andar hai, Bhagat gā rahe sundar hai̐, Gāyatrī kā mantar hai.	*It is an old temple. Inside the temple, there is Shiva's image. The devotees are singing the lovely Gayatri chant.*

LESSON 9
नौवाँ पाठ

INTRODUCTION TO SANDHI
COMPOUNDING OF VOWELS
स्वर संधि

When any two vowels come together,
they are compounded into one single long vowel
with the rules, shown in short, as follows :

	1st vowel	+	2nd vowel	= the Result
1	अ, आ	+	अ, आ	आ
	अ, आ	+	इ, ई	ए
	अ, आ	+	उ, ऊ	ओ
	अ, आ	+	ऋ	अर्
	अ, आ	+	ए, ऐ	ऐ
	अ, आ	+	ओ, औ	औ
2	इ, ई	+	अ,आ,उ,ऊ,ए,ऐ,ओ,औ	य,या,यु,यू,ये,यै,यो,यौ
	इ, ई	+	इ,ई	ई,ई
3	उ, ऊ	+	अ,आ,इ,ई,ए,ऐ,ओ,औ	व,वा,वि,वी,वे,वै,वो,वौ
	उ, ऊ	+	उ, ऊ	ऊ, ऊ
4	ए	+	अ,आ,इ,ई,उ,ऊ,ए,ऐ,ओ,औ	अय् + अ,आ,इ....औ
5	ऐ	+	अ,आ,इ,ई,उ,ऊ,ए,ऐ,ओ,औ	आय् + अ,आ,इ,ई,उ,ऊ,ए,ऐ,ओ,औ
	ओ	+	अ,आ,इ,ई,उ,ऊ,ए,ऐ,ओ,औ	अव् + अ,आ,इ,ई,उ,ऊ,ए,ऐ,ओ,औ
	औ	+	अ,आ,इ,ई,उ,ऊ,ए,ऐ,ओ,औ	आव् + अ,आ,इ,ई,उ,ऊ,ए,ऐ,ओ,औ

LESSON 10
दसवाँ पाठ

10.1 INTRODUCTION TO THE HINDI NUMERALS
हिंदी अंक

0	shūnya	0	शून्य	
1	ek	१	एक	One book. *ek kitāb* एक किताब।
2	do	२	दो	Two books. *dok kitābeँ* दो किताबें।
3	tīn	३	तीन	Three books. *tīn kitābeँ* तीन किताबें।
4	chār	४	चार	
5	pāñch	५	पाँच	
6	chhah	६	छह	
7	sāt	७	सात	
8	āṭh	८	आठ	
9	nau	९	नौ	
10	das	१०	दस	

EXERCISE 14 :

(1) Read the numbers in Hindī :
1 7 9 4 0 3 2 8 5 6

(2) Read the following Hindī numerals :
७ ४ १ ९ ६ 0 ५ ३ ८ २

(3) Read and Write the following Hindī numerals :
चार, सात, नौ, एक, शून्य, छह, आठ, पाँच, दो, दस

ANNOUNCEMENT : With the scientific and easy to follow tools given in this book, **just by mastering the use of tables 18, 23 and 25, you can start making and speaking your own sentences quickly and with confidence**.

10.2

COUNTING TO ONE HUNDRED

11 gyārah	ग्यारह	12 bārah	बारह	57 sattāvan	सत्तावन	58 aṭṭhāvan	अट्ठावन
13 terah	तेरह	14 chaudah	चौदह	59 unasaṭh	उनसठ	60 sāṭh	साठ
15 pandrah	पंद्रह	16 solah	सोलह	61 ikasaṭh	इकसठ	62 bāsaṭh	बासठ
17 satrah	सत्रह	18 aṭhārah	अठारह	63 tresaṭh	त्रेसठ	64 chauṅsaṭh	चौंसठ
19 unnīs	उन्नीस	20 bīs	बीस	65 paiṅsaṭh	पैंसठ	66 chhiyāsaṭh	छियासठ
21 ikkīs	इक्कीस	22 bāīs	बाईस	67 saḍasaṭh	सड़सठ	68 aḍasath	अड़सठ
23 teīs	तेईस	24 chaubīs	चौबीस	69 unahattar	उनहत्तर	70 sattar	सत्तर
25 pachchīs	पच्चीस	26 chhabbīs	छब्बीस	71 ikahattar	इकहत्तर	72 bahattar	बहत्तर
27 sattāīs	सत्ताईस	28 aṭṭhāīs	अट्ठाईस	73 tihattar	तिहत्तर	74 chauhattar	चौहत्तर
29 unatīs	उनतीस	30 tīs	तीस	75 pachahattar	पचहत्तर	76 chhihattar	छिहत्तर
31 ikatīs	इकतीस	32 battīs	बत्तीस	77 satahattar	सतहत्तर	78 aṭhahattar	अठहत्तर
33 taĩtīs	तैंतीस	34 chaũtīs	चौंतीस	79 unyāsī	उन्यासी	80 assī	अस्सी
35 paĩtīs	पैंतीस	36 chhattīs	छत्तीस	81 ikyāsī	इक्यासी	82 bayāsī	बयासी
37 saintīs	सैंतीस	38 aṭhattīs	अठत्तीस	83 tirāsī	तिरासी	84 chaurāsī	चौरासी
39 untālīs	उनतालीस	40 chālīs	चालीस	85 pachāsī	पचासी	86 chhiyāsī	छियासी
41 iktālīs	इकतालीस	42 bayālīs	बयालीस	87 sattāsī	सत्तासी	88 aṭṭhāsī	अट्ठासी
43 taiṅtālīs	तैंतालीस	44 chauvālīs	चौवालीस	89 nāvāsī	नवासी	90 nabbe	नब्बे
45 paĩtālīs	पैंतालीस	46 chhiyālīs	छियालीस	91 ikyānabe	इक्यानबे	92 bānabe	बानबे
47 saĩtālīs	सैंतालीस	48 aḍatālīs	अड़तालीस	93 tirānabe	तिरानबे	94 chaurānabe	चौरानबे
49 unachās	उनचास	50 pachās	पचास	95 pañchānabe	पन्चानबे	96 chhiyānabe	छियानबे
51 ikyāvan	इक्यावन	52 bāvan	बावन	97 sattānabe	सत्तानबे	98 aṭṭhānabe	अट्ठानबे
53 trepan	त्रेपन	54 chauwan	चौवन	99 ninyānabe	निन्यानबे	100 sau	सौ
55 pachapan	पचपन	56 chhappan	छप्पन				

HINDI NUMERALS:

०, १, २, ३, ४, ५, ६, ७, ८, ९, १०; ११, १२, १३, १४, १५, १६, १७, १८, १९, २०; २१, २२, २३, २४, २५, २६, २७, २८, २९, ३०; ३१, ३२, ३३, ३४, ३५, ३६, ३७, ३८, ३९, ४०; ४१, ४२, ४३, ४४, ४५, ४६, ४७, ४८, ४९, ५०; ५१, ५२, ५३, ५४, ५५, ५६, ५७, ५८, ५९, ६०; ६१, ६२, ६३, ६४, ६५, ६६, ६७, ६८, ६९, ७०; ७१, ७२, ७३, ७४, ७५, ७६, ७७, ७८, ७९, ८०; ८१, ८२, ८३, ८४, ८५, ८६, ८७, ८८, ८९, ९०; ९१, ९२, ९३, ९४, ९५, ९६, ९७, ९८, ९९, १००.

HINDI NUMERALS FROM 0 TO 99

	0	1	2	3	4	5	6	7	8	9
0	०	१	२	३	४	५	६	७	८	९
1	१०	११	१२	१३	१४	१५	१६	१७	१८	१९
2	२०	२१	२२	२३	२४	२५	२६	२७	२८	२९
3	३०	३१	३२	३३	३४	३५	३६	३७	३८	३९
4	४०	४१	४२	४३	४४	४५	४६	४७	४८	४९
5	५०	५१	५२	५३	५४	५५	५६	५७	५८	५९
6	६०	६१	६२	६३	६४	६५	६६	६७	६८	६९
7	७०	७१	७२	७३	७४	७५	७६	७७	७८	७९
8	८०	८१	८२	८३	८४	८५	८६	८७	८८	८९
9	९०	९१	९२	९३	९४	९५	९६	९७	९८	९९

LESSON 11

ग्यारहवाँ पाठ

MAKING YOUR OWN HINDI SENTENCES

11.1 MAKING SIMPLE SENTENCES - about a 'Present' event, with 'IS' (*hai* है)

Key words : I = मैं *(maĩ),* am = हूँ *(hū̃),* is = है *(hai),* are = हैं *(haĩ),* name = *nām* नाम।

my = मेरा *(merā),* your = आपका *(āp-kā),* his/her = उसका *(us-kā),* their = उनका *(un-kā)*

I	मैं *(maĩ)*	am	हूँ *(hū̃)*	I am	मैं हूँ	*maĩ hū̃*
You	आप *(āp)*	are	हैं *(haĩ)*	You are	आप हैं	*āp haĩ*
He, she, that	वह *(vah)*	is	है *(hai)*	He, she, that is	वह है	*vah hai*
This, it	यह *(yah)*	are	है *(hai)*	This, it is	यह है	*yah hai*

NOTE: The ँ sign is just a slight nasal tone added to the syllable below that ँ

TABLE 1 : Speaking a Present Event

	Subject (colloquial)	am	is	are (colloquial)
	I मैं *(maĩ)*	हूँ *(hū̃)*		
◦	He, that वह *(vah)* वो *(vo)*		है *(hai)*	
◦	She, that वह *(vah)* वो *(vo)*		है *(hai)*	
*	We हम *(ham)*			हैं *(haĩ)*
*	You आप *(āp)* Respect, formal			हैं *(haĩ)* हो *(ho)*
◦	You तुम *(tum)* Equal			हो *(ho)*
◦	You तू *(tū)* Informal, low			है *(hai)*
*	They वे *(ve)* वो *(vo)*			हैं *(haĩ)*
*	These ये *(ye)*			हैं *(haĩ)*

NOTE : **The above table shows that :**

(i) A Present Event is shown by suffix hū̃, hai, ho or haĩ (हूँ, है, हैं) = *h* + ū̃, *h* + ai, *h* + aĩ

(ii) In the suffixes hū̃, hai, ho, haĩ (हूँ, है, हो, हैं), the letter *'h'* (ह) stands for a 'Present' tense

(iii) letter *'ū̃'* (ऊँ) stands for 'first' person ◦singular subject 'I' (*h* + *ū̃* = *hū̃* ह + ऊँ = हूँ)

(iv) letter *'ai'* (ऐ) shows a second or third person ◦singular subject (you, he, she)

(*h + ai = hai* ह + ऐ = है)

(v) letter *'aĩ'* (ऐं) stands for all 'plural' *subjects. (*h + aĩ = haĩ* ह + ऐं = हैं)

TABLE 1A : Present Tense Suffixes SUMMARY

	Subject	Suffix	
◦	I	हूँ *(hũ)*	
◦	He/she	है *(hai)*	
*	We	हैं *(haĩ)*	
*	You *(āp)*	हैं *(haĩ)*	तुम हो *tum ho;* तू है *tū haĩ*
*	They	हैं *(haĩ)*	

Masuline			Feminine		
I am a boy	मैं लड़का हूँ	*maĩ laḍkā hũ*	I am a girl	मैं लड़की हूँ	*maĩ laḍkī hũ*
You are a boy	आप लड़का हैं	*āp laḍkā haĩ*	You are a girl	आप लड़की हैं	*āp laḍkī haĩ*
He, that is a boy	वह लड़का है	*vah laḍkā hai*	She, that is a girl	वह लड़की है	*vah laḍkī hai*
This is a boy	यह लड़का है	*yah laḍkā hai*	This is a girl	यह लड़की है	*yah laḍkī hai*

NOTE : Popular and difficult English words **may be used in Hindī** as if they are Hindī words.

EXERCISE 15 : Translate the English sentences into Hindī (Answers are given for help)

1. I am a man. *maĩ ādamī hũ.* मैं आदमी हूँ। I am a woman. *maĩ aurat hũ.* मैं औरत हूँ।
2. I am a dentist. *maĩ dentist hũ.* मैं *dentist* हूँ। I am a judge. *maĩ judge hũ.* मैं जज हूँ।
3. I am a brain surgeon. *maĩ brain surgeon hũ.* मैं *brain surgeon* हूँ।
4. I am taxi driver. *maĩ taxi driver hũ* मैं taxi driver हूँ। It is good. *yah achhā hai* यह अच्छा है।
5. I am an income-tax officer. *maĩ income-tax officer hũ.* मैं income-tax officer हूँ।
6. I am a traffic inspector. *maĩ traffic inspector hũ.* मैं traffic inspector हूँ।
7. She is a microbiologist. *vah microbiologist hai.* वह microbiologist है।
8. He is a conductor. *vah conductor hai.* वह conductor है। **My name is- *merā nām* मेरा नाम– है।**
9. Rāma is a tennis player. *Rāma tennīs khilāḍī hai.* राम टेनिस् खिलाड़ी है।
10. You are a poet. *āp kavi haĩ.* आप कवि हैं। I am alright (ok). *maĩ ṭhīk hũ.* मैं ठीक हूँ।

11.2 USING HINDI PLURAL WORDS

RATNAKAR'S FIRST THREE NOBLE TRUTHS : (Singular to Plural)

FIRST : If the word is Masculine ending in ā (आ), the ā (आ) changes to e (ए) in plural.

e.g. singular m◦ Boy लड़का *laḍkā* → plural m◦ Boys लड़के *laḍke*

SECOND: If the word is Feminine ans ends in a consonant or vowel ā (आ), then ẽ (एँ) is added to make it plural. e.g. singular f◦ Book किताब *kitāb* → plural f◦ Books किताबें *kitābẽ*

THIRD : If the word is Feminine ending in ī (ई), the ī (ई) changes to iyā̃ (इयाँ) in plural.

e.g. singular f◦ Girl लड़की *laḍkī* → plural f◦ Girls लड़कियाँ *laḍkiyā̃*

Dog (m◦) कुत्ता *(kuttā)* → Dogs कुत्ते *(kutte)*, Cat (f◦) बिल्ली (billī) → Cats बिल्लियाँ *(billiyā̃)*,

Car (f◦) गाड़ी *(gāḍī)* → Cars गाड़ियाँ *(gāḍiyā̃)*, *House (m◦) घर (ghar) → Houses घर *(ghar)*,

Thing (f◦) चीज *(chīz)* → Things चीजें *(chīzẽ)*, Cow (f◦) गाय (gāy) → Cows गाएँ *(gāẽ)*,

SINGULAR				PLURAL			
I	**मैं *(maĩ)***	**am**	**हूँ *(hũ)***	**We**	**हम *(ham)***	**are**	**हैं *(haĩ)***
You	**आप *(āp)***	**are**	**हैं *(haĩ)***	**You**	**आप *(āp)***	**are**	**हैं *(haĩ)***
He, she, that	**वह *(vah)***	**is**	**है *(hai)***	**They**	**वे *(ve)***	**are**	**हैं *(haĩ)***
This, it	**यह *(yah)***	**are**	**है *(hai)***	**These**	**ये *(ye)***	**are**	**हैं *(haĩ)***
I am	मैं हूँ	*maĩ hũ*		We are	हम हैं	*ham haĩ*	
You are	आप हैं	*āp haĩ*		You are	आप हैं	*āp haĩ*	
He, she, that is	वह है	*vah hai*		They are	वे हैं	*ve haĩ*	
This, it is	यह है	*yah hai*		These are	ये हैं	*ye haĩ*	

I am a boy	**मैं लड़का हूँ**	***maĩ laḍkā hũ***	**We are boys**	**हम लड़के हैं**	***ham laḍke haĩ***
You are a boy	**आप लड़का हैं**	***āp laḍkā haĩ***	**You are boys**	**आप लड़के हैं**	***āp laḍke haĩ***
He is a boy	**वह लड़का है**	***vah laḍkā hai***	**They are boys**	**वे लड़के हैं**	***ve laḍke haĩ***
This is a boy	**यह लड़का है**	***yah laḍkā hai***	**These are boys**	**ये लड़के हैं**	***ye laḍke haĩ***
I am a girl	मैं लड़की हूँ	*maĩ laḍkī hũ*	We are girls	हम लड़कियाँ हैं	*ham laḍkiyā̃ haĩ*
You are a girl	आप लड़की हैं	*āp laḍkī haĩ*	You are girls	आप लड़कियाँ हैं	*āp laḍkiyā̃ haĩ*
She is a girl	वह लड़की है	*vah laḍkī hai*	They are girls	वे लड़कियाँ हैं	*ve laḍkiyā̃ haĩ*
This is a girl	यह लड़की है	*yah laḍkī hai*	These are girls	ये लड़कियाँ हैं	*ye laḍkiyā̃ haĩ*

EXERCISE 16 : Translate the English sentences into Hindī (Answers are given for help)

1. We are men. *ham ādamī haĩ.* हम आदमी हैं। We are women. *ham auratẽ haĩ.* हम औरतें हैं।
2. This is a house. *yah ghar hai.* यह घर है। Those are houses. *ve ghar haĩ.* वे घर हैं।
3. This is a dog. *yah kuttā hai.* यह कुत्ता है। Those are dogs. *ve kutte haĩ.* वे कुत्ते हैं।
4. That is a cat. *vah billī hai.* वह बिल्ली है। These are cats. *ye billiyā̃ haĩ.* ये बिल्लियाँ हैं।
5. You are a painter. (*āp painter haĩ.* आप पेन्टर हैं)
6. These are Hindī books. (*ye Hindī kitābẽ haĩ.* ये हिंदी किताबें हैं)
7. This is a computer. (*yah computer hai.* यह computer है)
8. Those are red cars. (*ve lāl kārẽ haĩ. ve lāl gādiyā̃ haĩ.* वे लाल कारें हैं, वे लाल गाड़ियाँ हैं)
9. Those cars are red. (*ve kārẽ lāl haĩ. ve gādiyā̃ lāl haĩ.* वे कारें लाल हैं, वे गाड़ियाँ लाल हैं)
10. Rāma is a teacher. (*Rāma guruji hai.* राम गुरुजी है)
11. He is a Canadian. (*vah Canadian hai.* वह कनेडियन है)
12. She is Indian. (*vah Bhāratiya hai.* वह भारतीय है). You are American. (*āp Amrican haĩ.* आप अमरीकन हैं). They are Chinese. (*ve Chīnī haĩ.* वे चीनी हैं).

11.3 SPEAKING A PAST EVENT - WITH 'WAS' (था)

Key words : Here = *yahā̃* यहाँ। There = *vahā̃* वहाँ। Where? = *kahā̃?* कहाँ?

Rich = *amīr* अमीर। Poor = *garīb* गरीब। Do not = मत। Up to = *tak* तक ।

TABLE 2 : Speaking a Past Event

	Subject	was m◦	was f◦	were m◦	were f◦
	I मैं *(maĩ)*	था *(thā)*	थी (thī)		
◦	He वह *(vah)*	था *(thā)*			
◦	She वह *(vah)*	थी *(thī)*			
*	We हम *(ham)*			थे *(the)*	थीं *(thī̃)*
*	You आप *(āp)*			थे *(the)*	थीं *(thī̃)*
◦	You तुम *(tum)*			थे *(the)*	थी *(thī)*
◦	You तू *(tū)*			था *(thā)*	थी (thī)
*	They वे *(ve)*			थे *(the)*	थीं *(thī̃)*

NOTE : The above table shoes that :

(i) A Past Event is shown by a suffixs *thā, thī, the* or *thī̃* (था थी थे थीं) = *th*+ā, *th*+e, *th*+ī, th+ī̃

(ii) In these suffixes the letter *'th'* (थ) stands for a 'Past' tense

(iii) letter *'ā'* (आ) stands for masculine gender, singular subject (I, you, he)

(iv) letter *'ī'* (ई) shows a feminine singular subject (I, she)

(v) letter *'e'* (एं) stands for masculine plural subject (we, you, they)

(vi) letter *'ī̃'* (ईं) stands for feminine plural subject (we, you, they)

Masculine subject :

I was	मैं था	*maĩ thā*	We were	हम थे	*ham the*
You were	आप थे	*āp the*	You were	आप थे	*āp the*
He, that was	वह था	*vah thā*	They were	वे थे	*ve the*
This, it was	यह था	*yah thā*	These were	ये थे	*ye the*

I was here	मैं यहाँ था	*maĩ yahā̃ thā*	We were here	हम यहाँ थे	*ham yahā̃ the*
You were here	आप यहाँ थे	*āp yahā̃ the*	You were here	आप यहाँ थे	*āp yahā̃ the*
He was here	वह यहाँ था	*vah yahā̃ thā*	They were here	वे यहाँ थे	*ve yahā̃ the*
It was here	यह यहाँ था	*yah yahā̃ thā*	These were here	ये यहाँ थे	*ye yahā̃ the*

I was rich	मैं अमीर था	*maĩ amīr thā*	We were rich	हम अमीर थे	*ham amīr the*
You were rich	आप अमीर थे	*āp amīr the*	You were rich	आप अमीर थे	*āp amīr the*
He was rich	वह अमीर था	*vah amīr thā*	They were rich	वे अमीर थे	*ve amīr the*

Feminine subject :

I was	मैं थी	*maĩ thī*	We were	हम थीं	*ham thī̃*
You were	आप थीं	*āp thī̃*	You were	आप थीं	*āp thī̃*
She was	वह थी	*vah thī*	They were	वे थीं	*ve thī̃*

I was here	मैं यहाँ थी	*maĩ yahā̃ thī*	We were here	हम यहाँ थीं	*ham yahā̃ thī̃*
You were here	आप यहाँ थीं	*āp yahā̃ thī̃*	You were here	आप यहाँ थीं	*āp yahā̃ thī̃*
She was here	वह यहाँ थी	*vah yahā̃ thī*	They were here	वे यहाँ थीं	*yahā̃ thī̃*

I was rich	मैं अमीर थी	*maĩ amīr thī*	We were rich	हम अमीर थीं	*ham amīr thī̃*
You were rich	आप अमीर थीं	*āp amīr thī̃*	You were rich	आप अमीर थीं	*āp amīr thī̃*
She was rich	वह अमीर थी	*vah amīr thī*	They were rich	वे अमीर थीं	*ve amīr thī̃*

TABLE 2A : Past Tense Suffixes SUMMARY

	Subject	Suffix M◦	Suffix F◦
◦	I	था *(thā)*	थी *(thī)*
◦	He/she	था *(thā)*	थी *(thī)*
*	We	थे *(the)*	थी *(thī)*, थीं *(thī̃)*
*	You *(āp)*	थे *(the)*	थी *(thī)*, थीं *(thī̃)*
*	They	थे *(the)*	थी *(thī)*, थीं *(thī̃)*

EXERCISE 17 : Translate the English sentences into Hindī (Answers are given for help)

Key Words : Not = *nahī̃* नहीं। And = *aur* और। Or = *yā* या। Also = *bhī* भी। Only = *hī* ही।

1. I was an engineer. *main engineer thā.* मैं engineer था।
2. She was dentist. *vah dentist thī.* वह dentist थी। Where was she? *vah kahā̃ thī.* वह कहाँ थी।
3. He was a thief. *vah chor thā.* वह चोर था। They were thieves. *ve chor the.* वे चोर थे।
4. You were there. *āp vahā̃ the.* आप वहाँ थे।
5. Anitā is a chemical engineer. *Anitā chemical engineer hai.* अनिता केमिकल इंजिनियर है।

TABLE 3 : SUMMARY : What we learned so far, the 'cumulative learning'

Subject	am	is	are	was m◦	was f◦	were m◦	were f◦
1. I मैं *(maĩ)*	हूँ *(hū̃)*			था *(thā)*	थी (thī)		
2. He वह *(vah)*		है *(hai)*		था *(thā)*			
3. She वह *(vah)*		है *(hai)*		थी *(thī)*			
4. We हम *(ham)*			हैं *(haĩ)*			थे *(the)*	थीं *(thī̃)*
5. You आप *(āp)*			हैं *(haĩ)*			थे *(the)*	थीं *(thī̃)*
6. You तुम *(tum)*			हो *(ho)*			थे *(the)*	थी *(thi)*
7. You तू *(tū)*			हैं *(haĩ)*			था *(thā)*	थी *(thi)*
8. They वे *(ve)*			हैं *(haĩ)*			थे *(the)*	थीं *(thī̃)*

REVIEW : The above table shows that :

(i) A Present Event is shown by suffix hŭ̐, hai, ho or haĭ̐ (हूँ, है, हो, हैं) = *h* + ŭ̐, *h* + ai, *h* + aĭ̐

(ii) In the suffixes hŭ̐, hai, ho, haĭ̐ (हूँ, है, हो, हैं), the letter *'h'* (ह) stands for a 'Present' tense

(iii) letter *'ŭ̐'* (ऊँ) stands for 'first' person singular subject 'I'

(iv) letter *'ai'* (ऐ) shows a second or third person singular subject (you, he, she)

(v) letter *'aĭ̐'* (ऐं) stands for the 'plural' subjects.

(vi) Past Event is shown by a suffixs *thā, thī, the* or *thĭ̐* (था थी थे थीं) = *th*+ā, *th*+e, *th*+ī, th+ĭ̐

(vii) In these suffixes the letter *'th'* (थ) stands for a 'Past' tense

(viii) letter *'ā'* (आ) stands for masculine gender, singular subject (I, you, he)

(ix) letter *'ī'* (ई) shows a feminine singular subject (I, she)

(x) letter *'e'* (एं) stands for masculine plural subject (we, you, they)

(xi) letter *'ĭ̐'* (ईं) stands for feminine plural subject (we, you, they)

EXERCISE 18 : Read the Indian National Anthem.

Indian National Anthem

भारत का राष्ट्रगीत

जन गण मन अधिनायक जय हे! ।
भारत-भाग्य-विधाता ।।
पंजाब सिंध गुजरात मराठा ।
द्राविड उत्कल वंगा ।।
विंध्य हिमाचल यमुना गंगा ।
उच्छल जलधि तरंगा ।।
तव शुभ नामे जागे ।
तव शुभ आशिष मागे ।
गाहे तव जय गाथा ।।
जन गण मंगल दायक जय हे! ।
भारत-भाग्य-विधाता ।।
जय हे! जय हे! जय हे! ।
जय! जय! जय। जय हे! ।।

LESSON 12

TABLE 4 : HINDI PICTORIAL DICTIONARY

f◦ Woman
nārī नारी

m◦ child
bālak बालक

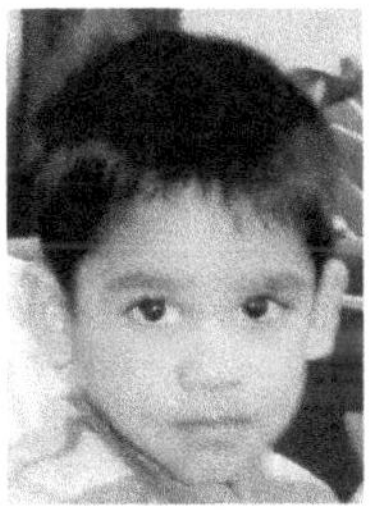
m◦ Face
cheharā चेहरा

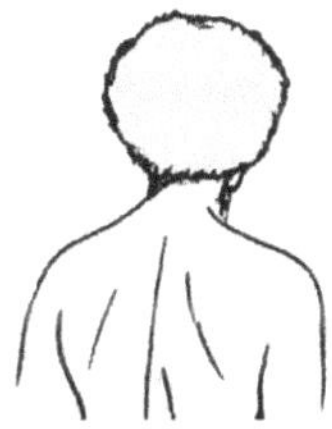
m◦ Head
sir सिर

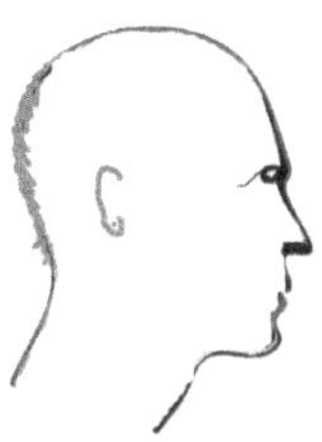
m◦ Bald
gañjā गंजा

f◦ Ponytail
choṭi चोटी

m◦ Hair
bāl बाल

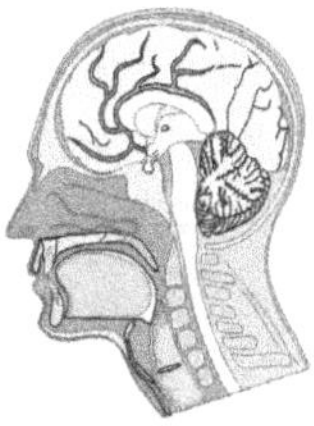
m◦ Brain
dināg दिमाग

f◦ Skull
khopaḍī खोपड़ी

f◦ Vision
nazar नज़र

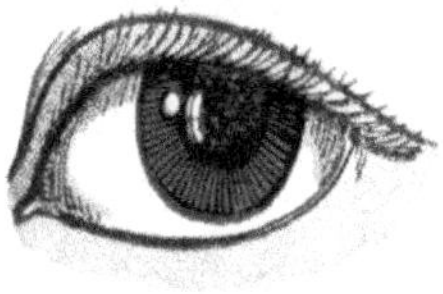
f◦ Eye
ā̇nkh आंख

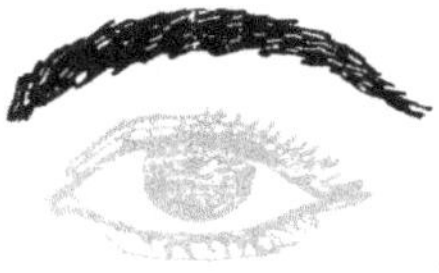
f◦ Eyebrow
bhõha भौंह

m◦ Tear
ā̃sū आँसू

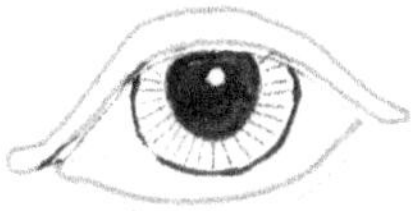
f◦ Eyeball
putalī पुतली

f◦ Eyelid
palak पलक

m◦ Cheek
gāl गाल

m◦ Forehead
lalāṭ ललाट

m◦ Mole
til तिल

m◦ Spilus
tilak तिलक

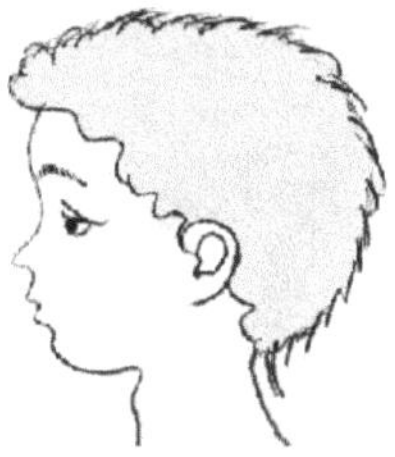
f◦ Neck
gardan गर्दन

f◦ Nose
nāk नाक

m◦ Mouth
mukh मुख

f◦ Mustache
mūchh मूछ

f◦ Beard
dādhī दाढ़ी

f◦ Chin
thuḍḍī ठुड्डी

m◦ Lip
Oṭh ओठ

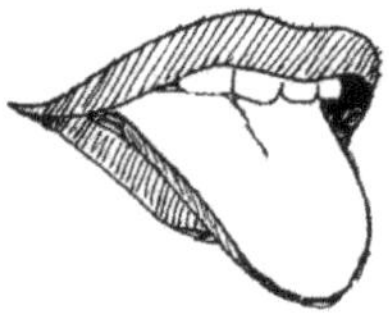

f◦ Tongue
jībh जीभ

m◦ Teeth
dānt दांत

m◦ Throat
galā गला

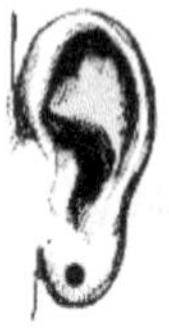

m◦ Ear
kān कान

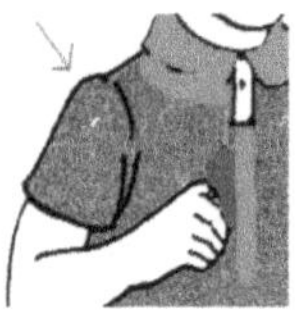

m◦ Shoulder
kandhā कंधा

m◦ Hand
hāth हाथ

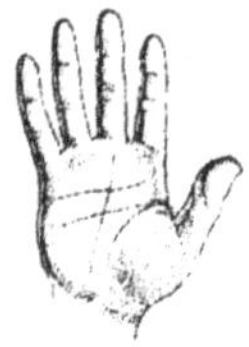

m◦ Palm
kartal करतल

m◦ Thumb
angūṭhā अंगूठा

f◦ Bone
haḍḍī हड्डी

f◦ Forefinger
tarjanī तर्जनी

f◦ Middle finger
madhyamā मध्यमा

f◦ Ring finger
anāmikā अनामिका

f◦ Little finger
kanakī कनीका

m◦ Nail
nākhūn नाखून

f◦ Elbow
kuhanī कुहनी

f◦ Wrist
kalāī कलाई

f◦ Fist
muṭṭhī मुट्ठी

f◦ Leg
ṭāṅg टाँग

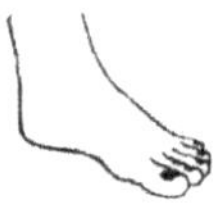

m◦ Foot
pā̐va पाँव

m◦ Sole
talavā तलवा

m◦ Knee
ghuṭnā घुटना

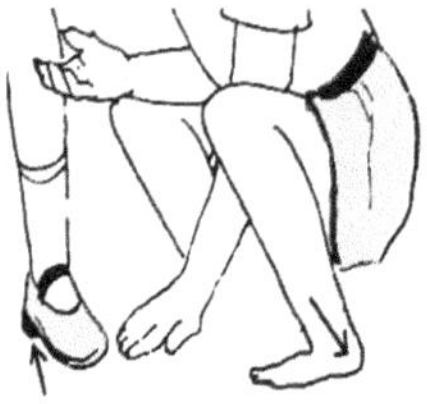

f◦ Heel
eḍī एड़ी

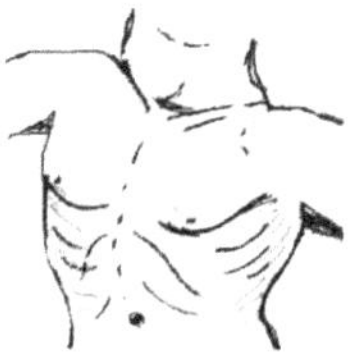

f◦ Chest
chhātī छाती

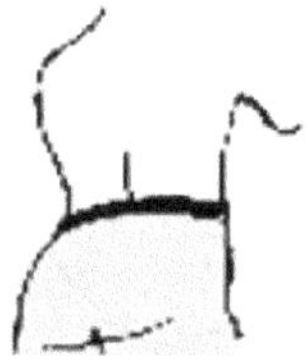

f◦ Waist
kamar कमर

m◦ Stomach
peṭ पेट

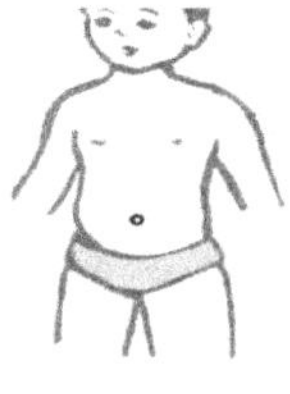

f◦ Bellybutton
nābhī नाभी

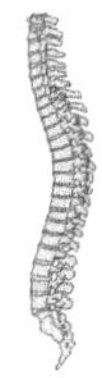

f◦ Spine
rīḍh रीढ़

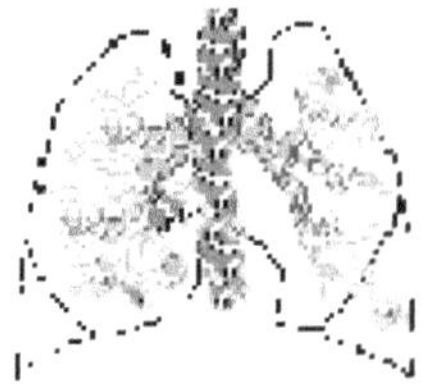

m◦ Lungs
fefade फेफडे

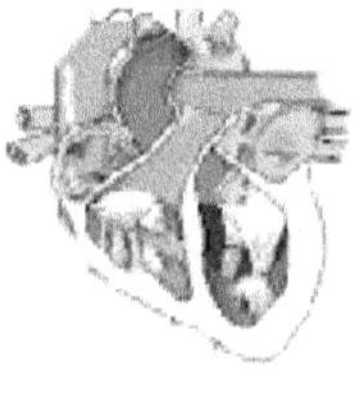

m◦ Heart
dil दिल

m◦ Hoof
khur खुर

m◦ Paw
pañjā पंजा

f◦ Trunk
sūṇḍ सूंड

f◦ Mane
ayāl अयाल

f◦ Wool
ūn ऊन

f◦ Tail
dum दुम

m◦ Horn
sing सिंग

f◦ Beak
choñch चोंच

m◦ Feather
paṅkh पंख

m◦ Egg
aṇḍā अंडा

m◦ Tree
peḍ पेड़

f◦ Vine
latā लता

m◦ Banyan
bargad बरगद

m◦ Faicus
pīpal पीपल

m◦ Mango
ām आम

m◦ Pine
devadār देवदार

m◦ Bamboo
bāṅs बांस

m◦ Palm
tāḍ ताड़

f◦ Grass
ghās घास

f◦ wood
lakaḍī लकड़ी

m◦ Leaf
pattā पत्ता

f◦ Branch
ḍālī डाली

f◦ Root
jaḍ जड़

m◦ Forest
Jungle जंगल

m◦ Mountain
pahāḍ पहाड़

m◦ Flower
fūl फूल

m◦ Lotus
kamal कमल

m◦ Rose
gulāb गुलाब

f◦ Jasmine
chamelī चमेली

f◦ Sunflower
sūrajmukhī सूरजमुखी

f◦ Bud
kalī कली

m◦ Fruit
fal फल

m◦ Banana
kelā केला

m◦ Grapes
angūr अंगूर

m◦ Apple
seb सेब

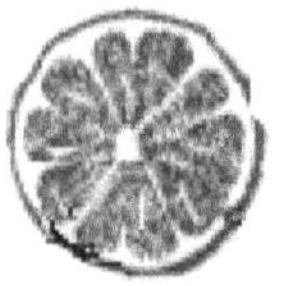

m◦ Lemon
nīmbū नींबू

m◦ Mango
ām आम

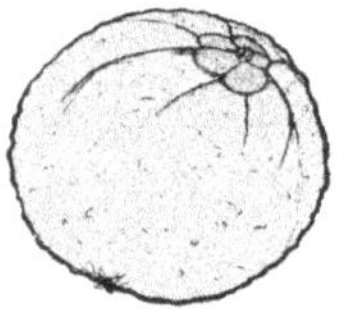

m◦ Orange
santrā संतरा

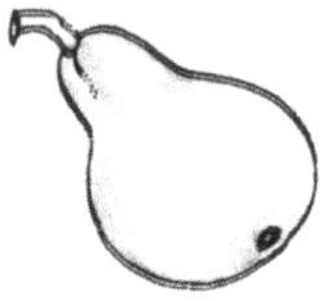

f◦ Pear
nāśapātī नाशपाती

m◦ Custard apple
sītāfal सीताफल

m◦ Papaya
paipitā पपिता

f◦ Pineapple
ananna!s अनन्नास

m◦ Pomegranate
anār अनार

m◦ Sugarcane
īkh ईख

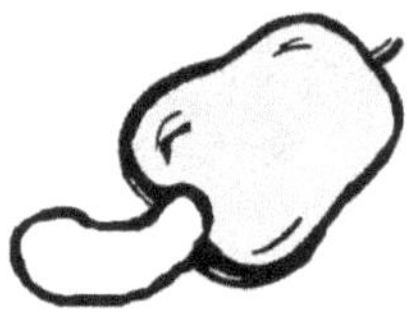

m◦ Cashew
kājū काजू

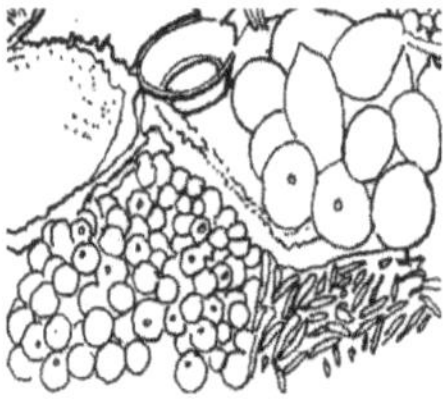

f◦ Vegetables
sabjī सब्जी

m◦ Beet
ćukandar चुकंदर

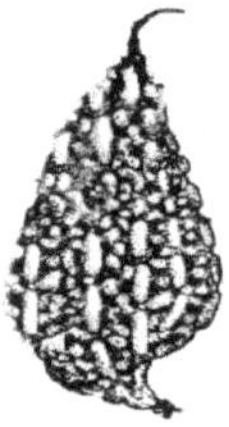

m◦ Bitter gourd
karelā करेला

f◦ Cabbage *pattā-*
gobhī पत्तागोभी

m◦ Watermelon
tarbūja तरबूज

f◦ Carrot
gājar गाजर

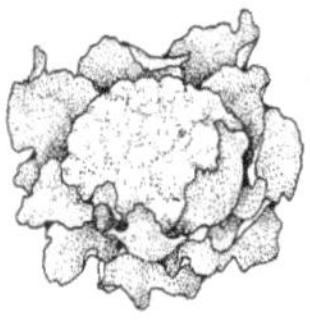

f◦ Cauliflower
fūl-gobhī फूलगोभी

m◦ Coriander
dhaniyā धनिया

f◦ Chili
mirchī मिरची

m◦ Plum
ber बेर

m◦ Tomato
ṭamāṭar टमाटर

m◦ Mint
pudinā पुदिना

f◦ Beans
sem सेम

f◦ Zucchini
turaī तुरई

m◦ Cocoanut
nāriyal नारियल

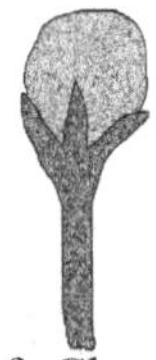
f◦ Clove
lavaṅg लवंग

f◦ Cardamom
ilāyacī इलायची

f◦ Almond
badām बदाम

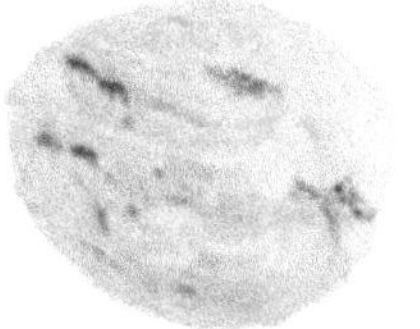
m◦ Walnut
akhroṭ अखरोट

f◦ Peanut
fali फली

m◦ Date
chhuārā छुआरा

m◦ Eggplant
baiṅgan बैंगन

m◦ Garlic
lahasun लहसुन

f◦ Ginger
adrak अद्रक

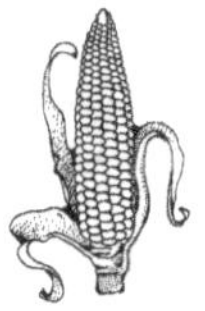
f◦ Corn
makkī मक्की

f◦ Okrā
bhinḍī भिंडी

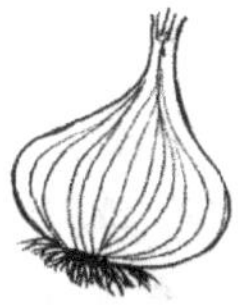
m◦ Onion
pyāj प्याज

m◦ Potato
ālu आलु

m◦ Peas
maṭar मटर

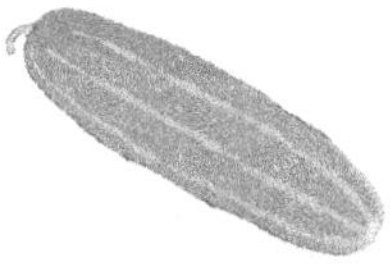
m◦ Cucumber
khīrā खीरा

m◦ Pumpkin
kaddu कद्दु

f◦ Radish
mūlī मूली

f◦ Spinach
pālak पालक

f◦ Tamarind
imlī इमली

m◦ Jackfruit
kaṭhal कटहल

f◦ Soup
dāl दाल

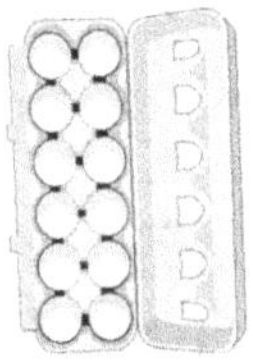
m◦ Eggs
aṇḍe अण्डे

m◦ Flour
āṭā आटा

m◦ Honey
shahad शहद

m◦ Oil
tel तेल

m◦ Breakfast
nāshtā नाश्ता

m◦ Butter
makkhan मक्खन

f◦ Catsup
Chaṭnī चटनी

m◦ Coffee
kahavā कहवा

f◦ Tea
Chāy चाय

f◦ *burfī*
बरफी

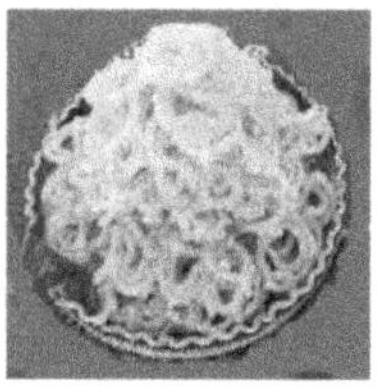

f◦ *jalebi*
जलेबी

m◦ *laḍḍu*
लड्डू

m◦ Milk
dūdh दूध

m◦ Clarified-butter
ghee घी

m◦ *parāṭhā*
पराठा

m◦ Cake
kek केक

m◦ Pickle
achār अचार

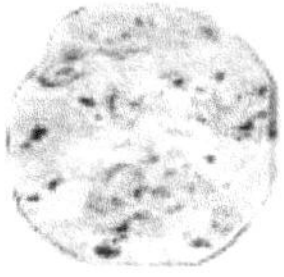

f◦ Bread
Roṭī रोटी

m◦ Rice
chāval चावल

f◦ Salad
salād सलाद

m◦ Salt
namak नमक

m◦ Spice
masālā मसाला

f◦ Wine
madirā मदिरा

f◦ Chicken
murgī मुर्गी

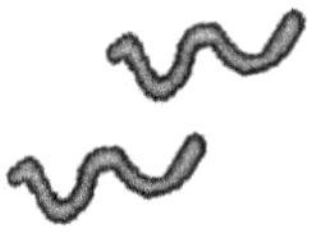

m◦ Worm
kīḍā कीड़ा

m◦ Animal
pashu पशु

m◦ Leopard
chītā चीता

m◦ Python
ajgar अजगर

m◦ Firefly
juganu जुगनु

f◦ Porcupine
sehī सेही

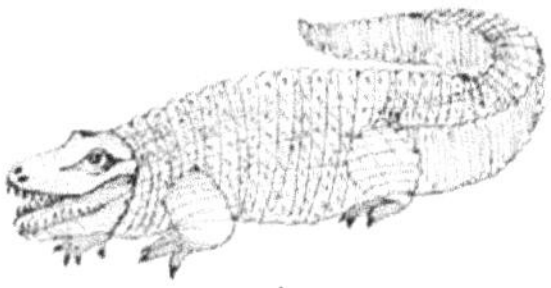

m◦ Alligator
ghaḍiyāl घड़ीयाल

f◦ Ant
chi̐ṇṭī चींटी

m◦ Bat
chamgīdaḍ चमगीदड़

m◦ Ape
ādimāna आदिमानव

m◦ Scorpion
bichchhu बिच्छु

f◦ Sheep
bheḍ भेड़

m◦ Snake
sām̐p सांप

f◦ Spider
makḍī मकड़ी

m◦ Turtle
kachhuā कछुआ

m◦ Deer
harin हरिन

m◦ Dog
kuttā कुत्ता

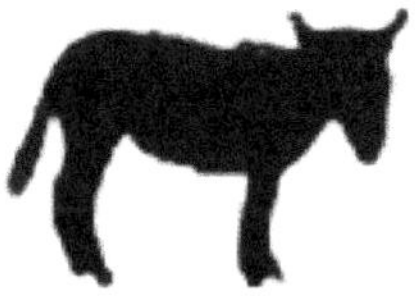
m◦ Donkey
gadhā गधा

m◦ Elephant
hāthī हाथी

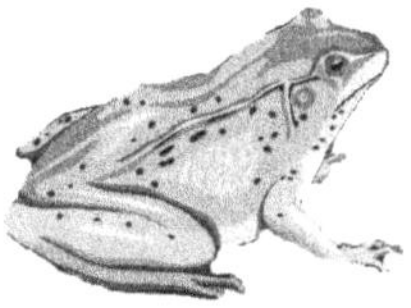
m◦ Frog
meṇḍhak मेंढक

m◦ Bear
bhālu भालु

f◦ Bee
makkhī मक्खी

f◦ Buffalo
bhaiṅs भैंस

f◦ Butterfly
titalī तितली

f◦ Fish
machhalī मछली

m◦ Camel
ūṇṭa ऊंट

f◦ Cat
billī बिल्ली

m◦ Cobra
nāg नाग

f◦ Cow
gāy गाय

f◦ Fox
lomaḍī लोमड़ी

f◦ Goat
bakarī बकरी

m◦ Hippo
kariyād करियाद

m◦ Horse
ghoḍā घोड़ा

m◦ Hyena
lakaḍbaggā लकड़बग्गा

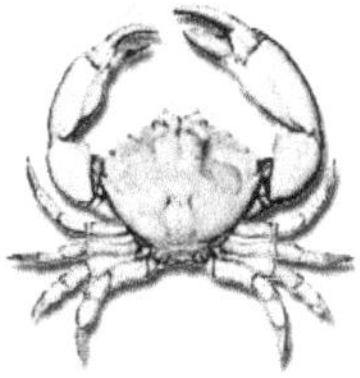
m◦ Crab
kekḍā केकड़ा

m◦ Lion
sim̐ha सिंह

f◦ Lizard
chhhipakalī छिपकली

m◦ Mongoose
nevlā नेवला

m◦ Monkey
bandar बंदर

m◦ Zebra
gorkhar गोरखर

m◦ Mosquito
machchhar मच्छर

m◦ Moth
pataṅg पतंग

m◦ Mouse
chūhā चूहा

m◦ Ox
bail बैल

f◦ Squirrel
gilharī गिलहरी

m◦ Pig
sūar सूअर

m◦ Rabbit
khargosh खरगोश

m◦ Roach
zingur झिंगुर

m◦ Rhino
genḍā गेंडा

m◦ Tiger
sher शेर

m◦ Bird
pakshi पक्षी

f◦ Cuckoo
koyal कोयल

m◦ Crow
kauvā कौवा

m◦ Duck
batakh बतख

m◦ Crane
bagulā बगुला

f◦ Eagle
chīl चील

f◦ Fly
makkhī मक्खी

f◦ Hen
murgī मुर्गी

m◦ Owl
ullū उल्लू

m◦ Falcon
bāj बाज

m◦ Parrot
totā तोता

m◦ Peacock
mor मोर

m◦ Pigeon
kabūtar कबूतर

m◦ Rooster
murgā मुर्गा

m◦ Pheasant
titar तीतर

m◦ Snail
ghonghā घोंघा

m◦ Swan
ham̐sa हंस

m◦ Vulture
gidh गिध

m◦ Woodpecker
kaṭhphoḍvā कठफोड़वा

m◦ Grasshopper
ṭiḍḍhā टिड्डा

m◦ Ostrich
Shuturmurg शुतुरमुर्ग

m◦ Flamingo
marāl मराल

f◦ Turkey
peru पेरु

m◦ Jay
bulbul बुलबुल

f◦ Quail
bater बटेर

m◦ Stove
chūlhā चूल्हा

m◦ Cup
pyālā प्याला

m◦ Glass
gilās गिलास

f◦ Plate
thālī थाली

f◦ Knife
chhurī छुरी

m◦ Knife
chākū चाकू

f◦ ladle
kaḍchī कडछी

m◦ *Spoon*
chammach चम्मच

f◦ Wok
kaḍāhī कड़ाही

f◦ Bucket
bālṭī बाल्टी

f◦ Book
kitāb किताब

m◦ Paper
kāgaz कागज़

f◦ Letter
chiṭṭhī चिठ्ठी

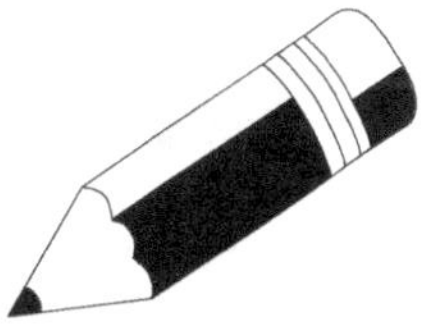

f◦ Pencil
lekhanī लेखनी

f◦ Pen
kalam कलम

m◦ Certificate
pramāṇ-patra प्रमाणपत्र

m◦ Money
paise पैसे

f◦ Ball
gend गेंद

f◦ Medicine
dawāī दवाई

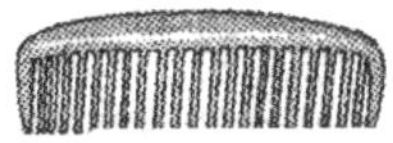

f◦ Comb
kanghī कंघी

m◦ Shirt
kurtā कुर्ता

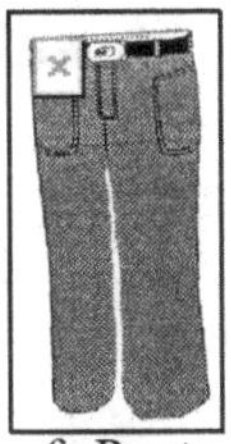

f◦ Pants
patlūn पतलून

m◦ Shoe
jūtā जूता

f◦ *sārī*
साड़ी

m◦ Brush
burus बुरुस

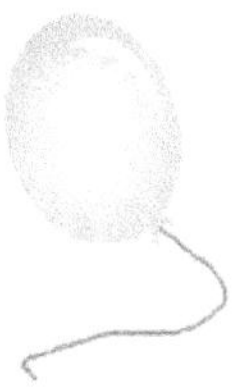

m◦ Balloon
gubbārā गुब्बारा

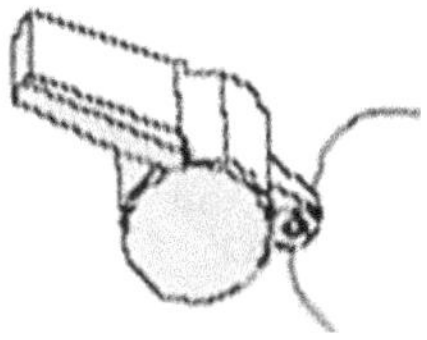

f◦ Whistle
sīṭī सीटी

f◦ Fan
paṅkhā पंखा

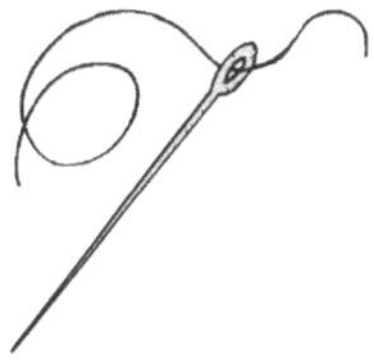

f◦ Needle
sūī सूई

f◦ Stick
chhaḍī छड़ी

f∘ Cap
ṭopī टोपी

m∘ Bag
thailā थैला

f∘ Umbrella
chhatrī छत्री

m∘ Glasses
chaṣmā चष्मा

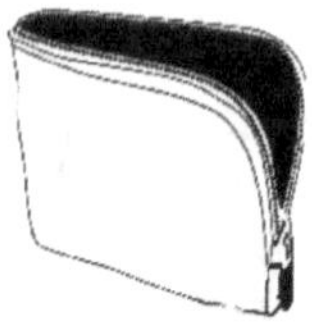

m∘ Wallet
baṭuā बटुआ

m∘ House
ghar घर

f∘ Key
chābī चाबी

m∘ Lock
tālā ताला

m∘ Door
darwājā दरवाजा

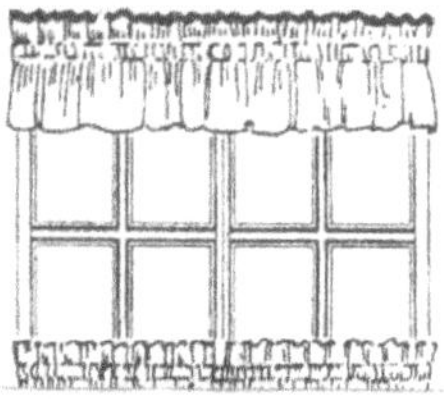

f∘ Window
khiḍakī खिड़की

f∘ Stool
chārpaī चारपाई

f∘ Chair
kursī कुर्सी

m∘ Broom
jhaḍū झाड़ू

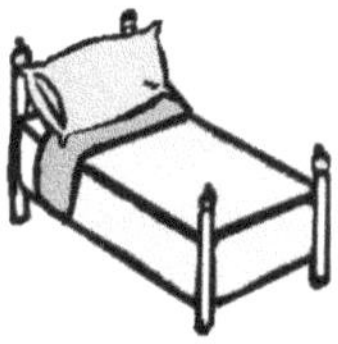

f∘ Bed
bistar बिस्तर

f∘ Electricity
bijlī बिजली

m∘ Pillow
takiyā तकिया

f∘ Mattress
gaddī गद्दी

m∘ Blanket
kambal कम्बल

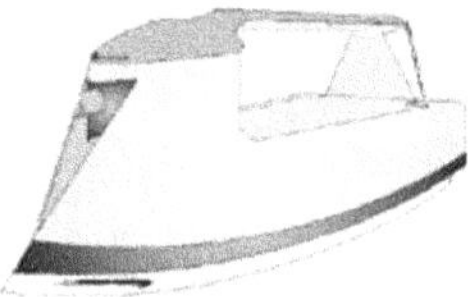

f∘ Iron
istarī इस्तरी

m∘ Lamp
dīyā दीया

f∘ Kettle
ketlī केतली

f∘ Rolling pin
belan बेलन

f∘ Jug
surāhī सुराही

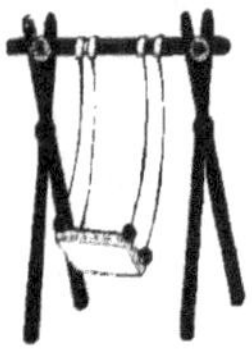

m∘ Swing
jhūlā झूला

m∘ Razor
ustarā उस्तरा

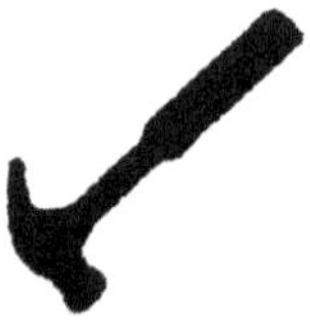

m∘ Hammer
hathauḍā हथौड़ा

m∘ Pliar
jamūr जमूर

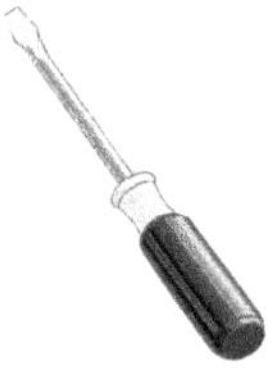

m∘ *Screwdriver*
pechkash पेचकश

f∘ Saw
ārī आरी

m∘ Wrench
pānā पाना

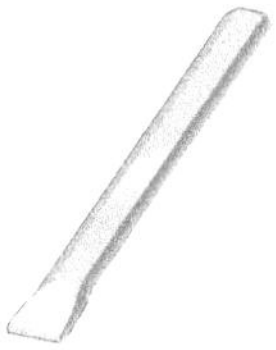
f◦ Chisel
chhenī छेनी

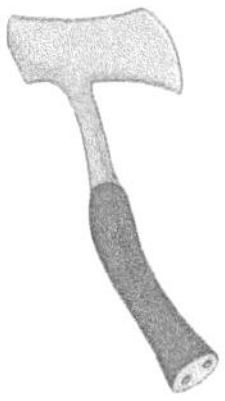
f◦ Ax
kulhāḍī कुल्हाड़ी

m◦ Shovel
fāvaḍā फावड़ा

m◦ Screw
pech पेच

f◦ Nail
kīl कील

m◦ Phone
dūrabhāsh दूरभाष

f◦ Cell जंगमदूरवाणी
jangamadūravānī

f◦ Radio *ākāśavāṇī*
आकाशवाणी

m◦ TV *dūradarśan*
दूरदर्शन

m◦ Computer
saṅgaṇak संगणक

f◦ Chess
śatranj शतरंज

f◦ Scissors
kainchī कैंची

m◦ Thread
dhāgā धागा

m◦ Broom
jhāḍū झाड़ू

f◦ Watch
ghaḍī घड़ी

m◦ Diamond
hīrā हीरा

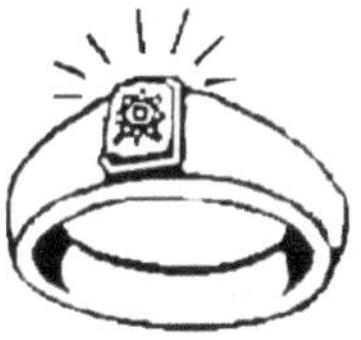
f◦ Ring
angūṭhī अंगूठी

m◦ Necklace
hār हार

m◦ Mirror
āīnā आईना

m◦ Paper
akhabār अखबार

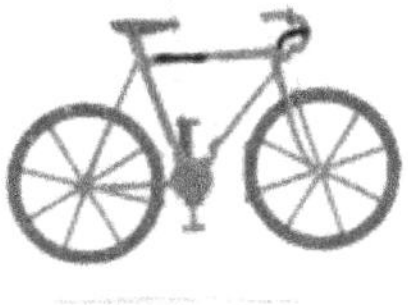
f◦ Bicycle
sāyakil सायकील

f◦ Car
gāḍī गाड़ी

m◦ Airplane
vimān विमान

f◦ Boat
nāv नाव

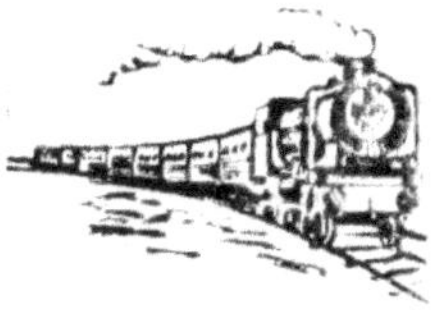
f◦ Rail
relgāḍī रेलगाड़ी

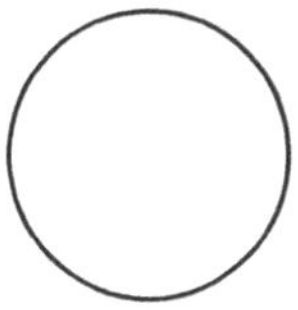
m◦ Circle
gol गोल

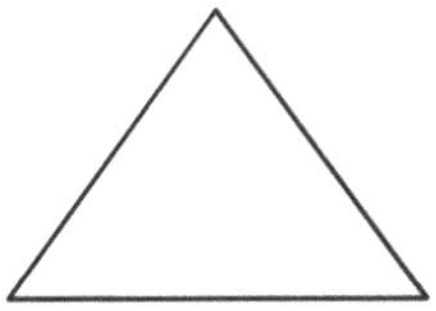
m◦ Triangle
trikoṇa त्रिकोण

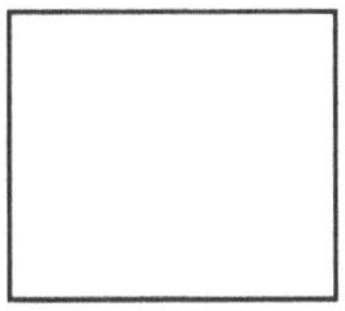
m◦ Square
chaturbhuj चतुर्भुज

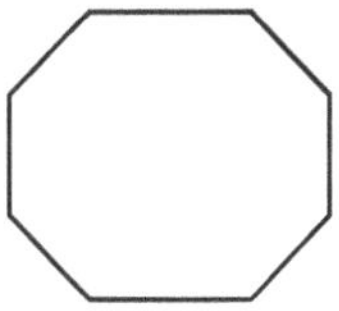
m◦ Hexagaon
shaṭkoṇa षट्कोण

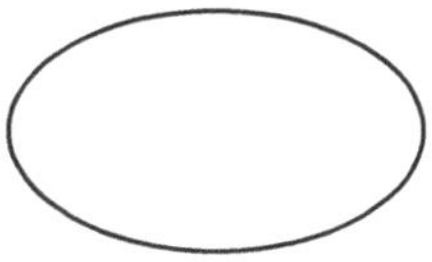
f◦ oval
aṇḍākritī अंडाकृति

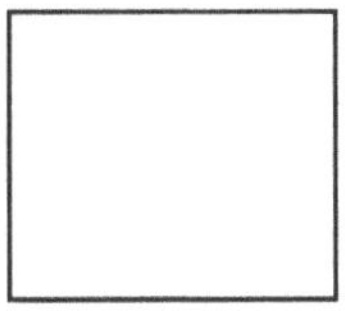

m◦ Accountant
munīm मुनीम

m◦ Bus-wālā
bus-wālā बसवाला

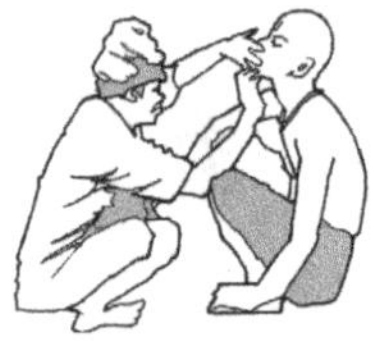
m◦ Barber
nāī नाई

m◦ Carpenter
baḍhaī बढ़ई

m◦ Boatman
kevaṭ केवट

f◦ Dancer
nartakī नर्तकी

m◦ Potter
kumhār कुम्हार

m◦ Farmer
kisān किसान

m◦ Labourer
majdūr मजदूर

m◦ Lawyer
vakīl वकील

m◦ Magician
jādūgar जादूगर

m◦ Musician
sangītakār संगीतकार

m◦ Painter
rangwālā रंगवाला

m◦ Goldsmith
sunār सुनार

m◦ Police
pulis पुलिस

m◦ Player
khilāḍī खिलाड़ी

m◦ Priest
pujārī पुजारी

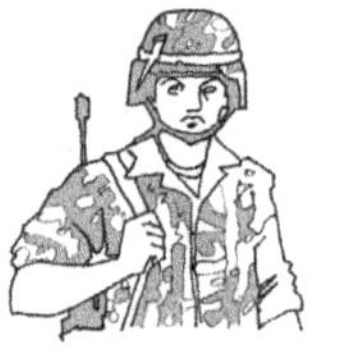
m◦ Soldie
jawān जवान

m◦ Snake charmer
saperā सपेरा

m◦ Tailor
darzī दर्ज़ी

f◦ Teacher
guruji गरुजी

m◦ Thief
chor चोर

f◦ Typist
ṭankiṇak टंकणक

m◦ Wrestler
pahalwān पहलवान

m◦ Swimmer
tairak तैरक

f◦ Nurse *parichārikā*
परिचारिका

m◦ Fruit vendor
sabzī-walī सब्ज़ीवाली

m◦ Ascetic
yogī योगी

m◦ Washerman
dhobī धोबी

m◦ Cricketer
ballebāz बल्लेबाज़

TABLE 5-A : COMMON HINDI ACTION WORDS, HINDI VERB STEMS (* = transitive verbs)

VERB STEMS			VERB STEMS			VERB STEMS		
आ	ā	come	जल	jal	burn (itself)	गिरा	girā	drop*
खा	khā	eat*	जला	jalā	burn*	छिप	chhip	hide (itself)
गा	gā	sing*	डर	dar	fear (self)	छिपा	chhipā	hide*
जा	jā	go (itself)	डरा	darā	scare*	मिल	mil	meet
पा	pā	get*	तल	tal	fry*	मिला	milā	mix*
ला	lā	bring*	पका	pakā	cook*	लिख	likh	write*
जी	jī	be alive	पढ़	paḍh	read*	हिल	hil	move (itself)
पी	pī	drink*	पढ़ा	padhā	teach*	हिला	hilā	move*
सी	sī	sew*	बता	batā	tell*	जीत	jīt	win*
छू	chhoo	touch*	बन	bana	become	सीख	sīkh	learn*
दे	de	give*	बना	banā	make*	चुरा	churā	steal*
ले	le	take*	मना	manā	celebrate*	खुल	khul	open (itself)
खो	kho	loose*	मर	mar	die	बुला	bulā	call*
पढ़	paḍh	read, learn*	मल	mal	rub*	कूद	kūd	jump
धो	dho	wash*	रह	rah	stay, live in	टूट	ṭūṭ	break (itself)
बो	bo	sow*	**सक**	**sak**	**be able, can**	भूल	bhụ̄l	forget
रो	ro	cry	सता	satā	bother*	रुक	ruk	stop
सो	so	sleep	काट	kāṭ	cut*	भेज	bhej	send*
हो	**ho**	**become**	चाट	chāṭ	lick*	सूँघ	sūngh	smell*
उड़	uḍ	fly (self)	**चाह**	**chāh**	**want***	बेच	bech	sell*
उड़ा	uḍā	fly*	छाप	chhāp	print*	तैर	tair	swim
कर	**kar**	**do***	जान	jān	know*	बैठ	baiṭh	sit
कह	kah	say*	भाग	bhāg	run	खोद	khod	dig*
खरीद	kharīd	buy*	मान	mān	agree*	खोल	khol	open*
चल	chal	walk	मार	mār	kill, hit*	तोड़	toḍ	break*
चला	chalā	drive*	गिर	gir	fall	बोल	bol	speak

NOTE : The underlined four are most important action words required for making sentences.

TABLE 5-B : ENGLISH ALPHABETICAL LIST, HINDI VERB STEMS (* = transitive verbs)

	VERB STEMS	
agree*	मान	*mān*
arrange*	रच	*rach*
become	**हो**	***ho***
become	बन	*ban*
bother*	सता	*satā*
break (self)	टूट	*ṭūṭ*
break*	तोड़	*toḍ*
bring*	ला	*lā*
burn (self)	जल	*jal*
burn*	जला	*jalā*
call*	बुला	*bulā*
can, be able	**सक**	***sak***
celebrate*	मना	*manā*
come	आ	*ā*
cook*	पका	*pakā*
cry	रो	*ro*
cut*	काट	*kāṭ*
die	मर	*mar*
dig*	खोद	*khod*
do*	**कर**	***kar***
drink*	पी	*pī*
drive*	चला	*chalā*
drop*	गिरा	*girā*
eat*	खा	*khā*
fall	गिर	*gir*
fear (self)	डर	*ḍar*
fly (self)	उड़	*uḍ*
fly*	उड़ा	*uḍā*
forget	भूल	*bhūl*
fry*	तल	*tal*
get*	पा	*pā*
give*	दे	*de*
go	जा	*jā*
hear*	सुन	*sun*
hide (self)	छिप	*chhip*
hide*	छिपा	*chhipā*
kill, hit*	मार	*mār*
know*	जान	*jān*
laugh	हँस	*hãs*
learn*	सीख	*sīkh*
live (alive)	जी	*jī*
loose*	खो	*kho*
make*	बना	*banā*
meet	मिल	*mil*
mix*	मिला	*milā*
move (self)	हिल	*hil*
move*	हिला	*hilā*
open (self)	खुल	*khul*
open*	खोल	*khol*
peel*	छील	*chhīl*
read*	पढ़	*paḍh*
rob*	लूट	*lūṭ*
rub*	मल	*mal*
run	भाग	*bhāg*
say*	कह	*kah*
show*	दिखा	*dikhā**
sell*	बेच	*bech*
sew*	सी	*sī*
sing*	गा	*gā*
sit	बैठ	*baiṭh*
sleep	सो	*so*
sow*	बो	*bo*
speak	बोल	*bol*
spread*	छा	*chhā*
stay, live	रह	*rah*
steal*	चुरा	*churā*
stop	रुक	*ruk*
sulk	रूठ	*rūṭh*
take*	ले	*le*
teach*	पढ़ा	*paḍhā*
tell*	बता	*batā*
think*	सोच	*soch*
touch*	छू	*chhoo*
walk	चल	*chal*
want, like*	**चाह**	***chāh***
wash*	धो	*dho*
weigh*	तोल	*tol*
win*	जीत	*jīt*
write*	लिख	*likh*

NOTE : The underlined four are most important action words required for making sentences.

LESSON 13

USING THE ACTION WORDS

FOR MAKING YOUR OWN SENTENCES

Let us learn **how to make our own sentences** in the following six ways

1. I normally 'do'	(you do; he, she, it does; we do, they do)	see - Table 6
2. I am 'doing'	(you are doing; he, she, it is doing; we, they are doing)	Table 7
3. I was 'doing'	(you were doing; he, she, it was doing; they were doing)	Table 8
4. I have 'already' done	(you have done; he, she, it has done; we, they have done)	Table 9
5. I had 'already' done	(you had done; he, she, it had done; we, they had done)	Table 10
6. I 'used to do'	(you used to do; he, she, it used to do; they used to do)	Table 12
SUMMARY	(do, doing, have done, has done, used to do)	Table 11

TABLE 6 : making sentences with - I do; you do; he, she, it does; we do; they do.

	Doer of the action Subject (colloquial)	drink verb	do, does 'do'	am, is, are, has, have am, is, are (colloquial)
∘	1. I मैं *maĩ*	पी *pī*	ता *tā*	हूँ *hũ*
∘	2. He वह *vah* (वो *vo*)	पी *pī*	ता *tā*	है *hai*
∘	3. She वह *vah* (वो *vo*)	पी *pī*	ती *tī*	है *hai*
*	4. We हम *ham*	पी *pī*	ते *te*	हैं *haĩ*
*	5. You आप *āp* = Respect, formal	पी *pī*	ते *te*	हैं *haĩ* (हो *ho*)
∘	5. You तुम *(tum)* = Equal	पी *pī*	ते *te*	(हो *ho*
∘	5. You तू *tū* = Informal, low	पी *pī*	ता *tā*	है *hai*
*	6. They वे *ve* (वो *vo*)	पी *pī*	ते *te*	हैं *haĩ*

NOTE : **The above table shows that :**

(i) A habitual mode 'do' is shown in Hindī with letter *'t'* (त) to which gender suffix *ā, e, ī* or *ĩ* (आ, ए, ई, ईं) is added. (त + आ = ता, त + ए = ते, त + ई = ती, त + ईं = तीं)

(ii) suffix 'ā' (आ) means masculine singular subject;

(iii) suffix 'e' (ए) means masculine plural subject;

(iv) suffix 'ī' (ई) means feminine singular subject;

(v) suffix 'ī̃' (ईं) means feminine plural subject;

TABLE 6A : Present Habitual Tense Suffixes SUMMARY

	Subject	Suffix M∘	Suffix F∘
∘	I	ता *(tā)*	ती *(tī)*
∘	He/she	ता *(tā)*	ती *(tī)*
*	We	ते *(te)*	ते *(te)*
*	You *(āp)*	ते *(te)*	ते *(te)*
*	They	ते *(te)*	ते *(te)*

EXERCISE 19 : Translate the English sentences into Hindī (Answers are given for help)

a. I drink. *maĩ pītā (pītī) hū̃.* मैं पीता (पीती) हूँ। You drink. *āp pīte haĩ.* आप पीते हैं। He drinks. *vah pītā hai.* वह पीता है। She drinks. *vah pītī hai.* वह पीती है। We drink. *ham pīte haĩ.* हम पीते हैं। They drink. *ve pīte haĩ.* वे पीते हैं।

b. I drink tea. *maĩ chāy pītā (pītī) hū̃.* मैं चाय पीता (पीती) हूँ। You drink tea. *āp chāy pīte haĩ.* आप चाय पीते हैं। He drinks tea. *vah chāy pītā hai.* वह चाय पीता है। She drinks tea. *vah chāy pītī hai.* वह चाय पीती है। We drink tea. *ham chāy pīte haĩ.* हम चाय पीते हैं। They drink tea. *ve chāy pīte haĩ.* वे चाय पीते हैं।

c. I drink hot tea. *maĩ garam chāy pītā (pītī) hū̃.* मैं गरम चाय पीता (पीती) हूँ। You drink hot tea. *āp garam chāy pīte haĩ.* आप गरम चाय पीते हैं। He drinks hot tea. *vah garamchāy pītā hai.* वह गरम चाय पीता है। She drinks hot tea. *vah garam chāy pītī hai.* वह गरम चाय पीती है। We drink hot tea. *ham garam chāy pīte haĩ.* हम गरम चाय पीते हैं। They drink hot tea. *ve garam chāy pīte haĩ.* वे गरम चाय पीते हैं।

2. They eat bananas. *ve kele khāte haĩ.* वे केले खाते हैं।

3. She sleeps. *vah sotī hai.* वह सोती है।

4. You write books. *āp kitābẽ likhte haĩ.* आप किताबें लिखते हैं।

5. He goes home. *vah ghar jātā hai.* वह घर जाता है।

DICTIONARY OF INFINITIVES

In order to form a verb from an infinitive, remove the last ना nā

In Hindī, the infinitives and verbal nouns end with the letter ना । eg◦ (i) do = √*kar* (कर) verb

(ii) to do (verb and verbal noun) = *karanā* करना.

Therefore, if you remove the suffix *nā* ना from any infinitive ot verbal noun, you get a basic root (√) verb.

Note that : (i) some verbs are only a single words, they are called Simple Verbs.

(ii) Some verbs have two words (the second word being *karanā, hona, jānā, denā* करना, होना, जाना, देना ...etc), these verbs are Compound Verbs (marked with * below)

to abandon *(√tyāga → tyāganā* त्यागना)

to accept *(√mān → mānanā* मानना)

to answer *(√jawāb de → jawāb denā* जवाब देना)*

to arrange *(√raća → raćanā* रचना)

to arrive *(√ā → ānā, pahũćanā* आना, पहुँचना)

to ask *(√pūćh → pūćhanā* पूछना)

to attain *(√prāpta kar → prāpta karanā* प्राप्त करना)*

to attempt *(√yatna kar → yatna karanā* यत्न करना)*

to bathe *(√nahā → nahānā* नहाना)

to be *(√rah, √ho → rahanā, honā* रहना, होना)*

to beg *(√yāćanā kar → yāćanā karanā* याचना करना)*

to bite, to cut *(√kāṭ → kāṭanā* काटना)

to break *(√ṭūṭ, toḍ → ṭūṭanā, toḍanā* टूटना, तोड़ना)

to blossom *(√khil → khilanā* खिलना)

to boil *(√ubal √ubāl → ubalanā, ubālanā* उबलना, उबालना)

to bring *(√lā → lānā* लाना)

to burn *(√jal, √jalā → jalanā, jalānā* जलना, जलाना)

to buy *(√kharīd → kharīdanā* खरीदना)

to call *(√bulā → bulānā* बुलाना)

to carry away *(√le jā → le jānā* ले जाना)*

to celebrate *(√manā → manānā* मनाना)

to clean *(√sāf-kar → sāf-karanā* साफ करना)*

to come *(√ā → ānā* आना)

to cook *(√pakā → pakānā* पकाना)

to count *(√gin → ginanā* गिनना)

to cover *(√ḍhak → ḍhakanā* ढकना)

to cross *(√pār kar → pār karanā* पार करना)*

to cry *(√ro → ronā* रोना)

to cut, to bite *(√kāṭ → kāṭanā* काटना)

to dance *(√nāć → nāćanā* नाचना)

to desire, to want *(√ćāh → ćāhanā* चाहना)

to die *(√mar → maranā* मरना)

to dig *(√khod → khodanā* खोदना)

to do *(√kar → karanā* करना)

to draw *(√nikāl → nikālanā* निकालना)

to drink *(√pī → pīnā* पीना)

to dry *(√sūkh→ sūkhanā* सूखना)

to dye, paint *(√ra̐gā → ra̐gānā* रँगाना)

to eat *(√khā → khānā* खाना)

to enter *(√praveś kar → praveś karanā* प्रवेश करना)*

to exist *(√rah → rahanā, honā* रहना, होना)

to explain *(√samajh → samajhānā* समझाना)

to fall *(√gir → giranā* गिरना)

to fear *(√ḍar → ḍaranā* डरना)

to fight *(√laḍ → laḍanā* लड़ना)

to fix *(√ṭhīk kar → ṭhīk karanā* ठीक करना)*

to fly *(√uḍa, √uḍā → uḍanā, uḍānā* उड़ना, उड़ाना)

to forget *(√bhūl → bhūlana* भूलना)

to forgive *(√māf kar → māf karanā* माफ करना)*

to free *(√ćhoḍ → ćhoḍanā* छोड़ना)

to fry *(√tal → talanā* तलना)

to get *(√pā → pānā* पाना)

to give *(√de → denā* देना)

to glow *(√ćamak → ćamakanā* चमकना)

to glue *(√ćipak → ćipakānā* चिपकाना)

to go *(√jā → jānā* जाना)

to grind *(√pīs → pīsanā* पीसना)

to grow *(√baḍh → baḍhanā* बढ़ना)

to hang *(√laṭak, √laṭakā → laṭakanā, laṭakānā* लटकना, लटकाना)

to happen, to have *(√ho → honā* होना)

to hear *(√sun → sunanā* सुनना)

to hide *(√ćhup, √ćhupā → ćhupanā, ćhupānā* छुपना, छुपाना)

to hit *(√mār → māranā* मारना)

to hold, catch *(√pakaḍ → pakaḍanā* पकड़ना)

to hum *(√gunagunā → gunagunānā* गुनगुनाना)

to hurt *(√dukhā → dukhānā)* (दुःखाना)

to increase *(√baḍh → baḍhanā* बढ़ना)

to join *(√mil, √milā → milanā, milānā* मिलना, मिलाना)

to jump *(√kūd → kūdanā* कूदना)

to keep *(√rakh → rakhanā* रखना)

to kill *(√mār → māranā* मारना)

to know *(√jān → jānanā* जानना)

to laugh *(√haँs → haँsanā* हँसना)

to lift *(√uṭhā → uṭhānā* उठाना)

to like *(√ćāh → ćāhanā* चाहना)

to live *(√jī → jīnā* जीना)

to lose *(√kho → khonā* खोना)

to love *(√pyār kar → pyār karanā* प्यार करना)*

to make (*√banā → banānā* बनाना)

to meet (*√mil → milanā* मिलना)

to melt (*√pighal → pighalanā* पिघलना)

to move (*√hil, √hilā → hilanā, hilānā* हिलना, हिलाना)

to open (*√khol → kholanā* खोलना)

to pick (*√uṭhā → uṭhānā* उठाना)

to play (*√khel* → khelanā खेलना)

to press (*√dabā → dabānā* दबाना)

to protect (*√rakṣā kar → rakṣā karanā* रक्षा करना)*

to pull (*√khīñć → khīñćanā* खींचना)

to punish (*√daṇḍa de → daṇḍa denā* दंड देना)*

to push (*√dhakel → dhakelanā* धकेलना)

to put, keep (*√rakh → rakhanā* रखना)

to rain (*√baras → barasanā* बरसना)

to read (*√paḍh → paḍhanā* पढ़ना)

to receive (*√pā → pānā* पाना)

to ride, to drive (*√ćalā → ćalānā* चलाना)

to roam (*√ghūm → ghūmanā* घूमना)

to rot (*√saḍ → saḍanā* सड़ना)

to run (*√bhāg → bhāganā* भागना)

to ripen (*√pak → pakanā* पकना)

to say (*√kah → kahanā)* (कहना)

to see (*√dekh → dekhanā* देखना)

to sell (*√beć → bećanā* बेचना)

to send (*√bhej → bhejanā* भेजना)

to serve (*√sevā kar → sevā karanā* सेवा करना)*

to sew (*√sī → sīnā* सीना)

to shine (*√tap, √tapā → tapanā, tapānā* तपना, तपाना)

to sing (*√gā → gānā* गाना)

to sink *(√ḍūb, √ḍubā → ḍūbanā, ḍubānā* डूबना, डुबाना)

to sit *(√baiṭh → baiṭhanā* बैठना)

to sleep (*√so* → sonā सोना)

to smell *(√sū̃gh → sū̃ghanā* सूँघना)

to smile *(√musakarā → musakarānā* मुसकराना)

to speak *(√bol → bolanā* बोलना)

to stop *(√ruk → rukanā* रुकना)

to study *(√paḍh → paḍhanā* पढ़ना)

to take *(√le → lenā* लेना)

to talk *(√bol → bolanā* बोलना)

to taste *(√ćakh → ćakhanā* चखना)

to tell *(√batā, √batalā → batānā, batalānā* बताना, बतलाना)

to think *(√soć → soćanā* सोचना)

to throw *(√fẽk → fẽkanā* फेंकना)

to tie *(√bāndh → bāndhanā* बाँधना)

to travel *(√safar kar → safar karanā* सफर करना)*

to understand *(√samajh → samajhanā* समझना)

to use *(√istemāl kar → istemal karanā* इस्तेमाल करना)*

to wake up *(√jāg → jāganā* जागना)

to walk *(√ćal → ćalanā* चलना)

to want *(√ćah → ćāhanā* चाहना)

to wash *(√dho → dhonā* धोना)

to waste *(√kharāb kar → kharāb karanā* खराब करना)*

to wear *(√pahan → pahananā* पहनना)

to win *(√jīt → jītanā* जीतना)

to wish *(√iććhā kar → iććhā karanā* इच्छा करना)*

to work *(√kām kar → kām karanā* काम करना)*

to worship *(√pūjā kar → pūjā karanā* पूजा करना)*

to write *(√likh → likhanā* लिखना) ...etc.

APPLICATION OF VERBS

1. I wish	*(mai̐ iććhā karatā hū̐)*	मैं इच्छा करता हूँ।
2. I wish	*(mai̐ iććhā karatī hū̐)*	मैं इच्छा करती हूँ।
3. We worship	*(ham pūjā karate hai̐*	हम पूजा करते हैं।
4. We worship	*(ham pūjā karatė hai̐*	हम पूजा करते हैं।
5. You work	*(āp kāma karate hai̐)*	आप काम करते हैं।
6. You work	*(āp kāma karatī hai̐)*	आप काम करती हैं।
7. He moves	*(vah hilatā hai)*	वह हिलता है।
8. He moves	*(vah hilātā hai)*	वह हिलाता है।
9. She moves	*(vah hilatī hai)*	वह हिलती है।
10. She moves	*(vah hilātī hai)*	वह हिलाती है।
11. It breaks	*(yah ṭūṭatā hai)*	यह टूटता है।
12. He breaks	*(vah toḍatā hai)*	वह तोड़ता है।
13. It dries	*(yah sūkhatā hai)*	यह सूखता है।
14. They dry	*(ve sukhāte hai̐)*	वे सुखाते हैं।
15. I dry	*(mai̐ sukhātā hū̐)*	मैं सुखाता हूँ।
16. I dry	*(mai̐ sukhātī hū̐)*	मैं सुखाती हूँ।
17. We hide	*(ham ćhupate hai̐)*	हम छुपते हैं।
18. We hide	*(ham ćhupatī hai̐)*	हम छुपती हैं।
19. We hide	*(ham ćhupāte hai̐)*	हम छुपाते हैं।
20. We hide	*(ham ćhupātī hai̐)*	हम छुपाती हैं।
21. I speak.	*(mai̐ bolatā hū̐, mai̐ bolatī hū̐)*	मैं बोलता हूँ, मैं बोलती हूँ।
22. Rām sits.	*(Rām baiṭhatā hai)*	राम बैठता है।
23. She sings.	*(vah gātī hai)*	वह गाती है।
24. They cook.	*(ve pakāte hai̐, ve pakātī hai̐)*	वे पकाते हैं, वे पकाती हैं।

25. You wish. *(āp ćāhate hai̐, āp ćāhatī hai̐)* आप चाहते हैं, आप चाहती हैं।

26. We write. *(ham likhate hai̐, ham likhatī hai̐)* हम लिखते हैं, हम लिखती हैं।

27. You cut. *(āp kāṭate hai̐, āp kāṭatī hai̐)* आप काटते हैं, आप काटती हैं।

28. They smile. *(ve ha̐sate hai̐, ve ha̐satī hai̐)* वे हँसते हैं, वे हँसती हैं।

29. Arvind paints a picture. *(Arvind ćitra ra̐gātā hai)* अरविंद चित्र रँगाता है।

30. We run. *(ham bhāgate hai̐, ham bhāgatī hai̐)* हम भागते हैं, हम भागती हैं।

(ham dauḍate hai̐, ham dauḍatī hai̐) हम दौड़ते हैं, हम दौड़ती हैं।

31. Rītā brings. *(Rītā lātī hai)* रीता लाती है।

32. Sunil takes a book. *(Sunīl letā hai)* सुनील पुस्तक लेता है।

33. He eats. *(vah bhojan karatā hai, vah khātā hai)* वह भोजन करता है, वह खाता है।

34. The boy cries. *(laḍakā rotā hai)* लड़का रोता है।

35. One boy cries. *(ek laḍakā rotā hai)* एक लड़का रोता है।

36. He sinks. *(vah ḍūbatā hai, vah ḍubātā hai)* वह डूबता है, वह डुबाता है।

37. They put, they keep. *(ve rakhate hai̐, ve rakhatī hai̐)* वे रखते हैं, वे रखती हैं।

38. We save. *(ham baćāte hai̐, ham baćātī hai̐)* हम बचाते हैं, हम बचाती हैं।

39. You sell. *(āp bećate hai̐, āp bećatī hai̐)* आप बेचते हैं, आप बेचती हैं।

40. She sends. *(vah bhejatī hai̐)* वह भेजती है।

41. She joins. *(vah milatī hai, vah milātī hai)* वह मिलती है, वह मिलाती है।

42. He throws. *(vah fe̐katā hai)* वह फेंकता है।

43. You jump. *(āp kūdate hai̐, āp kūdatī hai̐)* आप कूदते हैं, आप कूदती हैं।

44. I want money. *(mai̐ paise ćāhatā hu̐, mai̐ paise ćahatī hu̐)*
मैं पैसे चाहता हूँ, मैं पैसे चाहती हूँ।

45. I want to sleep. *(mai̐ sonā ćāhatā hu̐, mai̐ sonā ćahatī hu̐)*
मैं सोना चाहता हूँ, मैं सोना चाहती हूँ।

46. He wants to eat. *(vah khānā ćāhatā hai)* वह खाना चाहता है।

47. She wants to eat. *(vah khānā ćāhatī hai)* वह खाना चाहती है।

48. They want to go. *(ve jānā ćāhate hai̐, ve jānā ćāhatī hai̐)*
वे जाना चाहते हैं, वे जाना चाहती है।

TABLE 7 : Use of - I am doing; you are doing; he, she is doing; we are doing; they are doing

	Subject (colloquial) Doer of the action	verb drink	'-ing' doing	am, is, are I am, he is, they are
	1. I मैं *maĩ*	पी *pī*	रहा *rahā*	हूँ *hũ*
◦	2. He वह *vah* *(vo)*	पी *pī*	रहा *rahā*	है *hai*
◦	3. She वह *vah* *(vo)*	पी *pī*	रही *rahī*	है *hai*
*	4. We हम *ham*	पी *pī*	रहे *rahe*	हैं *haĩ*
*	5. You आप *āp* *(tum)*	पी *pī*	रहे *rahe*	हैं *haĩ* *(ho)*
*	6. They वे *ve* *(vo)*	पी *pī*	रहे *rahe*	हैं *haĩ*

NOTE : **The above table shows that :**

(i) A continuous (imperfect) mode '-ing' is shown in Hindī with letters *'rah'* (रह) to which gender suffix *ā, e,ī* or *ĩ* (आ, ए, ई, ईं) is added, as told in Table 6 ablve.

TABLE 7A : Present Continuous Tense Suffixes SUMMARY

	Subject	Suffix M◦	Suffix F◦
◦	I	रहा *(rahā)*	रही *(rahī)*
◦	He/she	रहा *(rahā)*	रही *(rahī)*
*	We	रहे *(rahe)*	रहे *(rahe)*
*	You *(āp)*	रहे *(rahe)*	रहे *(rahe)*
*	They	रहे *(rahe)*	रहे *(rahe)*

EXERCISE 20 : Translate the English sentences into Hindī (Answers are given for help)

1. I am drinking . *maĩ pī rahā (rahī) hũ.* मैं पी रहा (रही) हूँ। I am drinking tea. *maĩ chāy pī rahā (rahī) hũ.* मैं चाय पी रहा (रही) हूँ। I am drinking hot tea. *maĩ garam chāy pī rahā (rahī) hũ.* मैं गरम चाय पी रहा (रही) हूँ। You are drinking hot tea. *āp garam chāy pī rahe haĩ.* आप गरम चाय पी रहे हैं। He is drinking hot tea. *vah garam chāy pī rahā hai.* वह गरम चाय पी रहा है। She is drinking hot tea. *vah garam chāy pī rahī hai.* वह गरम चाय पी रही है। We are drinking hot tea. *ham garam chāy pī rahe haĩ.* हम गरम चाय पी रहे हैं। They are drinking hot tea. *ve garam chāy pī rahe haĩ.* वे गरम चाय पी रहे हैं।

2. They are eating bananas. *ve kele khā rahe haĩ.* वे केले खा रहे हैं।

3. She is sleeping. *vah so rahī hai.* वह सो रही है।

4. You are writing a book. *āp kitāb likh rahe haĩ.* आप किताब लिख रहे हैं।

5. He is going home. *vah ghar jā rahā hai.* वह घर जा रहा है।

TABLE 8 : I was doing; you were doing; he, she was doing; we were doing; they were doing

	Doer of the action	drink	-doing	Past tense
	Subject (colloquial)	verb	'-ing'	was, had
	1. I मैं *maĩ*	पी *pī*	रहा *rahā*	था *thā*
◦	2. He वह *vah* *(vo)*	पी *pī*	रहा *rahā*	था *thā*
◦	3. She वह *vah* *(vo)*	पी *pī*	रही *rahī*	थी *thī*
*	4. We हम *ham*	पी *pī*	रहे *rahe*	थे *the*
*	5. You आप *āp* *(tum)*	पी *pī*	रहे *rahe*	थे *the*
*	6. They वे *ve* *(vo)*	पी *pī*	रहे *rahe*	थे *the*

EXERCISE 21 : Translate the English sentences into Hindī (Answers are given for help)

1. I was drinking . *maĩ pī rahā thā (rahī thī)* मैं पी रहा था (रही थी) I was drinking tea. *maĩ chāy pī rahā thā (rahī thī).* मैं चाय पी रहा था (रही थी)। I was drinking hot tea. *maĩ garam chāy pī rahā thā (rahī thī).* मैं गरम चाय पी रहा था (रही थी)।

 You were drinking hot tea. *āp garam chāy pī rahe the.* आप गरम चाय पी रहे थे।

 He was drinking hot tea. *vah garam chāy pī rahā thā.* वह गरम चाय पी रहा था।

 She was drinking hot tea. *vah garam chāy pī rahī thī.* वह गरम चाय पी रही थी।

 We were drinking hot tea. *ham garam chāy pī rahe the.* हम गरम चाय पी रहे थे।

 They were drinking hot tea. *ve garam chāy pī rahe the.* वे गरम चाय पी रहे थे।

2. They were eating bananas. *ve kele khā rahe the.* वे केले खा रहे थे।

3. She was sleeping. *vah so rahī thī.* वह सो रही थी।

4. You were writing a book. *āp kitāb likh rahe the.* आप किताब लिख रहे थे।

5. He was going home. *vah ghar jā rahā thā.* वह घर जा रहा था।

TABLE 9 : I have 'already' done, you have done; he, she has done; we, they have done

	Doer of the action Subject (colloquial)	drink verb	already done *done*	am, is, has, have is, has
	1. I मैं *maĩ*	पी *pī*	चुका *chukā*	हूँ *hũ*
◦	2. He वह *vah* *(vo)*	पी *pī*	चुका *chukā*	है *hai*
◦	3. She वह *vah* *(vo)*	पी *pī*	चुकी *chukī*	है *hai*
*	4. We हम *ham*	पी *pī*	चुके *chuke*	हैं *haĩ*
*	5. You आप *āp*	पी *pī*	चुके *chuke*	हैं *haĩ*
*	6. They वे *ve* *(vo)*	पी *pī*	चुके *chuke*	हैं *haĩ*

NOTE : **The above table shoes that :**

(i) The 'already' done mode 'ed' is shown in Hindī with letters *'chuk'* (चुक) to which gender suffix *ā, e, ī* or *ĩ* (आ, ए, ई, ईं) is added, as shown above.

TABLE 9A : Already Done : Suffixes SUMMARY

	Subject	Suffix M◦	Suffix F◦
◦	I	चुका *(chukā)*	चुकी *(chukī)*
◦	He/she	चुका *(chukā)*	चुकी *(chukī)*
*	We	चुके *(chuke)*	चुके *(chuke)*
*	You *(āp)*	चुके *(chuke)*	चुके *(chuke)*
*	They	चुके *(chuke)*	चुके *(chuke)*

EXERCISE 22 : Translate the English sentences into Hindī (Answers are given for help)

1. I have already drunk hot tea. *maĩ garam chāy pī chukā (chukī) hũ.* मैं गरम चाय पी चुका (चुकी) हूँ। You have already drunk hot tea. *āp garam chāy pī chuke haĩ.* आप गरम चाय पी चुके हैं। He has already drunk hot tea. *vah garam chāy pī chukā hai.* वह गरम चाय पी चुका है। She has already drunk hot tea. *vah garam chāy pī chukī hai.* वह गरम चाय पी चुकी है। We have already drunk hot tea. *ham garam chāy pī chuke haĩ.* हम गरम चाय पी चुके हैं। They have already drunk hot tea. *ve garam chāy pī chuke haĩ.* वे गरम चाय पी चुके हैं।
2. They have already eaten bananas. *ve kele khā chuke haĩ.* वे केले खा चुके हैं।
3. She has already slept. *vah so chukī hai.* वह सो चुकी है।

4. You have already written a book. *āp kitāb likh chuke haĩ.* आप किताब लिख चुके हैं।

5. He has already gone home. *vah ghar jā chukā hai.* वह घर जा चुका है।

TABLE 10 : I had 'already' done, you had done; he, she had done; we, they had done

	Doer of the action: Subject (colloquial)	drink: verb	already done: *done*	Past tense: was, had
	1. I मैं *maĩ*	पी *pī*	चुका *chukā*	था *thā*
◦	2. He वह *vah* (*vo*)	पी *pī*	चुका *chukā*	था *thā*
◦	3. She वह *vah* (*vo*)	पी *pī*	चुकी *chukī*	थी *thī*
*	4. We हम *ham*	पी *pī*	चुके *chuke*	थे *the*
*	5. You आप *āp* (*tum*)	पी *pī*	चुके *chuke*	थे *the*
*	6. They वे *ve* (*vo*)	पी *pī*	चुके *chuke*	थे *the*

EXERCISE 23 : Translate the English sentences into Hindī (Answers are given for help)

1. I had already drunk hot tea. *maĩ garam chāy pī chukā thā (chukī thī).* मैं गरम चाय पी चुका था (चुकी थी)। You had already drunk hot tea. *āp garam chāy pī chuke the.* आप गरम चाय पी चुके थे। He had already drunk hot tea. *vah garam chāy pī chukā thā.* वह गरम चाय पी चुका था। She had already drunk hot tea. *vah garam chāy pī chukī thī.* वह गरम चाय पी चुकी थी। We had already drunk hot tea. *ham garam chāy pī chuke the.* हम गरम चाय पी चुके थे। They had already drunk hot tea. *ve garam chāy pī chuke the.* वे गरम चाय पी चुके थे।

TABLE 11 : SUMMARY, what we learned so far, the 'cumulative learning'

	Doer of the action: Subject			drink: verb	do, does......: 'do'	doing...............: '-ing'	.already done: done	am, is, has, have: is, has	Past tense: was, had
	I	मैं	*maĩ*	पी *pī*	ता *tā*	रहा *rahā*	चुका *chukā*	हूँ *hũ*	था *thā*
◦	He	वह	*vah*	पी *pī*	ता *tā*	रहा *rahā*	चुका *chukā*	है *hai*	था *thā*
◦	She	वह	*vah*	पी *pī*	ती *tī*	रही *rahī*	चुकी *chukī*	है *hai*	थी *thī*
*	We	हम	*ham*	पी *pī*	ते *te*	रहे *rahe*	चुके *chuke*	हैं *haĩ*	थे *the*
*	You	आप	*āp*	पी *pī*	ते *te*	रहे *rahe*	चुके *chuke*	हैं *haĩ*	थे *the*
*	They	वे	*ve*	पी *pī*	ते *te*	रहे *rahe*	चुके *chuke*	हैं *haĩ*	थे *the*

NOTE : The suffix *thā* (था) is comes in Hindī sentence ONLY when there is 'was, had or used to' in the English sentence. Exception is : verb 'want' *chāh* चाह। e.g. I wanted. मैं चाहता था।

TABLE 12 : I used to do; you used to do; he, she used to do; we used to do; they used to do

	Doer of the action Subject (colloquial)	drink verb	used to (drink) used to
	1. I मैं *maı̃*	पी *pī*	ता था *tā thā*
◦	2. He वह *vah* *(vo)*	पी *pī*	ता था *tā thā*
◦	3. She वह *vah* *(vo)*	पी *pī*	ती थी *tī thī*
*	4. We हम *ham*	पी *pī*	ते थे *te the*
*	5. You आप *āp*	पी *pī*	ते थे *te the*
*	6. They वे *ve* *(vo)*	पी *pī*	ते थे *te the*

EXERCISE 24 : Translate the English sentences into Hindī (Answers are given for help)

1. I used to drink tea. *maı̃ chāy pītā thā (pītī thī).* मैं चाय पीता था, पीती थी। You used to drink tea. *āp chāy pīte the.* आप चाय पीते थे। He used to drink tea. *vah chāy pītā thā.* वह चाय पीता था। She used to drink tea. *vah chāy pītī thī.* वह चाय पीती थी। We used to drink tea. *ham chāy pīte the.* हम चाय पीते थे। They used to drink tea. *ve chāy pīte the.* वे चाय पीते थे।
2. They used to eat bananas. *ve kele khāte the.* वे केले खाते थे। 3. She used to sleep. *vah sotī thī.* वह सोती थी। 4. You used to write books. *āp kitābẽ likhte the.* आप किताबें लिखते थे।

EXERCISE 25 : Translate the Hindī sentences into English (Answers are given for help)

Key Words : O Clock, at O Clock = *baje* बजे। Today = *āj* आज। Tomorrow, Yesterday = *kal* कल। Now = *ab* अब। Then = *tab* तब। When? = *kab* कब? What = *kyā* क्या। Work = *kām* काम।

1. Anjalī is coming at two O Clock. *añjalī do baje ā rahī hai.* अंजली दो बजे आ रही है।
2. They are not working today. *ve āj kām nahı̃ kar rahe haı̃.* वे आज काम नहीं कर रहे हैं।
3. Yesterday she was eating two *Roties. Vah kal do roṭiyā̃ khā rahī thī.* वह कल दो रोटियाँ खा रही थी।
4. What Vishāl was saying yesterday? *Vishāl kal kyā kah rahā thā.* विशाल कल क्या कह रहा था?
5. Mīrā was singing Hindī songs. (song = *gānā*) *mīrā Hindī gāne gā rahī thī.* मीरा हिंदी गाने गा रही थी।
6. Rādhā wants a cup of tea. *Rādhā ek kap chāy chāhatī hai.* राधा एक कप चाय चाहती है।
7. Rītā is now going home. *Rītā ab ghar jā rahī hai.* रीता अब घर जा रही है।
8. Nītā can run 10 km. *Nītā das kilo-mitar bhāg saktī hai.* नीता दस किलो-मिटर भाग सकती है।

9. You can not walk one km. *āp ek km. nahī̃ chal sakte haĩ.* आप एक कि.मी. नहीं चल सकते।

10. Yesterday a house was burning. *kal ek ghar jal rahā thā.* कल एक घर जल रहा था।

11. Gopāl has already fried the Samosās. *Gopāl samose tal chukā hai.* गोपाल समोसे तल चुका है।

12. Monā had already brought the books. *Monā kitābẽ lā chukī thī.* मोना किताबें ला चुकी थी।

13. Vijay reads at 7 O Clock. *Vijay sāt baje paḍhtā hai.* विजय सात बजे पढ़ता है।

14. I used to drink only coffee, now I drink tea also. *maĩ kāfī hī pītā thā, ab maĩ chāy bhī pītā hū̃.* मैं काफी ही पीता था, अब मैं चाय भी पीता हूँ।

15. We used to walk five km., now we walk only three km. *ham pā̃ch km. chalte the, ab ham tīn hī km. chalte haĩ.* हम पाँच कि.मि. चलते थे, अब हम तीन ही किलो मिटर चलते हैं।

16. They had already eaten bananas. *ve kele khā chuke the.* वे केले खा चुके थे।

17. She had already slept. *vah so chukī thī.* वह सो चुकी थी।

18. You had already written a book. *āp kitāb likh chuke the.* आप किताब लिख चुके थे।

19. He had already gone home. *vah ghar jā chukā thā.* वह घर जा चुका था।

13.1 MAKING SENTENCES FOR **FUTURE EVENTS**

The future events are generally of three kinds, viz॰ :

1. I will do   (you will do; he, she, it will do; we, they will do)   see - Table 13
2. I should do, I may do   (you should do; he, she do; we, we should do, they should do)
3. Should I do? May I do?   (should you do? should he do? she should do? should they do?)

TABLE 13 : Future and Subjunctive actions : I will do, I should-may do...etc.

Doer of the action	drink	will	will	I should, I may	should I ? may I?
Subject	verb	I will m॰	I will f॰	Suffix m॰ f॰	Should I? m॰ f॰
I मैं *maĩ*	पी *pī*	ऊँगा *ūngā*	ऊँगी *ūngī*	ऊँ *ū̃*	ऊँ क्या? *ū̃ kyā?*
He वह *vah*	पी *pī*	एगा *egā*	--	ए *e*	ए क्या? *e kyā?*
She वह *vah*	पी *pī*	--	एगी *egī*	ए *e*	ए क्या? *e kyā?*
We हम *ham*	पी *pī*	एँगे *enge*	एँगी *engī*	एँ *ẽ*	एँ क्या? *ẽ kyā?*
You आप *āp*	पी *pī*	एँगे *enge*	एँगी *engī*	एँ *ẽ*	एँ क्या? *ẽ kyā?*
They वे *ve*	पी *pī*	एँगे *enge*	एँगी *engī*	एँ *ẽ*	एँ क्या? *ẽ kyā?*

NOTE : **The above table shows that :**

(i) A Future Event (will) is shown in Hindī with letter *'g'* (ग) to which :

(ii) add the 'person' operative *ũ̐, e, ẽ* (ऊँ, ए, एँ), as described earlier, and then

(iii) add the 'gender' operative ā, e, ī, ī̐ (आ ए ई ईं), as said earlier in Table 6:

NOTE : (a) suffix 'ā' (आ) means masculine singular subject

(b) suffix 'e' (ए) means masculine plural subject

(c) suffix 'ī' (ई) means feminine singular subject

(d) suffix 'ī̐' (ईं) means feminine plural subject

TABLE 13A : Future Tense Suffixes SUMMARY

	Subject	Suffix M◦	Suffix F◦
◦	I	ऊँगा *(ungā)*	ऊँगी *(ungī)*
◦	He/she	एगा *(egā)*	एगी *(egī)*
*	We	एँगे *(enge)*	एँगे *(enge)*/ एँगी *(engī)*
*	You *(āp)*		
*	They		

NOTE : **masculine plural** एँगे *(enge)* is commonly used for **feminine plural** also.

EXERCISE 26 : Translate the English sentences into Hindī (Answers are given for help)

(a). **FUTURE TENSE** : I will drink. *maĩ piũngā (piũngī).* मैं पीऊँगा (पीऊँगी)। You will drink. *āp pieṅge.* आप पीएँगे। He will drink. *vah piegā.* वह पीएगा। She will drink. *vah piegī.* वह पीएगी। We will drink. *ham pieṅge.* हम पीएँगे। They will drink. *ve pieṅge.* वे पीएँगे।

(b). THE **POTENTIAL** MOOD (should, may) : I should drink. *maĩ piũ̐.* मैं पीऊँ। You should drink. *āp pieṅ.* आप पीएँ। He should drink. *vah pie.* वह पीए। She should drink. *vah pie.* वह पीए। We should drink. *ham pieṅ.* हम पीएँ। They should drink. *ve pieṅ.* वे पीएँ।

NOTICE THE SIMILARITY BETWEEN FUTURE TENSE AND THE POTENTIAL MOOD

(c). THE **INTERROGATIVE** MOOD : Should I drink? *maĩ piũ kyā?* मैं पीऊँ क्या? Should you drink? *āp piẽ kyā?* आप पीएँ क्या? Should he drink. *vah pie kyā.* वह पीए क्या? Should she drink. *vah pie kyā.* वह पीए क्या? Should we drink? *ham piẽ kyā?* हम पीएँ क्या? Should they drink? *ve piẽ kyā?* वे पीएँ क्या?

(d). Will I drink? *maĩ pīūngā (pīūngī) kyā?* मैं पीऊँगा (पीऊँगी) क्या? Will you drink? *āp pīenge kyā?* आप पीएँगे (पीएँगी) क्या? Will he drink? *vah pīegā kyā?* वह पीएगा क्या? Will she drink? *vah pīegī kyā?* वह पीएगी क्या? Will we drink? *ham pīenge kyā?* हम पीएँगे क्या? Will they drink? *ve pīenge kyā?* वे पीएँगे क्या?

RATNAKAR'S FOURTH NOBLE TRUTH : (Potential Mood)

A Verb in Potential Mood needs only a suffix indicating 'Person' (i.e. 1st, 2nd or 3rd; singular or plural). That is, it does not need any tense suffix (ह, थ, ग), mode suffix (त, रह, चुक) or a gender suffix (आ, ए, ई, ईं). e.g. (m॰ f॰) I should drink. *maĩ pīū̃ (pī + ū̃).* मैं पीऊँ।

RATNAKAR'S FIFTH NOBLE TRUTH : *(kyā)*

Whem '*kyā*' (क्या) comes at the beginning or at the end of a sentence, *kyā* (क्या) = a question mark (?). But, when *kyā* (क्या) comes anywhere in the sentence, then this *kyā* (क्या) = what?

(e). What will I drink? *maĩ kyā pīūngā (pīūngī)?* मैं क्या पीऊँगा (पीऊँगी)? What will you drink? *āp kyā pīenge?* आप क्या पीएँगे (पीएँगी)? What will he drink? *vah kyā pīegā?* वह क्या पीएगा? What will she drink? *vah kyā pīegī?* वह क्या पीएगी? What will we drink? *ham kyā pīenge?* हम क्या पीएँगे? What will they drink? *ve kyā pīenge?* वे क्या पीएँगे?

EXERCISE 27 : Translate the Hindī sentences into English (Answers are given for help)

Key Words : Everyday = *roz* रोज। Never = *kabhī nahī̃* कभी नहीं। Always = *hameshā* हमेशा।
Someone = *koī* कोई। Sometimes = *kabhī* कभी। Anytime = *kabhī bhī* कभी भी।
Some, Something = *kuchh* कुछ। Anything, Whatever = *kuchh bhī* कुछ भी।
where = *kahā̃* कहाँ। Somewhere = *kahī̃* कहीं। Anywhere = *kahī̃ bhī* कहीं भी।

1. Neil will come home at two O Clock. *Neil do baje ghar āegā.* नील दो बजे घर आएगा।
2. Rānī will not work today. *Rānī āj kām nahī̃ karegī.* रानी आज काम नहीं करेगी।
3. Yesterday Nīrā was sewing a dress. *kal Nīrā dress sī rahī thī.* कल नीरा ड्रेस सी रही थी।
4. What should Vijay say? *Vijay kyā kahe?* विजय क्या कहे?
5. What will Mīnā say? *Mīnā kyā kahegī?* मीना क्या कहेगी?
6. Rājā will want a cup of tea. *Rājā ek kap chāy chāhegā.* राजा एक कप चाय चाहेगा।
7. Should Rīkkī go home now. *Rīkkī ab ghar jāe kyā?* रीक्की अब घर जाए क्या?

8. Nīrū should go home now. *Nīrū ab ghar jāe.* नीरू अब घर जाए।

9. What should David write? *David kyā likhe?* डेविड क्या लिखे?

10. What was burning yesterday? *kal kyā jal rahā thā.* कल क्या जल रहा था।

11. Govind had already washed the dishes. *Govind thāliyā̐ dho chukā thā.* गोविंद थालियाँ धो चुका था।

12. Mohan should not sleep here today. *Mohan āj yahā̐ nahī̐ soye.* मोहन आज यहाँ नहीं सोए।

13. Vimalā reads something everyday. *Vimalā roz kuchh paḍhatī hai.* विमला रोज कुछ पढ़ती है।

14. Sunīl will be a TV star. *Sunīl TV star (sitārā) hogā.* सुनील टीवी स्टार (सितारा) होगा।

15. Vikās should win there. *Vikās vahā̐ jīte.* विकास वहाँ जीते।

16. Nobody wins always. *koī bhī hameshā nahī̐ jītatā hai.* कोई भी हमेशा नहीं जीतता है।

17. Somebody was here. *koī yahā̐ thā.* यहाँ कोई था।

18. Was anyone here? *kyā koī yahā̐ thā?* क्या कोई यहाँ था? *koī yahā̐ thā kyā ?* कोई यहाँ था क्या?

13.2 MAKING A REQUEST
the Imperative Sentences

Making a Request, Suggestion or giving an Order, is an Imperative Mood. A Request, Suggestion or an Order is made by a person (1st person) to a person whom he is talking to (2nd person). These three functions are done in three respective ways :

(A) MAKING A Respectful REQUEST :

A request is normally made in a respectful manner, using the word *āp* (आप) for you. For making such request word "please" is used in English, hut in Hindi the **imperative suffix *iye* (इये) is added to the verb**, which has please built in it. Therefore, you will ogten not see Hindi people using the word "please" in their sentences, unless it is an earnest or a formal request. The word the word *āp* (आप) you, may not be actually used, because it is always understood.

TABLE 13.2A : Suffix for making a REQUEST

Sentence	Subject (optional)	VERB आ *(ā) = come*	Suffix इये *(iye)*	Hindi Sentence
Please come!	You *āp* (आप)	आ *(ā)*	इये *(iye)*	आइये! *(āiye!)*

EXAMPLES :

IMPORTANT NOTE : The Hindi Learning books will tell you that the Hindi word verb "eat" is khjānā (खाना), but that is wrong. Khānā (खाना) is not a verb. It is (i) an finitive (to eat), or (ii) a verbal noun (food), or (iii) a gerund (eating). The Hindi verb (or verb stem or root verb) is **khā** (खा) to which you add any suffix. Please remember this note in order to learn Hindi easily and properly.

1. (you) please come! = *āp* आप + *āiye* आइये! = आप आइये! = *āp āiye* = आइये! = *āiye!*
2. Please speak! (Speak = *bol* बोल) *boliye* = बोलिये!
3. Please eat! (Eat = *khā* खा) *khāiye* = खाइये!
4. Please sleep! (Sleep = *so* सो) *soiye* = सोइये!
5. Please walk! (Walk = *chal* चल) *chaliye* = चलिये! It also means, "let's go."

TABLE 13.2B : The four **IRREGULAR** imperative VERBS

	Verb	Hindi	Changes to	Suffix जिये *jiye* is added	Imperative form
1	Take	ले *le*	ली *lī*	जिये *jiye*	लीजिये *lījiye*
2	Give	दे *de*	दी *dī*	जिये *jiye*	दीजिये *dījiye*
3	Do	कर *kar*	की *kī*	जिये *jiye*	कीजिये *kījiye*
4	Drink	पी *pī*	पी *pī**	जिये *jiye*	पीजिये *pījiye*
	* The verb पी *pī* does not change but the suffix इये *iye* changes from to जिये *jiye*				

(B) MAKING A Formal SUGGESTION :

A suggestion is also made in a respectful manner, using the word *āp* (आप) or *tum* (तुम) for you. For making such suggestion word "please" is used in English, hut in Hindi the **imperative suffix *o* (ओ) is added to the verb**, which has please built in it. Therefore, you will ogten not see Hindi people using the word "please" in their sentences. The word the word *āp* (आप) or *tum* (तुम) for you, may not be actually used, because it is always understood.

TABLE 13.2C : Suffix for making a SUGGESTION

Sentence	Subject (optional)	VERB सुन *(sun) = listen*	Suffix ओ *(o)*	Hindi Sentence
Please listen!	You *tum* (तुम)	सुन *(sun)*	ओ *(o)*	सुनो! *(suno!)*

EXAMPLES :

1. Please stop! (Stop = *ruk* रुक) *ruko!* = रुको!
2. Please go! (Go = *jā* जा) *jāo* = जाओ!
3. Please say! (Say = *kah* कह) *kaho* = कहो!
4. Please don't do! (Don't do = *mat kar* मत कर) *mat karo* = मत करो!
5. Please run! (Run = *bhāg* भाग) *bhāgo* = भागो!

(C) GIVING AN ORDER :

A n order is given aa a command, in which respects may not be there. Here, the word *tū* (तू) may be used for "you." For making such order word "please" is not used in English, and in Hindi, no imperative suffix is added to the verb. Just the plain verb is used, instead.

TABLE 13.2D : Suffix for giving an ORDER

Sentence	Subject (optional)	VERB बैठ *(baiṭh) = sit*	No suffix	Hindi Sentence
Sit!	You *tū* (तू)	बैठ *(baiṭh)*		बैठ *(baiṭh!)*

EXAMPLES :

1. Get out! (Get out = *nikal* निकल) *nikal!* = निकल!
2. Shut up! (Sut up = *chup kar* चुप कर) *chup kar* = चुप कर!
3. Don't move! (Don't move = *hil mat* हिल मत) *hil mat* = हिल मत!
4. Show (it to me)! (Show = *dikhā* दिखा) *dikhā* = दिखा!
5. Take a hike! (Take a hike = *bhāg* भाग) *bhāg* = भाग!

EXERCISE 28 : Read the following lines fron the Gita :

Bhagavad Gita

भगवद्गीता

कुतस्त्वा कश्मलमिदं विषमे समुपस्थितम् ।
अनार्यजुष्टमस्वर्ग्यमकीर्तिकरमर्जुन ।।

LESSON 14

MAKING SENTENCES FOR COMPLETED ACTIONS

A perfected or completed action indicates what you did, have done or had done.

(i) suffix (m◦) *ā* (आ) or (f◦) *ī* (ई) is attached to the verb that ends in a consonant or a short vowel.

e.g. verb *chal* चल (to walk) →

(1) walked *chal + ā = chalā;*

(2) I walked m◦ *maĩ chalā,* f◦ *maĩ chalī.* चल + आ = चला, (m◦) मैं चला, (f◦) मैं चली।

TABLE 14A : The **Perfect** Action Suffix for verbs ending in short vowels

	Verb	SUFFIX	
		Singular	Plural
1	Masculine	आ *ā*	ए *e*
2	Feminine	ई *ī*	ईं *ĩ* (or यी *yī*)

(ii) suffix *yā (y + ā)* या or *yī (y + ī)* यी is attached to the verb that ends in a long vowel such as *ā, ī* or *o* (आ, ई, ओ). e.g. verb *so* सो (sleep) → (slept) m◦ *so + y + ā = soyā,* I slept m◦ *maĩ soyā,* f◦ *maĩ soyī.* सो + या = सोया, (m◦) मैं सोया, (f◦) मैं सोयी।

TABLE 14B : The **Perfect** Action Suffix for verbs ending in long vowels

	Verb	SUFFIX	
		Singular	Plural
1	Masculine	या *yā*	ये *ye*
2	Feminine	यी *yī*	यीं *yĩ* (or यी *yī*)

(iii) If a completed action is Transitive, the suffix *ne* (ने) is attached to the subject. e.g. verb *khā* खा (eat) → (ate) *khā + yā = khāyā,* (I ate) *maĩne khāyā.* खा + या = खाया, मैंने खाया। *pī* पी (drink) → (drank) *pī + yā = pīyā,* (I drank) *maĩne pīyā.* पी + या = पीया, मैंने पीया।

(iv) When suffix *ne* (ने) is attached to a subject, the verb changes according to the Object (the thing on which the action is done). Now the Subject has no effect on the verb.

e.g. m◦ and f◦ subject → I ate a banana. *maĩ ne kelā khāyā* मैंने केला खाया। I ate bananas. *maĩ ne kele khāye* मैंने केले खाये। I ate a roṭī *maĩ ne roṭī khāyī* मैंने रोटी खायी। I ate roṭīs *maĩ ne roṭiyā̃ khāyī̃* मैंने रोटियाँ खायीं।

TABLE 14C : The **Perfect** Tense, **Transitive** suffix ने *ne*

Subject	Singular	Plural
I /we	मैंने *maĩ-ne*	हमने *ham-ne*
He/she/they	उसने *us-ne*	उन्हों ने *unhõ ne*
You आप *(āp)*	आपने *āp-ne*	आपने *āp-ne*
You तुम *(tum)*	तुमने *tum-ne*	तुमने *tum-ne*
You तू *(tū)*	तूने *tū-ne*	तुमने *tum-ne*
Rām	राम ने *Rām ne*	
Sītā	सीता ने *Sītā ne*	

RATNAKAR'S SIXTH NOBLE TRUTH : (Perfect tense)

If an action is completed on a transitive verb, suffix *ne* (ने) is attached to the subject.

(a) Completed or perfected action = I did, I have done, I had done ...etc.

(b) Transitive action is where the the action is performed on an object, not on the subject. e.g. I (the subject) ate (the verb) a mango (the object), I drank tea, I wrote a book ...etc.

(c) Intransitive action is where the action is performed by the doer (subject) on him/herself, i.e. the action is not transferred to any external object. e.g. I (the subject) went, Bob slept, John walked, dog ran, cat died, they stayed, we came, you lived, baby cried, water leaked, house burnt, Sonia won, she swam, he sat, monkey jumped, sun rose, rain fell.

The perfect (completed) actions are mainly of three kinds, such as :

1. I did (you did; he, she, it did; we did; they did) see - Table 14
2. I have done (you have done; he, she has done; we have done; they have done)
3. I had done (you had done; he, she had done; we had done; they had done)

TABLE 14 : I did; you did; he, she, it did; we did; they did ...etc.

	Doer of the action		Intransitive actions------			Transitive actions --					
	Subject		intransitive action	suffix		transitive action suffix	verb type 1 consonant end	suffix		verb type 2 Long vowel	suffix
	I मैं *maĩ*		*chal* चल	*ā* आ		*maĩ ne* मैंने	*kah* कह	*ā* आ		पी *pī*	*yā* या
◦	He वह *vah*		*chal* चल	*ā* आ		*usne* उसने	*kah* कह	*ā* आ		पी *pī*	*yā* या
◦	She वह *vah*		*chal* चल	*ī* ई		*usne* उसने	*kah* कह	*ā* आ		पी *pī*	*yā* या
*	We हम *ham*		*chal* चल	*e* ए		*hamne* हमने	*kah* कह	*ā* आ		पी *pī*	*yā* या
*	You आप *āp*		*chal* चल	*e* ए		*āpne* आपने	*kah* कह	*ā* आ		पी *pī*	*yā* या
*	They वे *ve*		*chal* चल	*e* ए		*unhõne* उन्होंने	*kah* कह	*ā* आ		पी *pī*	*yā* या

EXERCISE 29 : Translate the English sentences into Hindī (Answers are given for help)

NOTE : Many people use masculine plural tenses for feminine plural tenses also.

(a). **Intransitive** actions, such as I came , I went, I fell, I walked :

I walked *maĩ chalā (chalī)* मैं चला (चली)। You fell *āp gire* आप गिरे। He came *vah āyā.* वह आया। She went *vah gayaī* वह गयी। We slept *ham soye* हम सोये। They stayed *ve rahe.* वे रहे।

(b). Intransitive actions, such as I have come, I have gone, I have fallen, I have walked :

I have walked. *maĩ chalā (chalī) hũ.* मैं चला (चली) हूँ। You have fallen. *āp gire haĩ.* आप गिरे हैं। He has come. *vah āyā hai.* वह आया है। She has gone. *vah gayaī hai.* वह गयी है। We have slept. *ham soye haĩ.* हम सोये हैं। They have stayed. *ve rahe haĩ.* वे रहे हैं।

(c). Intransitive actions, such as I had come, I had gone, I had fallen, I had walked :

I had walked. *maĩ chalā thā (chalī thī).* मैं चला था (चली थी)। You had fallen. *āp gire the.* आप गिरे थे। He had come. *vah āyā thā.* वह आया था। She had gone. *vah gayaī thī.* वह गयी थी। We had slept. *ham soye the.* हम सोये थे। They had stayed. *ve rahe the.* वे रहे थे।

(d). **Transitive** actions, such as I did, I wrote, I drank, I saw :

I ate. *maĩ ne khāyā.* मैंने खाया। I ate a mango. *maĩ ne ām khāyā.* मैंने आम खाया। I ate one banana. *maĩ ne ek kelā khāyā.* मैंने एक केला खाया। I ate two bananas. *maĩ ne do kele khāye.* मैंने दो केले खाये। I ate one Roṭī. *maĩ ne ek Roṭī khāyī.* मैंने एक रोटी खायी। I ate two Roṭīs.

maĩ ne do Roṭiyā̃ khāyī̃. मैंने दो रोटियाँ खायीं।

You drank tea. *āp ne chāy pī.* आपने चाय पी (पीयी)। Jack washed hands. *Jack ne hāth dhoye.* जैक ने हाथ धोये। Sunitā touched TV. *Sunita ne TV chhūā.* सुनीता ने टीवी छूआ। We peeled bananas. *hamne kele chhīle.* हमने केले छीले। Rām and Shyām did the work. *Rām aur Shyām ne kām kiyā.* राम और शाम ने काम किया।

(e). Transitive actions, such as - I have done, I have written, I have drunk, I have seen :
I have eaten. *maĩ ne khāyā hai.* मैंने खाया है। I have eaten a mango. *maĩ ne ām khāyā hai.* मैंने आम खाया है। I have eaten one banana. *maĩ ne ek kelā khāyā hai.* मैंने एक केला खाया है। I have eaten two bananas. *maĩ ne do kele khāye hai.* मैंने दो केले खाये है। I have eaten one roṭī. *maĩ ne ek roṭī khāyī hai.* मैंने एक रोटी खायी है। I have eaten two roṭīs. *maĩ ne do roṭiyā̃ khāyī̃ haĩ.* मैंने दो रोटियाँ खायीं हैं।

You have drunk tea. *āp ne chāy pī hai.* आपने चाय पी है। Jack has washed hands. *Jack ne hāth dhoye haĩ.* जैक ने हाथ धोये हैं। Sunitā has touched TV. *Sunita ne TV chhūā hai.* सुनीता ने टीवी छूआ है। We have peeled bananas. *hamne kele chhīle haĩ.* हमने केले छीले हैं। Rām and Shyām have done the work. *Rām aur Shyām ne kām kiyā hai.* राम और शाम ने काम किया है।

(f). Transitive actions, such as - I had done, I had written, I had drunk, I had seen :
I had eaten. *maĩ ne khāyā thā.* मैंने खाया था। I had eaten a mango. *maĩ ne ām khāyā thā.* मैंने आम खाया था। I had eaten one banana. *maĩ ne ek kelā khāyā thā.* मैंने एक केला खाया था। I had eaten two bananas. *maĩ ne do kele khāye the.* मैंने दो केले खाये थे। I had eaten one roṭī. *maĩ ne ek roṭī khāyī thī.* मैंने एक रोटी खायी थी। I had eaten two roṭīs. *maĩ ne do roṭiyā̃ khāyī thī̃.* मैंने दो रोटियाँ खायी थीं।

You had drunk tea. *āp ne chāy pī thī.* आपने चाय पी थी। Jack had washed hands. *Jack ne hāth dhoye the.* जैक ने हाथ धोये थे। Sunitā had touched TV. *Sunita ne TV chhūā thā.* सुनीता ने टीवी छूआ था। We had peeled bananas. *hamne kele chhīle the.* हमने केले छीले थे। Rām and Shyām had done the work. *Rām aur Shyām ne kām kiyā thā.* राम और शाम ने काम किया था।

RATNAKAR'S SEVENTH NOBLE TRUTH : (The Suffixes) **The 18 SUFFIXES :**

(1) Present tense = 'h' (ह); (2) Past tense = 'th' (थ); (3) Future tense = 'g' (ग); (4) Habitual 'do' mode = 't' (त); (5) Continuous (imperfect) '-ing' mode = 'rah' (रह); (6) Already 'done' mode = 'chuk' (चुक); (7) Masculine singular= 'ā ' (आ); (8) Masculine plural = 'e' (ए); (9) Feminine singular = 'ī ' (ई); (10) Feminine plural = 'iyā̃' (इयाँ); (11) First person singular (I) = 'ū̃ ' (ऊँ); (12) Third person singular (he, she) = 'ai' (ऐ); (13) Any Third person plural (we, you, they) = 'aĩ ' (एँ) ; (14) Any Perfect action = 'ā ' (आ); (15) Transitive Perfect action = 'ne' (ने). ALSO : (16) am = 'hū̃ ' (हूँ); (17) is, has, have = 'hai' (है); (18) was, had = 'thā ' (था).

IN DEPTH VIEW OF THE PERFECT (COMPLETED) ACTIONS

TABLE 15 : (completed Intransitive actions) I walked, I have walked, I had walked ...etc.

Doer of the action   Intransitive actions --

	Subject	action type 1 end in consonant	suffix		action type 2 Long vowel	suffix		HAVE		HAD
	I मैं *maĩ*	*chal* चल	*ā* आ		सो *so*	*yā* या		हूँ *hū̃*		*thā* था
◦	He वह *vah*	*chal* चल	*ā* आ		सो *so*	*yā* या		है *hai*		*thā* था
◦	She वह *vah*	*chal* चल	*ī* ई		सो *so*	*yī* यी		है *hai*		*thī* थी
*	We हम *ham*	*chal* चल	*e* ए		सो *so*	*ye* ये		हैं *haĩ*		*the* थे
*	You आप *āp*	*chal* चल	*e* ए		सो *so*	*ye* ये		हैं *haĩ*		*the* थे
*	They वे *ve*	*chal* चल	*e* ए		सो *so*	*ye* ये		हैं *haĩ*		*the* थे

TABLE 16 : (Presently completed actions) I have written, I have eaten ...etc. *** for m◦ object**

Doer of the action   Transitive actions --

Subject	transitive action suffix	verb type 1 consonant end	suffix	present action (have) suffix		verb type 2 Long vowel	suffix	present action (have) suffix
I मैं *maĩ*	*ne* ने	*likh* लिख	*ā* आ*	है *hai*		*khā* खा	*yā* या*	है *hai*
He *उस *us*	*ne* ने	*likh* लिख	*ā* आ*	है *hai*		*khā* खा	*yā* या*	है *hai*
She *उस *us*	*ne* ने	*likh* लिख	*ā* आ*	है *hai*		*khā* खा	*yā* या*	है *hai*
We हम *ham*	*ne* ने	*likh* लिख	*ā* आ*	है *hai*		*khā* खा	*yā* या*	है *hai*
You आप *āp*	*ne* ने	*likh* लिख	*ā* आ*	है *hai*		*khā* खा	*yā* या*	है *hai*
They *उन्हों *unhõ*	*ne* ने	*likh* लिख	*ā* आ*	है *hai*		*khā* खा	*yā* या*	है *hai*

NOTES : (i) For the changes from *vah* वह to *us* उस and *ve* वे to *un* उन, see Tables 23-24 (ii) * In tables 16-17, m◦ object is default.

TABLE 17 : (Previously completed actions) I had written, I had eaten ...etc. *** for m◦ object**

Doer of the action   Transitive actions --

Subject	transitive action suffix	verb type 1 consonant end	suffix	past action (had) suffix		verb type 2 Long vowel	suffix	past action (had) suffix
I मैं *maĩ*	*ne* ने	*likh* लिख	*ā* आ*	*thā* था*		*khā* खा	*yā* या*	*thā* था*
He *उस *us*	*ne* ने	*likh* लिख	*ā* आ*	*thā* था*		*khā* खा	*yā* या*	*thā* था*
She *उस *us*	*ne* ने	*likh* लिख	*ā* आ*	*thā* था*		*khā* खा	*yā* या*	*thā* था*
We हम *ham*	*ne* ने	*likh* लिख	*ā* आ*	*thā* था*		*khā* खा	*yā* या*	*thā* था*
You आप *āp*	*ne* ने	*likh* लिख	*ā* आ*	*thā* था*		*khā* खा	*yā* या*	*thā* था*
They *उन्हों *unhõ*	*ne* ने	*likh* लिख	*ā* आ*	*thā* था*		*khā* खा	*yā* या*	*thā* था*

NOTES : (i) For the changes from *vah* वह to *us* उस and *ve* वे to *un* उन, see Tables 23-24 (ii) * In tables 16-17, m◦ object is default.

EXPLANATION OF TABLES 15, 16 and 17

(Perfect or completed actions)

Intransitive actions, I did xxx (Table 15)

1. I did walk or I walked. *maĩ chalā.* मैं चला। He did walk or he walked. *vah chalā.* वह चला। She did walk or she walked. *vah chalī.* वह चली। We did walk or we walked. *ham chale.* हम चले। You did walk or You walked. *āp chale.* आप चले। They did walk or They walked. *ve chale.* वे चले। * I did sleep or I slept. *maĩ soyā.* मैं सोया। He did sleep or he slept. *vah soyā.* वह सोया। She did sleep or she slept. *vah soyī.* वह सोयी। We did sleep or we slept. *ham soye.* हम सोये। You did sleep or You slept. *āp soye.* आप सोये। They did sleep or They slept. *ve soye.* वे सोये।

2. I **have** walked. *maĩ chalā hũ.* मैं चला हूँ। He has walked. *vah chalā hai.* वह चला है। She has walked. *vah chalī hai.* वह चली है। We have walked. *ham chale haĩ.* हम चले हैं। You have walked. *āp chale haĩ.* आप चले हैं। They have walked. *ve chale haĩ.* वे चले हैं। * I have slept. *maĩ soyā hũ.* मैं सोया हूँ। He has slept. *vah soyā hai.* वह सोया है। She has slept. *vah soyī hai.* वह सोयी है। We have slept. *ham soye haĩ.* हम सोये हैं। You have slept. *āp soye haĩ.* आप सोये हैं। They have slept. *ve soye haĩ.* वे सोये हैं। They have slept now. *ve ab soye haĩ.* वे अब सोये हैं। They have slept right now. *ve abhi soye jaĩ.* वे अभी सोये हैं।

3. I **had** walked. *mai͂ chalā thā.* मैं चला था। He had walked. *vah chalā thā.* वह चला था। She had walked. *vah chalī thī.* वह चली थी। We had walked. *ham chale the.* हम चले थे। You had walked. *āp chale the.* आप चले थे। They had walked. *ve chale the.* वे चले थे। * I had slept. *mai͂ soyā thā.* मैं सोया था। He had slept. *vah soyā thā.* वह सोया था। She had slept. *vah soyī thī.* वह सोयी थी। We had slept. *ham soye the.* हम सोये थे। You had slept. *āp soye the.* आप सोये थे। They had slept. *ve soye the.* वे सोये थे।

Transitive actions, I have done xxx (Table 16)

4. I **did** write or I wrote. *mai͂-ne likhā.* मैंने लिखा। He did write or he wrote. *us-ne likhā.* उसने लिखा। She did write or she wrote. *us-ne likhā.* उसने लिखा। We did write or we wrote. *ham-ne likhā.* हमने लिखा। You did write or You wrote. *āp-ne likhā.* आपने लिखा। They did write or They wrote. *unho͂-ne likhā.* उन्होंने लिखा। * I did eat or I ate. *mai͂-ne khāyā.* मैंने खाया। He did eat or he ate. *us-ne khāyā.* उसने खाया। She did eat or she ate. *us-ne khāyā.* उसने खाया। We did eat or we ate. *ham-ne khāyā.* हमने खाया। You did eat or You ate. *āp-ne khāyā.* आपने खाया। They did eat or They ate. *unho͂-ne khāyā.* उन्होंने खाया।

5. I **have** written. *mai͂-ne likhā hai.* मैंने लिखा है। He has written. *us-ne likhā hai.* उसने लिखा है। She has written. *us-ne likhā hai.* उसने लिखा है। We have written. *ham-ne likhā hai.* हमने लिखा है। You have written. *āp-ne likhā hai.* आपने लिखा है। They have written. *unho͂-ne likhā hai.* उन्होंने लिखा है। * I have eaten. *mai͂-ne khāyā hai.* मैंने खाया है। He has eaten. *us-ne khāyā hai.* उसने खाया है। She has eaten. *us-ne khāyā hai.* उसने खाया है। We have eaten. *ham-ne khāyā hai.* हमने खाया है। You have eaten. *āp-ne khāyā hai.* आपने खाया है। They have eaten. *unho͂ne khāyā hai.* उन्होंने खाया है।

Transitive actions, I had done xxx (Table 17)

6. I **had** written. *mai͂-ne likhā thā.* मैंने लिखा था। He had written. *us-ne likhā thā.* उसने लिखा था। She had written. *us-ne likhā thā.* उसने लिखा था। We had written. *ham-ne likhā thā.* हमने लिखा था। You had written. *āp-ne likhā thā.* आपने लिखा था। They had written. *unho͂-ne likhā thā.* उन्होंने लिखा था। * I had eaten. *mai͂-ne khāyā thā.* मैंने खाया था। He had eaten. *us-ne khāyā thā.* उसने खाया था। She had eaten. *us-ne khāyā thā.* उसने खाया था। We had eaten. *ham-ne khāyā thā.* हमने खाया था। You had eaten. *āp-ne khāyā thā.* आपने खाया था। They had eaten. *unho͂-ne khāyā thā.* उन्होंने खाया था।

ADVANCED PRACTICAL USE OF THE ABOVE PERFECT ACTIONS

Intransitive actions, as given in Table 15

(For Masculine, Feminine, Singular, Plural - refer to the Picture Dictionary and first three Noble Truths)

7. I **did** walk or I walked ten k.m. *maĩ das k.m. chalā.* मैं दस कि.मि. चला। He walked up to temple. *vah mandir tak chalā.* वह मंदिर तक चला। She walked yesterday. *vah kal chalī.* वह कल चली। We walked slowly. *ham dhīre chale.* हम धीरे चले। You walked fast. *āp tej chale.* आप तेज चले। They walked more. *ve jyādā chale.* वे ज्यादा चले। * I slept less. *maĩ kam soyā.* मैं कम सोया। He did not sleep. *vah nahĩ soyā.* वह नहीं सोया। She did sleep. *vah soyī.* वह सोयी। We slept enough. *ham kāfī soye.* हम काफी सोये। You slept a lot. *āp bahut soye.* आप बहुत सोये। They slept a little bit. *ve jarā (thoḍā) soye.* वे जरा (थोड़ा) सोये।

8. I **have** always walked. *maĩ hameshā chalā hũ.* मैं हमेशा चला हूँ। He has never walked. *vah kabhī nahĩ chalā hai.* वह कभी नहीं चला है। She has walked sometimes. *vah kabhī kabhī chalī hai.* वह कभी कभी चली है। We have walked ahead. *ham āge chale haĩ.* हम आगे चले हैं। You have walked behind. *āp pīchhe chale haĩ.* आप पीछे चले हैं। They have walked together. *ve sāth sāth chale haĩ.* वे साथ साथ चले हैं।

9. I **had** walked outside. *maĩ bāhar chalā thā.* मैं बाहर चला था। He had walked inside. *vah andar chalā thā.* वह अंदर चला था। She had walked in front. *vah sāmane chalī thī.* वह सामने चली थी। We had walked today. *ham āj chale the.* हम आज चले थे।

Transitive actions, I have done xxx (Table 16)

10. I **did** write or I wrote a letter. *maĩ-ne patra likhā.* मैंने पत्र लिखा। He wrote letters. *us-ne patra likhe.* उसने पत्र लिखे। She wrote a letter. *us-ne patra likhā.* उसने पत्र लिखा। We wrote a letter. *ham-ne chiṭṭhī likhī.* हमने चिट्ठी लिखी (*patra likhā.* मैंने पत्र लिखा)। You wrote letters. *āp-ne chiṭṭhiyā̃ likhī.* आपने चिट्ठियाँ लिखी (*patra likhe.* मैंने पत्र लिखे)। They wrote books. *unhõ-ne kitābẽ likhī.* उन्होंने किताबें लिखी। * I ate a banana. *maĩ-ne kelā khāyā.* मैंने केला खाया। He ate bananas. *us-ne kele khāyā.* उसने केले खाया। She ate a roṭī. *us-ne roṭī khāyī.* उसने रोटी खायी। We ate roṭīs. *ham-ne roṭiyā̃ khāyī.* हमने रोटियाँ खायी। You ate a mango. *āp-ne ām khāyā.* आपने आम खाया। They ate mangos. *unhõ -ne ām khāye.* उन्होंने आम खाये।

11. I **have** written a book. *maĩ-ne kitāb likhī hai.* मैंने किताब लिखी है। He has written a book. *us-ne kitāb likhī hai.* उसने किताब लिखी है। She has written a letter. *us-ne khat likhā hai.* उसने खत लिखा है (*patra likhā hai.* मैंने पत्र लिखा है)। We have written letters. *ham-ne khat likhe haĩ.* हमने खत लिखे हैं (*patra likhe haĩ.* मैंने पत्र लिखे हैं)। You have written Hindī. *āp-ne hindī likhā hai.* आपने हिंदी लिखा है। They have written Hindī. *unhõ-ne hindī likhā hai.* उन्होंने हिंदी लिखा है। * I have eaten two apples. *maĩ-ne do seb khāye haĩ.* मैंने दो सेब खाये हैं। He has eaten three Samosas. *us-ne tīn samose khāye haĩ.* उसने तीन समोसे खाये हैं। She has eaten four Paraṭhās. *us-ne chār parāṭhe khāye haĩ.* उसने चार पराठे खाये हैं। We have eaten five grapes. *ham-ne pāñch angūr khāye haĩ.* हमने पाँच अंगूर खाये हैं। You have eaten six chillies. *āp-ne chhah mirchiyā̃ khāyī haĩ.* आपने छह मिरचियाँ खायी हैं। They have eaten seven tomatos. *unhõne sāt tamāṭar khāye haĩ.* उन्होंने सात टमाटर खाये हैं।

Transitive actions, I had done xxx (Table 17)

12. I **had** eaten sugarcane. *maĩ-ne īkh khāyā thā.* मैंने ईख खाया था। He had eaten eight pomegranates. *us-ne āṭh anār khāye the.* उसने आठ अनार खाये थे। She had eaten nine lemons. *us-ne nau nīmbū khāye the.* उसने नौ नींबू खाये थे। We had eaten ten dates. *ham-ne das chhuāre khāye the.* हमने दस छूआरे खाये थे। You had not eaten garlic. *āp-ne lahsun nahĩ khāyā thā.* आपने लहसुन नहीं खाया था। They had eaten a little. *unhõ -ne thoḍā khāyā thā.* उन्होंने थोड़ा खाया था।

TABLE 18 : SUMMARY OF SUFFIXES FOR ALL TEN ACTIONS WE LEARNED SO FAR in Tables 1-17

TABLE 18-A : FOR MASCULINE SUBJECTS

REMEMBER : For Transitive Perfect Actions you have to add *ne* (ने) to the subject, and change the verb according to the gender and number of the object.

Doer of the action------		to Drink	Habitual	Imperfect	Already done	Present•	Past•	Future•	Request	Question	Completed Intransitive Actions --------------		
Masc-uline	subject	verb	do	-doing	done	am, is	was, had	will do	I should	should I?	did	have done	had done
I (m•)	मैं *maĩ*	पी *pī*	ता *tā*	रहा *rahā*	चुका *chukā*	हूँ *hū̃*	था *thā*	ऊँगा *ū̃gā*	ऊँ *ū̃*	ऊँ *ū̃ ?*	आ *ā*	आ हूँ *ā hū̃*	आ था *ā thā*
He	वह *vah*	पी *pī*	ता *tā*	रहा *rahā*	चुका *chukā*	है *hai*	था *thā*	एगा *egā*	ए *e*	ए *e ?*	आ *ā*	आ है *ā hai*	आ था *ā thā*
We	हम *ham*	पी *pī*	ते *te*	रहे *rahe*	चुके *chuke*	हैं *haĩ*	थे *the*	एंगे *ẽge*	एं *ẽ*	एं *ẽ ?*	ए *e*	ए हैं *e haĩ*	ए थे *e the*
You	आप *āp*	पी *pī*	ते *te*	रहे *rahe*	चुके *chuke*	हैं *haĩ*	थे *the*	एंगे *ẽge*	एं *ẽ*	एं *ẽ ?*	ए *e*	ए हैं *e haĩ*	ए थे *e the*
They	वे *ve*	पी *pī*	ते *te*	रहे *rahe*	चुके *chuke*	हैं *haĩ*	थे *the*	एंगे *ẽge*	एं *ẽ*	एं *ẽ ?*	ए *e*	ए हैं *e haĩ*	ए थे *e the*
			1	2	3		4	5	6	7	8	9	10

Remember : In Transitive Completed actions, suffix ने (*ne*) is added to the Subject; NOW the verb is controlled by theGender and Number of the Object.

The suffixes for : (i) m• singular = आ *ā* (ii) f• sing• = ई *ī* (iii) plural• = ए *e*. Shown above are the suffixes only for actions with m• singular Object.

TABLE 18-B : FOR FEMININE SUBJECTS

REMEMBER : For Transitive Perfect Actions you have to add *ne* (ने) to the subject, and change the verb according to the gender and number of the object.

Doer of the action------		to Drink	Habitual	Imperfect	Already done	Present•	Past•	Future•	Request	Question	Completed Intransitive Actions --------------		
Femin-ine	subject	verb	do	-doing	done	am, is	was, had	will do	I should	should I?	did	have done	had done
I (f•)	मैं *maĩ*	पी *pī*	ती *tī*	रही *rahī*	चुकी *chukī*	हूँ *hū̃*	थी *thī*	ऊँगी *ū̃gī*	ऊँ *ū̃*	ऊँ *ū̃ ?*	ई *ī*	ई हूँ *ī hū̃*	ई थी *ī thī*
She	वह *vah*	पी *pī*	ती *tī*	रही *rahī*	चुकी *chukī*	है *hai*	थी *thī*	एगी *egī*	ए *e*	ए *e ?*	ई *ī*	ई है *ī hai*	ई थी *ī thī*
We	हम *ham*	पी *pī*	तीं *tī̃*	रहीं *rahī̃*	चुकीं *chukī̃*	हैं *haĩ*	थीं *thī̃*	एंगे *ẽge*	एं *ẽ*	एं *ẽ ?*	ईं *ī̃*	ई हैं *ī̃ haĩ*	ई थीं *ī̃ thī̃*
You	आप *āp*	पी *pī*	तीं *tī̃*	रहीं *rahī̃*	चुकीं *chukī̃*	हैं *haĩ*	थीं *thī̃*	एंगे *ẽge*	एं *ẽ*	एं *ẽ ?*	ईं *ī̃*	ई हैं *ī̃ haĩ*	ई थीं *ī̃ thī̃*
They	वे *ve*	पी *pī*	तीं *tī̃*	रहीं *rahī̃*	चुकीं *chukī̃*	हैं *haĩ*	थीं *thī̃*	एंगे *ẽge*	एं *ẽ*	एं *ẽ ?*	ईं *ī̃*	ई हैं *ī̃ haĩ*	ई थीं *ī̃ thī̃*
			1	2	3		4	5	6	7	8	9	10

Remember : In Transitive Completed actions, suffix ने (*ne*) is added to the Subject; NOW the verb is controlled by the Gender and Number of the Object.

The suffixes for : (i) m• singular = आ *ā* (ii) f• sing• = ई *ī* (iii) plural• = ए *e*. Shown above are the suffixes only for actions with m• singular Object.

NOTES : (i) He, she, that = वह, *वो (*vah*, * *vo*); (ii) Those = वे, *वो (*ve*, **vah* * *vo*); (iii) It, this, these = यह, *ये (*yah*, **ye*); *colloquial

For detailed expansion and extended variations of these pronouns, see Table 25

EXPLANATION OF TABLES 18 and 18-A
THE TEN MOST COMMON WAYS OF USING ACTION-WORDS

13. PRESENT HABITUAL, 'do' mode (suffixes ता, ती, ते *tā, tī, te*): I walk or I do walk. (m∘) *maiँ chaltā hūँ.* मैं चलता हूँ। (f∘) *maiँ chaltī hūँ.* मैं चलती हूँ। He walks, he does walk. *vah chaltā hai.* वह चलता है। She walks, she does walk. *vah chaltī hai.* वह चलती है। We walk, we do walk. *ham chalte haiँ.* हम चलते हैं। You walk, you do walk. *āp chalte haiँ.* आप चलते हैं। They walk, they do walk. *ve chalte haiँ.* वे चलते हैं।

14. CONTINUOUS, 'doing' mode (suffixes रहा, रही, रहे *rahā, rahī, rahe*): I **am** walking. (m∘) *maiँ chal rahā hūँ.* मैं चल रहा हूँ। (f∘) *maiँ chal rahī hūँ.* मैं चल रही हूँ। He is walking. *vah chal rahā hai.* वह चल रहा है। She is walking. *vah chal rahī hai.* वह चल रही है। We are walking. *ham chal rahe haiँ.* हम चल रहे हैं। You are walking. *āp chal rahe haiँ.* आप चल रहे हैं। They are walking. *ve chal rahe haiँ.* वे चल रहे हैं। * I **was** walking. (m∘) *maiँ chal rahā thā.* मैं चल रहा था। (f∘) *maiँ chal rahī thī.* मैं चल रही थी। He was walking. *vah chal rahā thā.* वह चल रहा था। She was walking. *vah chal rahī thī.* वह चल रही थी। We were walking. (m∘) *ham chal rahe the.* हम चल रहे थे। (f∘) *ham chal rahī thīँ.* हम चल रही थीं। You were walking. (m∘) *āp chal rahe the.* आप चल रहे थे। (f∘) *āp chal rahī thīँ.* आप चल रहे थीं। They were walking. (m∘) *ve chal rahe the.* वे चल रहे थे। (f∘) *ve chal rahī thīँ.* वे चल रहीं थीं।

15. ALREADY COMPLETED, 'already done' mode (suffixes चुका, चुकी, चुके *chukā, chukī, chuke*): I **have** already walked. (m∘) *maiँ chal chukā hūँ.* मैं चल चुका हूँ। (f∘) *maiँ chal chukī hūँ.* मैं चल चुकी हूँ। He has already walked. *vah chal chukā hai.* वह चल चुका है। She has already walked. *vah chal chukī hai.* वह चल चुकी है। We have already walked. *ham chal chuke haiँ.* हम चल चुके हैं। You have already walked. *āp chal chuke haiँ.* आप चल चुके हैं। They have already walked. *ve chal chuke haiँ.* वे चल चुके हैं। * I **had** already walked. (m∘) *maiँ chal chukā thā.* मैं चल चुका था। (f∘) *maiँ chal chukī thī.* मैं चल चुकी थी। He had already walked. *vah chal chukā thā.* वह चल चुका था। She had already walked. *vah chal chukī thī.* वह चल चुकी थी। We had already walked. *ham chal chuke the.* हम चल चुके थे। You had already walked. *āp chal chuke the.* आप चल चुके थे। They had already walked. *ve chal chuke the.* वे चल चुके थे।

16. PAST HABITUAL : 'used to do' mode (suffixes ता था, ती थी, ते थे *tā thā, tī thī, te the*): I used to walk. (m∘) *maiँ chal tā thā.* मैं चलता था। (f∘) *maiँ chal tī thī.* मैं चलती थी। He used to walk. *vah chal tā thā.* वह चलता था। She used to walk. *vah chal tī thī.* वह चलती थी। We used to walk. *ham chal te the.* हम चलते थे। You used to walk. *āp chal te the.* आप चलते थे। They used to walk. *ve chal te the.* वे चलते थे।

17. **FUTURE, 'will' mode** (suffixes ऊँगा, ऊँगी, एगा, एगी, एंगे *ū̐gā, ū̐gī, egā, egī, enge*): I will walk. (m◦) *maĩ chalū̐gā.* मैं चलूँगा। (f◦) *maĩ chalū̐gā.* मैं चलूँगी। He will walk. *vah chalegā.* वह चलेगा। She will walk. *vah chalegī.* वह चलेगी। We will walk. *ham chalenge.* हम चलेंगे। You will walk. *āp chalenge.* आप चलेंगे। They will walk. *ve chalenge.* वे चलेंगे।

18. **POTENTIAL, 'should or may' mode** (suffixes ऊँ, ए, एं *ū̐, e, ẽ, enge*): I (m◦ and f◦) should walk. *maĩ chalū̐.* मैं चलूँ। He or she should walk. *vah chale.* वह चले। We should walk. *ham chalẽ.* हम चलें। You should walk. *āp chalẽ.* आप चलें। They should walk. *ve chalẽ.* वे चलें।

19. **INTERROGATIVE, 'should I? or may I?' mode** (suffixes ऊँ? ए? एं? *ū̐? e? ẽ? enge?*): Should I walk. (m◦ and f◦) *maĩ chalū̐?* मैं चलूँ? *maĩ chalū̐ kyā?* मैं चलूँ क्या? Should he or she walk. *vah chale?* वह चले? *vah chale kyā?* वह चले क्या? Should we walk. *ham chalẽ?* हम चलें? *ham chalẽ kyā?* हम चलें क्या? Will you walk. *āp chalenge?.* आप चलेंगे? *āp chalenge kyā?.* Will they walk? *ve chalenge?* वे चलेंगे?∗ *ve chalenge kyā?* वे चलेंगे क्या?

20. **SIMPLE PERFECT, 'did' mode** (suffixes आ, या, ई, यी *ā. yā, ī, yī*): I did walk or I walked. (m◦) *maĩ chalā.* मैं चला। (f◦) *maĩ chalī.* मैं चली। He did walk or he walked. *vah chalā.* वह चला। She did walk or she walked. *vah chalī.* वह चली। We did walk or we walked. *ham chale.* हम चले। You did walk or you walked. *āp chale.* आप चले। They did walk or they walked. *ve chale.* वे चले।

21. **Transitive Actions (As said before, refer Tables 23-24 for changes to pronouns *vah* वह and *ve* वे)** I (m◦ and f◦) did eat or I ate a banana. *maĩne kelā khāyā.* मैंने केला खाया। I ate two bananas. *maĩne do kele khāye.* मैंने दो केले खाये। I ate a roṭī. *maĩne roṭī khāyī.* मैंने रोटी खायी। I ate two roṭīs. *maĩne do roṭiyā̐ khāyī̐.* मैंने दो रोटियाँ खायीं। ∗ He or she ate a banana. *usne kelā khāyā.* उसने केला खाया। He or she ate two bananas. *usne do kele khāye.* उसने दो केले खाये। He ate a roṭī. *usne roṭī khāyī.* उसने रोटी खायी। He ate two roṭīs *usne do roṭiyā̐ khāyī̐.* उसने दो रोटियाँ खायीं। ∗ We ate a banana. *hamne kelā khāyā.* हमने केला खाया। We ate two bananas. *hamne do kele khāye.* हमने दो केले खाये। We ate a roṭī. *hamne roṭī khāyī.* हमने रोटी खायी। We ate two roṭīs *hamne do roṭiyā̐ khāyī̐.* हमने दो रोटियाँ खायीं। ∗ You (m◦ and f◦) ate a banana. *āpne kelā khāyā.* आपने केला खाया। You ate two bananas. *āpne do kele khāye.* आपने दो केले खाये। You ate a roṭī. *āpne roṭī khāyī.* आपने रोटी खायी। You ate two roṭīs *āpne do roṭiyā̐ khāyī̐.* आपने दो रोटियाँ खायीं। ∗ They (m◦ and f◦) ate a banana. *unhõne kelā khāyā.* उन्होंने केला खाया। They ate two bananas. *unhõne do kele khāye.* उन्होंने दो केले खाये। They ate a roṭī. *unhõne roṭī khāyī.* उन्होंने रोटी खायी। They ate two roṭīs *unhõne do roṭiyā̐ khāyī̐.* उन्होंने दो रोटियाँ खायीं।

22. **PRESENT PERFECT, 'have done' mode** (sucffixes आ है, ई है, ए हैं *ā hai, ī hai, e haĩ*): I have walked. (m◦) *maĩ chalā hū̃.* मैं चला हूँ। (f◦) *maĩ chalī hū̃.* मैं चली हूँ। He has walked. *vah chalā hai.* वह चला है। She has walked. *vah chalī hai.* वह चली है। We have walked. *ham chale haĩ.* हम चले हैं। You have walked. *āp chale haĩ.* आप चले हैं। They have walked. *ve chale haĩ.* वे चले हैं।

23. **Transitive Actions: (As said before, refer Tables 23-24 for changes to pronouns he, she, and they)** I (m◦ and f◦) have eaten a banana. *maĩne kelā khāyā hai.* मैंने केला खाया है। I have eaten two bananas. *maĩne do kele khāye haĩ.* मैंने दो केले खाये हैं। I have eaten a roṭī. *maĩne roṭī khāyī hai.* मैंने रोटी खायी है। I have eaten two roṭīs. *maĩne do roṭiyā̃ khāyī haĩ.* मैंने दो रोटियाँ खायी हैं। * He or she has eaten a banana. *usne kelā khāyā hai.* उसने केला खाया है। He or she has eaten two bananas. *usne do kele khāye haĩ.* उसने दो केले खाये हैं। He or she has eaten a roṭī. *usne roṭī khāyī hai.* उसने रोटी खायी है। He or she has eaten two roṭīs *usne do roṭiyā̃ khāyī haĩ.* उसने दो रोटियाँ खायी हैं। * We, you or they have eaten a banana. *hamne, āpne, unhõne kelā khāyā hai.* हमने, आपने, उन्होंने केला खाया है। We, you or they have eaten two bananas. *hamne, āpne, unhõne do kele khāye haĩ.* हमने आपने, उन्होंने दो केले खाये हैं। We, you or they have eaten a roṭī. *hamne, āpne, unhõne roṭī khāyī hai.* हमने आपने, उन्होंने रोटी खायी है। We, you or they have eaten two roṭīs *hamne, āpne, unhõne do roṭiyā̃ khāyi haĩ.* हमने आपने, उन्होंने दो रोटियाँ खायी हैं।

24. **PAST PERFECT, 'had done' mode** (suffixes आ था, ई थी, ए थे *ā thā, ī thī, e the*): I had walked. (m◦) *maĩ chalā thā.* मैं चला था। (f◦) *maĩ chalī thī.* मैं चली थी। He had walked. *vah chalā thā.* वह चला था। She had walked. *vah chalī thī.* वह चली थी। We had walked. *ham chale the.* हम चले थे। You had walked. *āp chale the.* आप चले थे। They had walked. *ve chale the.* वे चले थे।

25. **Transitive Actions (As said before, refer Tables 23-24 for changes to pronouns *vah* वह and *ve* वे)** I (m◦ and f◦) had eaten a banana. *maĩne kelā khāyā thā.* मैंने केला खाया था। I had eaten two bananas. *maĩne do kele khāye the.* मैंने दो केले खाये थे। I had eaten a roṭī. *maĩne roṭī khāyī thī.* मैंने रोटी खायी थी। I had eaten two roṭīs. *maĩne do roṭiyā̃ khāyī thĩ.* मैंने दो रोटियाँ खायी थीं। * He or she had eaten a banana. *usne kelā khāyā the.* उसने केला खाया थे। He or she had eaten two bananas. *usne do kele khāye the.* उसने दो केले खाये थे। He or she had eaten a roṭī. *usne roṭī khāyī hai.* उसने रोटी खायी थी। He or she had eaten two roṭīs *usne do roṭiyā̃ khāyī thĩ.* उसने दो रोटियाँ खायी थीं। * We, had eaten a banana. *hamne kelā khāyā thā.* हमने केला खाया था। You had eaten two bananas. *āpne do kele khāye the.* आपने दो केले खाये थे। They had eaten a roṭī. *unhõne roṭī khāyī thī.* उन्होंने रोटी खायी थी। They had eaten two roṭīs *unhõne do roṭiyā̃ khāyi thĩ.* उन्होंने दो रोटियाँ खायी थीं।

These three pages show the intrinsic guts of Hindi Syntax to the Teachers of Hindi

RATNAKAR'S BRAIN SURGERY OF THE HINDI GRAMMAR

From the charts of tenses we studied in previous lessons, **following facts can be discovered :**

(1) I drink hot tea = *mai̐ garam chāy pītā hū̐* = mai̐ garam chāy pī t ā h ū̐

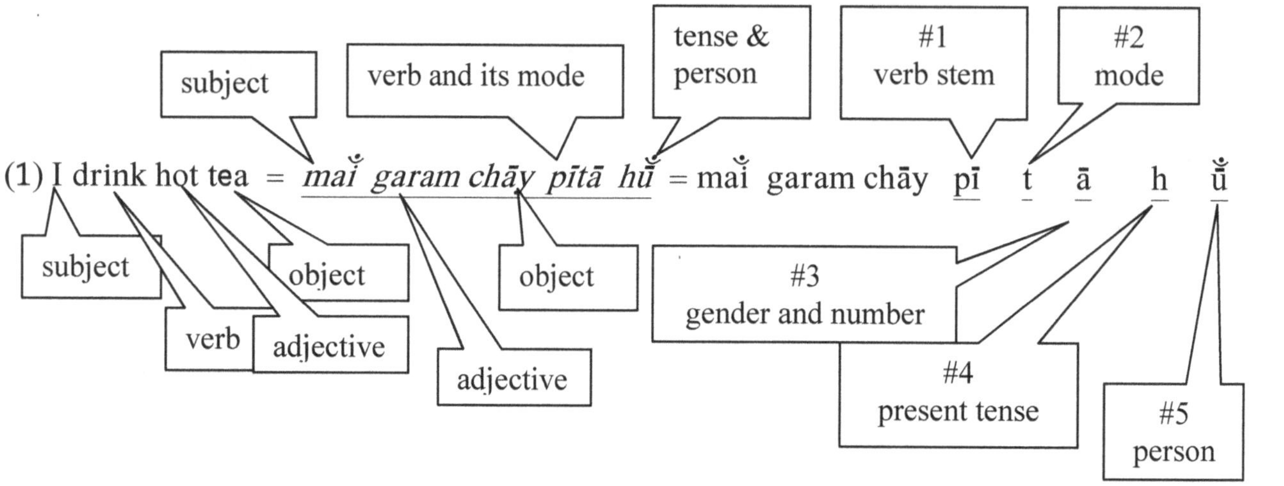

Note: #2 *'t'* = habitual mode (do), *rah* = incomplete mode (-ing), *chuk* = 'already done' mode.

#3 *ā* = m∘ singular; *ī* = f∘ singular, *e* = m∘ plural; *ī̐* = f∘ plural.

#5 *ū̐* = 1st person singular; *ai, e* = second and third person singular; *ai̐, e̐* = plural.

(2) I was drinking tea = *mai̐ chāy pī rahā thā* = mai̐ chāy pī rah ā th ā

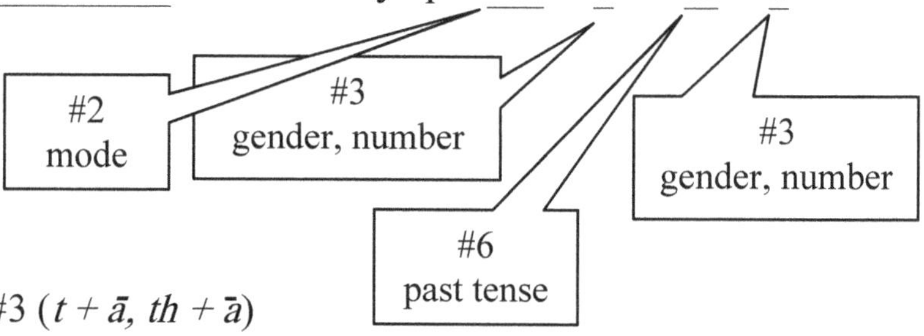

Note : #6 *'th'* = was, had, *used to

* used to = #2 + #3 and #6 + #3 (*t + ā, th + ā*)

Therefore, m∘ (i) Was = *thā* था, (ii) Had = *thā* था, (iii) Used to = *tā thā* ता था।

(3) I will drink tea = *mai̐ chāy piū̐gā* = mai̐ chāy pī ū̐ g ā

Note : #7 for future tense, logically the Tense operative *'g'* goes <u>after</u> #5 Person indicator.

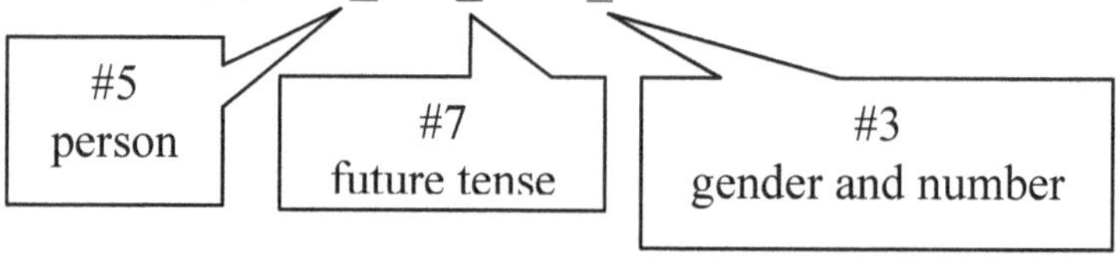

(4) I should drink tea (the Potential mood) = *mai̐ chāy piū̐* = mai̐ chāy pī ū̐

Note : Potential mood needs only #5. It does not need any tense operative such as, *h* for present, *th* for past or *g* for future tense.

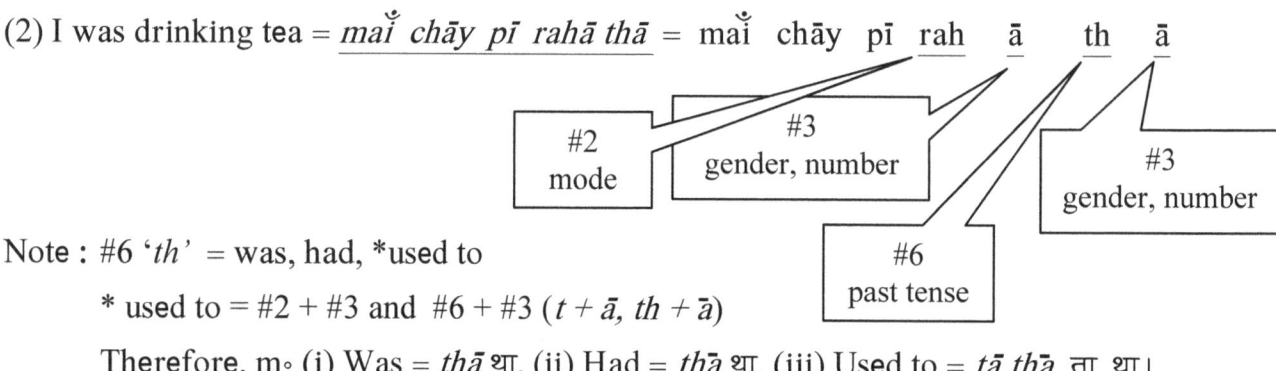

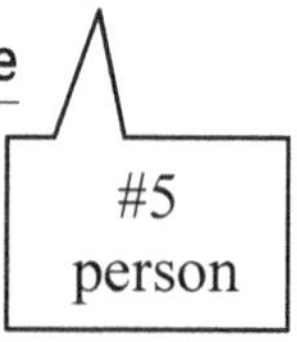

> These three pages show the intrinsic guts of Hindi Syntax to the Teachers of Hindi

(5) I walked = I did walk = *maĩ chalā* = maĩ chal ā

- perfect, intransitive verb
- indefinite, perfect action
- subject
- intransitive verb
- #3 perfect tense suffix, gender and number See the Note below

Note : #3 The perfect tense suffix **ā (आ)** changes with gender (m∘ ā आ, f∘ ī ई) and number (pl∘ e ए, ī̃ ईं). Also, when the verb ends with a long vowel, (such as ā, ī, o आ, ई, ओ) letter *y* य is prefixed to the perfect tense suffix **ā (आ)** e.g. (1) 'chal' ā = chalā. (2) 'so' y + ā = soyā

(6) I have walked slowly = *maĩ dhīre chalā hū̃* = maĩ dhīre chal ā h ū̃

- present
- perfect action
- subject
- adverb
- adverb
- intransitive verb
- #3 perfect tense suffix, *yā* for a long vowel
- #4 present tense
- #5 person

Note : The first-person Present-perfect-tense indicator 'have' translates into Hindī as '*hū̃*' हूँ

(7) I had walked = *maĩ chalā thā* = maĩ chal ā th ā

- past
- perfect action
- subject
- intransitive verb
- #3 perfect tense suffix, *yā* for a long vowel
- #3 gender and number
- #6 past
- #4 present tense

Note : **#6** Past tense suffix '*th*' थ is added is added to the verb ONLY when there is '<u>was</u>,' '<u>had</u>' or '<u>used to</u>' in the sentence.

(8) I saw (have seen, had seen) = *maĩ ne dekhā (hai, thā)* = maĩ ne dekh ā (hai, thā)

- perfect, transitive action
- present tense
- past tense
- #8 transitive perfect action suffix
- #3 perfect tense suffix, *yā* for a long vowel
- #6 past

Note : #8 When the <u>action is transitive and perfected</u> (present, past or future), <u>suffix '*ne*' (ने) is attached to the verb</u>. With suffix *ne* (ने), the Subject has no effect on the verb. Now, the Object affects the verb. e.g. (1) m∘ *Rām chāy pītā hai*, f∘ *Sītā chāy pītī hai.* (2) perfect actions (object f∘ *chāy*, m∘ *ām*) *Rām ne chāy pī, Sītā ne chāy pī, Rām ne ām khāyā, Sītā ne ām khāyā.*

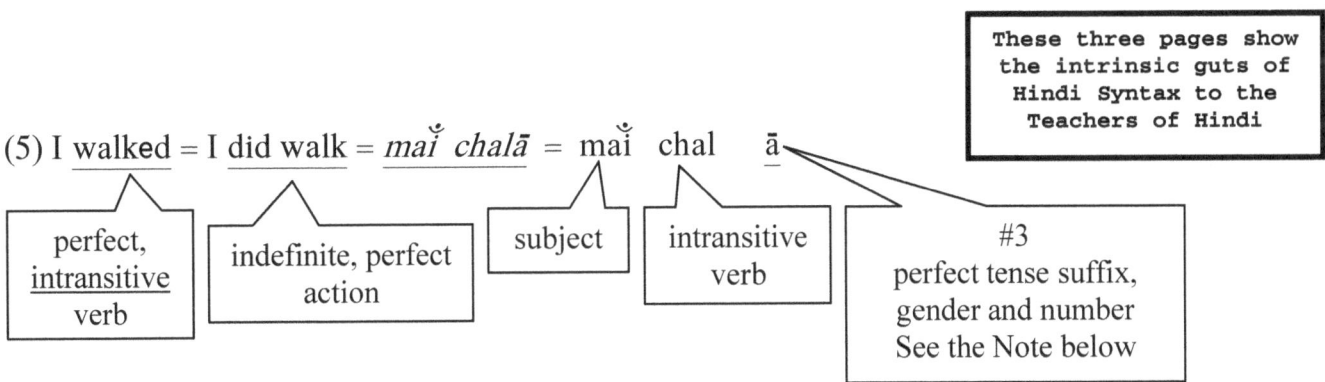

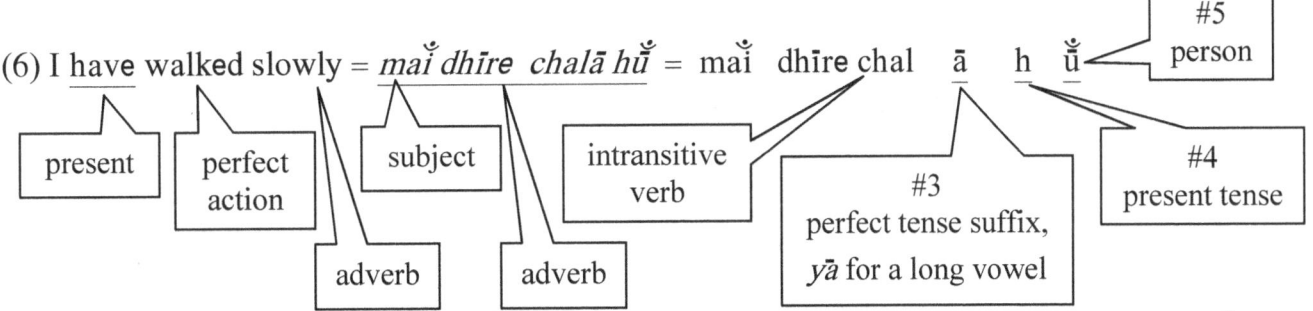

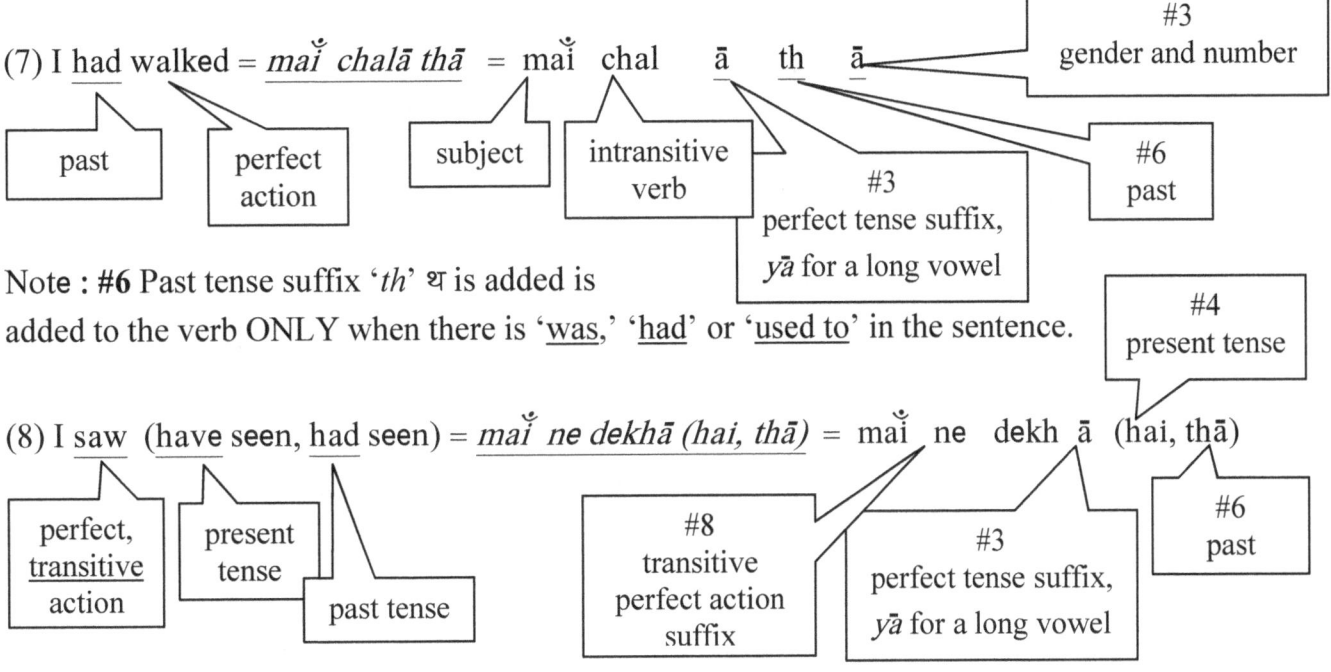

These three pages are created to show the intrinsic guts of the Hindi Syntax to the Teachers of Hindi Language

THE X-Ray VISION, SEEING THROUGH THE HINDI SYNTAX

From the charts given on previous two pages following structural skeleton can be seen through the Hindī Syntax :

eg. I drink hot tea slowly, I eat a sweet banana, I eat sweet bananas, I eat sweet roṭī, I eat sweet rotīs ...etc

English syntax: I (subject) drink (verb + tense) hot (adjective) tea (object) slowly (adverb)

Hindī syntax: *maĩ* (subject) *garam* (adj◦) *chāy* (object) *dhīre* (adverb) *pītā hū̃* (verb + tense, gender, number, person)

main *mīṭhā (mīṭhī) kelā (roṭī)* *khātā-khatī hū̃*

m◦, f◦; singular, pl◦	m◦, f◦; singular, pl◦	m◦, f◦; singular, pl◦	transitive, intransitive		do, -ing, -ed	masculine, feminine	present, past, future	1st., 2nd, 3rd	singular, plural
subject	adjective	object	verb	+	mode,	gender,	tense,	person,	number
maĩ	*mīṭhā (mīṭhī)*	*kelā (roṭī)*	*khā*	+					

subject (*maĩ*):

I	*maĩ*
you	*āp*
he, that	*vah*
she, that	*vah*
it, this	*yah*
we	*ham*
you	*āp*
they, those	*ve*
these	*ye*
m◦ *laḍkā*	f◦ *laḍkī*

adjective (*mīṭhā (mīṭhī)*): Gender

m◦ sg◦ = आ *'ā'*
m◦ pl◦ = ए *'e'*
f◦ sg◦ = ई *'ī'*
f◦ pl◦ = ईं *'ī̃'*

object (*kelā (roṭī)*): Gender

m◦ sg◦ = आ *'ā'*
m◦ pl◦ = ए *'e'*
f◦ sg◦ = ई *'ī'*
f◦ pl◦ = इयाँ *'īyā̃'*

Mode + Gender

'do' = त *'t'*
'ing' = रह *'rah'*
'ed' = चुक *'chuk'*

Gender
m◦ sg◦ = आ *'ā'*
m◦ pl◦ = ए *'e'*
f◦ sg◦ = ई *'ī'*
f◦ pl◦ = ईं *'ī̃'*

Tense

past = थ *'th'*
future = ग *'g'*
present = ह *'h'*

Gender (past, future)
m◦ sg◦ = आ *'ā'*
m◦ pl◦ = ए *'e'*
f◦ sg◦ = ई *'ī'*
f◦ pl◦ = ईं *'ī̃'*

Present:
1st◦ person sg◦ = ऊँ *'ū̃'*
1st◦ person pl◦ = ऐं *'aĩ'*
2nd◦ person sg◦ = ऐ *'ai'*
2nd◦ person pl◦ = ऐं *'aĩ'*
3rd◦ person sg◦ = ऐ *'ai'*
3rd◦ person pl◦ = ऐं *'aĩ'*

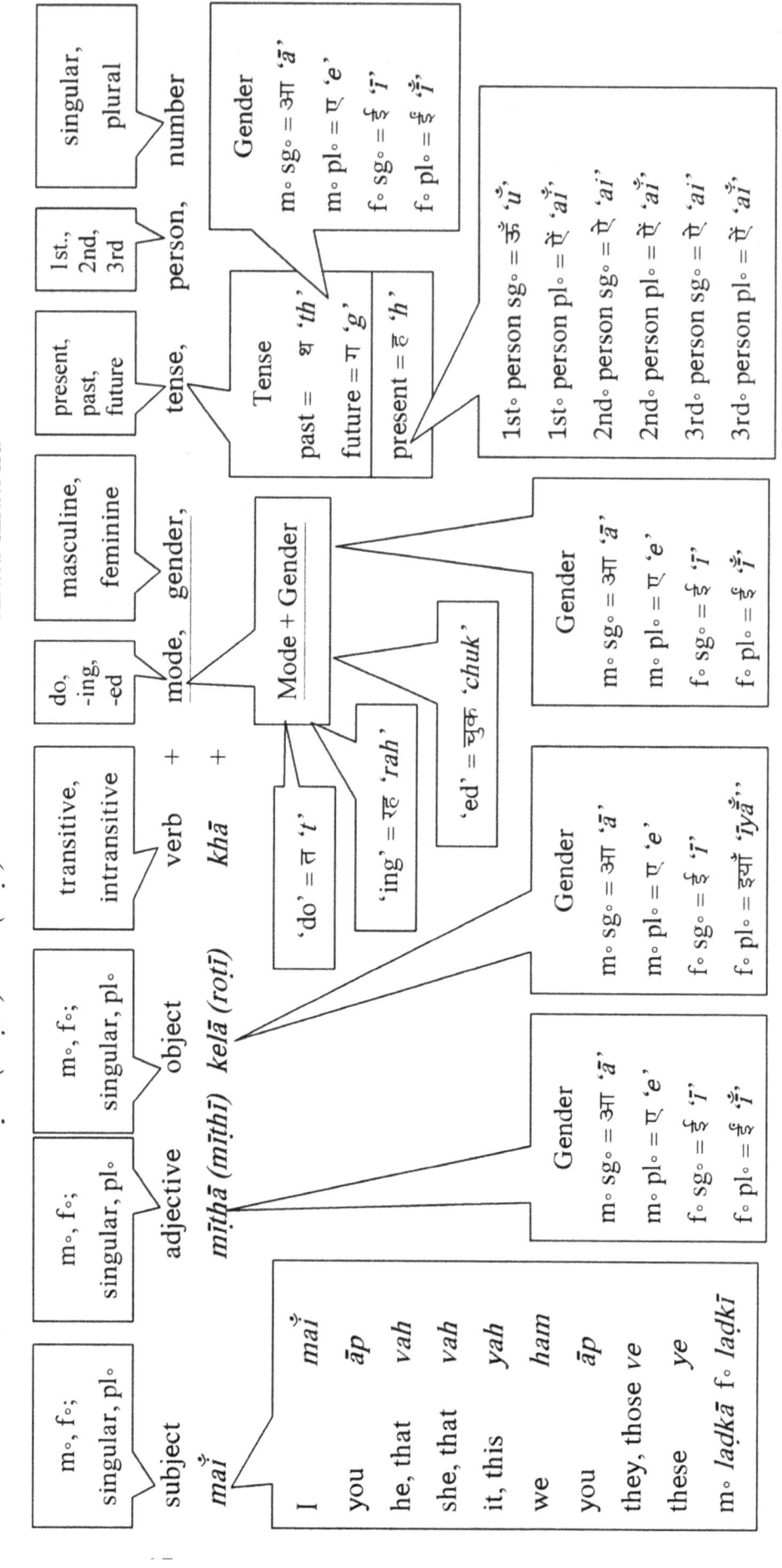

14.1 THE HINDI IRREGULR VERBS

Take, Give, Do, Drink, Become and Go

The table 18 is the Maste Table of the comple Hindi Grammar, for the Hindi syntax and Hindi verb usage.

However, the following four tables show that, six verbs namely "**Take, Give, Do, Drink, Become** and **Go**" have irregular inflections in the :

(i) Perfect Tense,

(ii) Imperative Mood,

(iii) Future Tenas and

(iv) Potential Mood.

(i). **PERFECT TENSE :** Prefect Simple, Perfect present, Perfect past and Perfect future

Irregular verbs : "Take, Give, Do, Become, Go"

TABLE 14.1A : Irreguar verbs in the Perfect Ternse

	Verb	**becomes**	Suffix		Perfect Tense	Example
			m∘	f∘		m∘ f∘
1	Take : ले le	**लि li / ली lī**	या yā	यी yī	लिया liyā लियी/ली liyi or lī	पानी लिया pānī liyā चाय ली chāy lī
2	Give : दे de	**दि di / दी dī**	या yā	यी yī	दिया diyā दियी/दी diyi or dī	पानी दिया pānī diyā चाय दी chāy dī
3	Do : कर kar	**कि ki / की kī**	या yā	यी yī	किया kiyā कयी/की liyi or lī	काम किया kām kiyā शादी की shadī kī
4	Be Become : हो ho	**हु hu**	आ yā	ई ī	हुआ huā हुई hulī	काम हुआ kām huā शादी हुई shadī huī
5	Go : जा ja	**ग ga**	या yā	यी yī	गया gayā गयी gayi	राम गया Rām gayā सीता गयी Sītā gaylī

(ii). **IMPERATIVE MOOD :**

Irregular verbs : "Take, Give, Do, Drink"

TABLE 14.1B : Irreguar verbs in the Imperative Mood

	Verb	**becomes**	Suffix	Imperative	Example
					m∘ f∘
1	Take : ले le	**ली lī**	जिये jiye	लीजिये lījiye	पानी लीजिये pānī lījiye
2	Give : दे de	**दी dī**	जिये jiye	दीजिये dījiye	पानी दीजिये pānī dījiye
3	Drink : पी pī	**पी pī**	**जिये jiye**	पीजिये lījiye	पानी पीजिये pānī pijiye
4	Do : कर kar	**की kī**	जिये jiye	कीजिये kījiye	काम कीजिये kām kījiye

(iii). **FUTURE TENSE : First Person, Singular only : I Will xxx**

Irregular verbs : "Take, Give, Become"

TABLE 14.1C : Irreguar verbs in the Future Tense (First Person, Singular - I मैं)

	Verb	**becomes**	Suffix	Future Tense	Example
					m∘ f∘
1	Take : ले le	**लू lū**	ऊँगा ūngā ऊँगी ūngī	लूँगा lūngā लूँगी lūngī	पानी लूँगा pānī lūngā पानी लूँगी pānī lūngī
2	Give : दे de	**दू dū**	ऊँगा ūngā ऊँगी ūngī	दूँगा dūngā दूँगी dūngī	पानी दूँगा pānī dūngā पानी दूँगी pānī dūngī
3	Become : हो ho	**हू hū**	ऊँगा ūngā ऊँगी ūngī	हूँगा hūngā हूँगी hūngī	सफल हूँगा safal hūngā सफल हूँगी safal hūngī

(iv). **POTENTIAL MOOD : First Person, Singular only : I should xxx**

Irregular verbs : "Take, Give, Become"

TABLE 14.1D : Irreguar verbs in the Potential Mood (First Person, Singular - I मैं)

	Verb	**becomes**	Suffix	Future Tense	Example : m∘ f∘ both
1	Take : ले le	**लू lū**	ऊँ ū̐	लूँ lū̐	पानी लूँ pānī lū̐
2	Give : दे de	**दू dū**	ऊँ ū̐	दूँ dū̐	पानी दूँ pānī dū̐
3	Become : हो ho	**हू hū**	ऊँ ū̐	हूँ hū̐	सफल हूँगा safal hū̐

LESSON 15
बारहवाँ पाठ

USING THE RELATIONAL SUFFIXES
English : **PREPOSITIONS**, Hindi : **POSTPOSITIONS**

USE OF THE SUFFIXES *ko* (को), *se* (से), *mẽ* (में), *par* (पर)

ko (को) = to; *se* (से) = with, by, from; *mẽ* (में) = in; *par* (पर) = on, at

RATNAKAR'S EIGHTH NOBLE TRUTH : (attaching Case suffixes)

(i) When ANY SUFFIX (*ko* को, *se* से, *mẽ* में, *par* पर or any other suffix) comes after a MASCULINE SINGULAR noun ending in *ā* (आ), this *ā* (आ) is changed to *e* (ए).

e.g. m◦ boy *laḍkā* लड़का + *ko* को = *laḍke ko* लड़के को।

TABLE 2 : Adding a **Postposition** to a **SINGULAR** Noun/Adjective

M◦ Singular Noun/Adj. **ending in *ā* (आ)**	***ā* (आ)** changed to ***e* (ए)**	+ Suffix ***ko* (को)**	to a boy
Boy = laḍkā लड़का	laḍke लड़के	*ko* को	laḍke ko लड़के को
Dog = kuttā कुत्ता	kutte कुत्ते	*ko* को	kutte ko कुत्ते को

(ii) When ANY SUFFIX comes after ANY PLURAL NOUN, particle *õ* (ओं) must be added to that noun, before attaching the suffix.

TABLE 2 : Adding a **Postposition** to a **PLURAL** Noun/Adjective

Plural Noun/Adj.	**Plural**	plural + ***õ***	+ postposition	= to the boys to the girls
Boy = laḍkā लड़का	laḍke लड़के	laḍkõ लड़कों	*ko* को	laḍkõ ko लड़के को
Girl = laḍkī लड़की	laḍkiyā̃ लड़कियाँ	laḍkiyõ लड़कियों	*ko* को	laḍkiyõ ko लड़कियों को

e.g. m॰ Houses *ghar* + *o̐ + ko* = *gharo̐ ko* घर + ओं + को = घरों को ।

   f॰ books *kitāb* + *o̐ + ko* = *kitābo̐ ko* किताब + ओं + को = किताबों को ।

RATNAKAR'S NINTH NOBLE TRUTH (change in pronouns, see Tables 23-24) :

I = *maĩ* मैं । He, she, that = *vah* वह । It, this = *yah* यह । They, those = *ve* वे । These = *ye* ये ।
When any suffix is attached to these pronouns : (i) *maĩ* मैं changes to → *muz* मुझ । (ii) *vah* वह changes to → *us* उस । (iii) *yah* यह changes to → *is* इस । (iv) *ve* वे changes to → *un* उन । and (v) *ye* ये changes to → *in* इन ।

(15.1) Use of *ko* को (to) :

1. I am giving a book to Līlā. *main Līlā ko kitāb de rahā hū̐.* मैं लीला को किताब दे रहा हूँ।

2. He is giving books to Mālā. *vah Mālā ko kitābe̐ de rahā hai.* वह माला को किताबें दे रहा है।

3. She is giving keys to Mīnā. *vah Mīnā ko chābiyā̐ de rahī hai.* वह मीना को चाबियाँ दे रही है।

4. A boy is giving a banana to a monkey. *laḍkā bandar ko kelā de rahā hai.* लड़का बंदर को केला दे रहा है।

5. A boy is giving bananas to a monkey. *laḍkā bandar ko kele de rahā hai.* लड़का बंदर को केले दे रहा है।

6. A boy is giving bananas to the monkeys. *laḍkā bandaro̐ ko kele de rahā hai.* लड़का बंदरों को केले दे रहा है।

7. The boys are giving bananas to the monkeys. *laḍke bandaro̐ ko kele de rahe hai̐.* लड़के बंदरों को केले दे रहे हैं।

(15.2) Use of *se* से (with, by or from) :

(i) *se* से = WITH or BY

1. I go by car. *maĩ car se jātā hū̐.* मैं कार से जाता हूँ। We are going by car. *ham car se jā rahe hai̐.* हम कार से जा रहे हैं।

2. I cut bananas with a knife. *maĩ chākū se kele kāṭatā hū̐.* मैं चाकू से केले काटता हूँ। Shīlā was cutting two bananas with two knives. *Shīlā do chākuo̐ se do kele kāṭ rahī thī.* शीला दो चाकुओं से दो केले काट रही थी।

3. Jitū should go by train. *Jitū relgāḍī se jāe.* जीतू रेल गाड़ी से जाए।

(ii) ***se* से** = **FROM**

1. I came from Singāpur. *maĩ Singāpur se āyā.* मैं सिंगापुर से आया। Amit went from Mumbaī to Nāgpur. *Amit Mumbaī se Nāgpur gayā.* अमित मुंबई से नागपुर (को) गया।
2. I am here from four O Clock. *maĩ yahā̃ chār baje se hū̃.* मैं यहाँ चार बजे से हूँ।
3. Ritū takes money from the room. *Rītū kamre se paise letī hai.* रीतू कमरे से पैसे लेती है।

(15.3) Use of *mẽ* में (in) and *par* पर (on, at) :

(i) ***mẽ*** **में** = **IN**

1. There is no water in the glass. *gilās mẽ pānī nahī̃ hai.* गिलास में पानी नहीं है। Ajay is in the room. *Ajay kamre mẽ hai.* अजय कमरे में है।
2. The dog is not in the house. *kuttā ghar mẽ nahī̃ hai.* कुत्ता घर में नहीं है।
3. The key is in the lock. *chābī tāle mẽ hai.* चाबी ताले में है।

(ii) ***par* पर** = **ON, AT**

1. The cup is on the dish. *cup thālī par hai.* कप थाली पर है।
2. There are leaves on the tree. *peḍ par patte haĩ.* पेड़ पर पत्ते हैं।
3. Rām is at the station. *Rām station par hai.* राम स्टेशन पर है।

(15.4) Use of *kā, kī* (का, की)

m∘ *kā* (का), f∘ *kī* (की) = of

The English preposition 'OF' becomes postposition *kā* (का) or *kī* (की) in Hindī. For showing the possessive relationship of a Masculine Object, suffix *kā* (का) is added to the possessor, and for a Feminine Object, suffix *kī* (की) is added.

EXAMPLES :

1. Shobhā's brother. *Shobhā kā bhaī.* शोभा का भाई। Gītā's sister. *Gītā kī bahin.* गीता की बहिन।
2. This is Rola's car. *yah Rolā ki cār hai.* यह रोला की कार है।
3. Those are Anitā's books. *ve Anitā kī kitābẽ haĩ.* वे अनिता की किताबें हैं।
4. Where are Tarā's cats? *Tārā kī billiyā̃ kahā̃ haĩ?* तारा की बिल्लियाँ कहाँ हैं?
5. That is Savitā's coffee. *vah Savitā kī kāfī hai.* वह सविता की काफी है।

6. He is Dīpak's Brother. *vah Dīpak kā bhāī hai.* वह दीपक का भाई है।

7. I eat *burfī* made of milk. *maĩ dūdh kī burfī khātā hũ.* मैं दूध की बर्फी खाता हूँ।

8. This is Monika's house. *yaha Monikā kā ghar hai.* यह मोनिका का घर है।

NOTE : For first person ('my' and 'our'), suffixes *rā, rī* रा, री *are used in place of the suffixes kā, kī* का, की।

EXAMPLES :

Our house. *hamārā ghar.* हमारा घर। My mother. *merī mā̃* मेरी माँ। My dogs. *mere kutte.* मेरे कुत्ते। Our dogs. *hamāre kutte.* हमारे कुत्ते। Our dog. *hamārā kuttā.* हमारा कुत्ता। Our cat. *hamārī billī.* हमारी बिल्ली। Our cats. *hamārī billiyā̃.* हमारी बिल्लियाँ। My cats. *merī billiyā̃.* मेरी बिल्लियाँ।

(15.5) Use of suffixes *ke sāth* (के साथ), *ke pās* (के पास), *ke liye* (के लिये)

ke sāth (के साथ) = together with; *ke pās* (के पास) = near, have; *ke liye* (के लिये) = for

(A) *ke sāth* के साथ = with, together with :

(1) I am going with Sunīl. *maĩ Sunīl ke sāth jā rahā/rahī hũ* मैं सुनील के साथ जा रहा/रही हूँ।

(2) I am drinking milk with you. *maĩ āp ke sāth dūdh pī rahā hũ.* मैं आपके साथ दूध पी रहा हूँ।

(3) Jim will go to Washington with Suman. *Jim Suman ke sāth Washington ko jāegā.* जिम सुमन के साथ वाशिंगटन को जाएगा।

(B) *ke pās* के पास = with, near, have, has, had :

(1) The book is with Rājā. *kitāb Rājā ke pās hai.* किताब राजा के पास है।

(2) Ramesh has ten Rupees. *Ramesh ke pās das rupaye haĩ.* रमेश के पास दस रुपये हैं।

(3) Śrī Laṅkā is near India. *Śrī Lakṅkā Bhārat ke pās hai.* श्रीलंका भारत के पास है।

(15.6) Use of suffixes *kījiye* (कीजिये) *and chāhiye* (चाहिये)

***kījiye* (कीजिये) = please do. *chāhiye* (चाहिये) = require, want, need**

(1) In Hindī, a request is made to other person by adding suffix इए, or इये (*ie, iye*) to the verb.

(2) The suffix इए, इये (*ie, iye*) includes the expression of 'please' in it, and thus, you do not have to add please (*kṛpayā* कृपया) in each sentence. Even the 'orders' should be respectful.

NOTE : However, in informal Hindī, *'o'* (ओ) is used in place of this *'iye'* (इये) suffix.

eg. *jāiye* (जाइये) = *jāo* (जाओ).

EXCEPTION : For the verbs that already end in vowel *ī* (ई) :

The की, दी, पी and ली are the interrogative forms of the **irregular** verbs कर (do), दे (give), पी (drink), ले (take). For the these verbs, (do √*kī*, give √*dī*, drink √*pī*, take √*lī*) की (do), दी (give), पी (drink), ली (take) - suffix जिए or जीये is attached in place of the suffix इए or इये। e.g. *kījiye* (please do), *dījiye* (please give), *pījiye* (please drink), *lījiye* (please take) = कीजिये (please do), दीजिये (please give), पीजिये (please drink), लीजिये (please take).

Some people casually use the informal 'order' suffix *o* (ओ) in place of *iye* (इये). e.g. आओ for आइये, जाओ for जाइये, खाओ for खाइये, लाओ for लाइये, पीओ for पीजिये ...etc.

EXERCISE 30 :

Translate the Hindī sentences into English (Answers are provided for your help)

1. INVITATION : (Please) come to our house. *hamāre ghar āīye.* हमारे घर आइये।
2. SUGGESTION : (Please) sit here. *yahā̃ baiṭhiye.* यहाँ बैठिये।
3. ORDER : Do not come here. *yahā̃ mat āīye.* यहाँ मत आइये। (do not, don't = मत *mat*)
4. REQUEST : (Please) have tea. *kṛpayā chāy lījiye.* कृपया चाय लीजिये, पीजिये।
6. CONSOLATION : (Please) do not cry. *mat roīye.* मत रोइये।
7. INSTRUCTION : (Please) do work properly. *kām ṭhīk se kījiye.* काम ठीक से कीजिये।

NOTE : In the Charts of Cases on the following seven pages :

1N◦ = **Nominative** case, the DOER of the action (the subject)

2A◦ = **Accusative** case, the OBJECT of the action

3I◦ = **Instrumental** case, the INSTRUMENT with/by which action is done

4D◦ = **Dative** case, FOR WHOM the action is performed

5A◦ = **Ablative** case, the place FROM WHERE the action starts

6P◦ = **Possessive** case, the RELATIONSHIP OF the object in a sentence

7L◦ = **Locative** case. the LOCATION of the object.

TABLE 19 - CHART OF SUFFIXES FOR MASCULINE NOUNS

THE Hindī Chart (The English Chart is on the Next Page)

NOTES : (i) ए *(e)* is added to m◦ singular nouns ending in आ *(ā)* and (ii) ओं *(ō̃)* is added to all **plural** nouns m◦ and f◦, before attaching any suffix.

			m◦ (i) a child,	m◦ (ii) a boy,	m◦ (iii) a saint,	m◦ (iv) a saint
Words ending in →			(i) अ (बालक)	(ii) आ (लड़का)	(iii) इ (योगी)	(iv) उ (साधु)
with suffix ने		singular→	बालक ने	लड़के ने	योगी ने	साधु ने
1N◦ (Perfect, transitive)		plural→	बालकों ने	लड़कों ने	यागियों ने	साधुओं ने
2 A◦	to को	singular→	बालक को	लड़के को	योगी को	साधु को
		plural→	बालकों को	लड़कों को	योगियों को	साधुओं को
3 I◦	with, by से	singular→	बालक से	लड़के से	योगी से	साधु से
		plural→	बालकों से	लड़कों से	योगियों से	साधुओं से
4 D◦	for के लिये	singular→	बालक के लिये	लड़के के लिये	योगी के लिये	साधु के लिये
		plural→	बालकों के लिये	लड़कों के लिये	योगियों के लिये	साधुओं के लिये
5 A◦	from से	singular→	बालक से	लड़के से	योगी से	साधु से
		plural→	बालकों से	लड़कों से	योगियों से	साधुओं से
6 P◦	of का	singular→	बालक का	लड़के का	योगी का	साधु का
		plural→	बालकों का	लड़कों का	योगियों का	साधुओं का
7 L◦	in में	singular→	बालक में	लड़के में	योगी में	साधु में
		plural→	बालकों में	लड़कों में	योगियों में	साधुओं में
	on, at पर	singular→	बालक पर	लड़के पर	योगी पर	साधु पर
		plural→	बालकों पर	लड़कों पर	योगियों पर	साधुओं पर

TABLE 20 - CHART OF CASES, MASCULINE NOUNS

The English Chart (The Hindī Chart is on the Previous Page)

NOTES : (i) ए *(e)* is added to m◦ singular nouns ending in आ *(ā)* and (ii) ओं *(o̐)* is added to all **plural** nouns m◦ and f◦, before attaching any suffix.

			m◦ a child,	m◦ a boy,	m◦ a saint,	m◦ a saint
Word ending in →			(i) *a (bālak)*	(ii) *ā (laḍkā)*	(iii) *ī (yogī)*	(iv) *u (sādhu)*
with suffix	*ne*	singular→	*bālak ne*	*laḍke ne*	*yogī ne*	*sādhu ne*
1N◦ (Perfect, transitive)		plural→	*bālako̐ ne*	*laḍko̐ ne*	*yogiyo̐ ne*	*sādhuo̐ ne*
2 A◦	to *ko*	singular→	*bālak ko*	*laḍke ko*	*yogī ko*	*sādhu ko*
		plural→	*bālako̐ ko*	*laḍko̐ ko*	*yogiyo̐ ko*	*sādhuo̐ ko*
3 I◦	with, by *se*	singular→	*bālak se*	*laḍke se*	*yogī se*	*sādhu se*
		plural→	*bālako̐ se*	*laḍko̐ se*	*yogiyo̐ se*	*sādhuo̐ se*
4 D◦	for *ke liye*	singular→	*bālak ke liye*	*laḍke ke liye*	*yogī ke liye*	*sādhu ke liye*
		plural→	*bālako̐ ke liye*	*laḍko̐ ke liye*	*yogiyo̐ ke liye*	*sādhuo̐ ke liye*
5 A◦	from *se*	singular→	*bālak se*	*laḍke se*	*yogī se*	*sādhu se*
		plural→	*bālako̐ se*	*laḍko̐ se*	*yogiyo̐ se*	*sādhuo̐ se*
6 P◦	of *kā*	singular→	*bālak kā*	*laḍke kā*	*yogī kā*	*sādhu kā*
		plural→	*bālako̐ kā*	*laḍko̐ kā*	*yogiyo̐ kā*	*sādhuo̐ kā*
7 L◦	in *me̐*	singular→	*bālak me̐*	*laḍke me̐*	*yogī me̐*	*sādhu me̐*
		plural→	*bālako̐ me̐*	*laḍko̐ me̐*	*yogiyo̐ me̐*	*sādhuo̐ me̐*
	on, at *par*	singular→	*bālak par*	*laḍke par*	*yogī par*	*sādhu par*
		plural→	*bālako̐ par*	*laḍko̐ par*	*yogiyo̐ par*	*sādhuo̐ par*

TABLE 21 - CHART OF CASES : FEMININE NOUNS

The Hindī Chart (The English Chart is on the Next Page)

NOTES : (i) To make plural of a femimine noun ending in a consonant , add एं *(ẽ)* to it.

(ii) ओं *(õ)* is added to all **plural** nouns (m◦ and f◦), before attaching any suffix.

			f◦ a book,	f◦ a girl,	f◦ a girl,	f◦ a thing
Words ending in →			(i) अ (किताब)	(ii) आ (बालिका)	(iii) ई (लड़की)	(iv) उ (वस्तु)
with suffix ने		singular→	किताब ने	बालिका ने	लड़की ने	वस्तु ने
1N◦ (Perfect, transitive)		plural→	किताबों ने	बालिकाओं ने	लड़कियों ने	वस्तुओं ने
2 A◦	to को	singular→	किताब को	बालिका को	लड़की को	वस्तु को
		plural→	किताबों को	बालिकाओं को	लड़कियों को	वस्तुओं को
3 I◦	with, by से	singular→	किताब से	बालिका से	लड़की से	वस्तु से
		plural→	किताबों से	बालिकाओं से	लड़कियों से	वस्तुओं से
4 D◦	for के लिये	singular→	किताब के लिये	बालिका के लिये	लड़की के लिये	वस्तु के लिये
		plural→	किताबों के लिये	बालिकाओं के लिये	लड़कियों के लिये	वस्तुओं के लिये
5 A◦	from से	singular→	किताब से	बालिका से	लड़की से	वस्तु से
		plural→	किताबों से	बालिकाओं से	लड़कियों से	वस्तुओं से
6 P◦	of का	singular→	किताब का	बालिका का	लड़की का	वस्तु का
		plural→	किताबों का	बालिकाओं का	लड़कियों का	वस्तुओं का
7 L◦	in में	singular→	किताब में	बालिका में	लड़की में	वस्तु में
		plural→	किताबों में	बालिकाओं में	लड़कियों में	वस्तुओं में
	on, at पर	singular→	किताब पर	बालिका पर	लड़की पर	वस्तु पर
		plural→	किताबों पर	बालिकाओं पर	लड़कियों पर	वस्तुओं पर

TABLE 22 - CHART OF CASES : FEMININE NOUNS

The English Chart (Hindī Chart is on the Previous Page)

NOTES : (i) To make plural of a femimine noun ending in a consonant , add एं *(e̐)* to it.

(ii) ओं *(o̐)* is added to all **plural** nouns m◦ and f◦, before attaching any suffix.

			f◦ a book,	f◦ a girl,	f◦ a girl,	f◦ a thing
Word ending in →			(i) *a (kitāb)*	(ii) *ā (bālikā)*	*ī (laḍkī)*	*u (vastu)*
with suffix	*ne*	singular→	*kitāb ne*	*bālikā ne*	*laḍkī ne*	*vastu ne*
1N◦ (Perfect, transitive)		plural→	*kitābo̐ ne*	*bālikao̐ ne*	*laḍkiyo̐ ne*	*vastuo̐ ne*
2 A◦	to *ko*	singular→	*kitāb ko*	*bālikā ko*	*laḍkī ko*	*vastu ko*
		plural→	*kitābo̐ ko*	*bālikāo̐ ko*	*laḍkiyo̐ ko*	*vastuo̐ ko*
3 I◦	with, by *se*	singular→	*kitāb se*	*bālikā se*	*laḍkī se*	*vastu se*
		plural→	*kitābo̐ se*	*bālikāo̐ se*	*laḍkiyo̐ se*	*vastuo̐ se*
4 D◦	for *ke liye*	singular→	*kitāb ke liye*	*bālikā ke liye*	*laḍkī ke liye*	*vastu ke liye*
		plural→	*kitābo̐ ke liye*	*bālikāo̐ ke liye*	*laḍkiyo̐ ke liye*	*vastuo̐ ke liye*
5 A◦	from *se*	singular→	*kitāb se*	*bālikā se*	*laḍkī se*	*vastu se*
		plural→	*kitābo̐ se*	*bālikāo̐ se*	*laḍkiyo̐ se*	*vastuo̐ se*
6 P◦	of *kā*	singular→	*kitāb kā*	*bālikā kā*	*laḍkī kā*	*vastu kā*
		plural→	*kitābo̐ kā*	*bālikāo̐ kā*	*laḍkiyo̐ kā*	*vastuo̐ kā*
7 L◦	in *me̐*	singular→	*kitāb me̐*	*bālikā me̐*	*laḍkī me̐*	*vastu me̐*
		plural→	*kitābo̐ me̐*	*bālikāo̐ me̐*	*laḍkiyo̐ me̐*	*vastuo̐ me̐*
	on, at *par*	singular→	*kitāb par*	*bālikā par*	*laḍkī par*	*vastu par*
		plural→	*kitābo̐ par*	*bālikāo̐ par*	*laḍkiyo̐ par*	*vastuo̐ par*

THE PRONOUNS

DEFINITIONS :

(1)The word used in place of a noun (in order to avoid its repetition) is called a *Pronoun.*

(2) If a pronoun qualifies a noun, then the pronoun is called a *Pronominal or Possessive Adjective.*

EXPLANATION :

(i) See this sentence :

Rām is going to Rām's school to see Rām's teacher and to return Rām's teacher Rām's teacher's books.

राम राम के शिक्षक को मिलने और राम के शिक्षक की पुस्तकें राम के गुरुजी को लौटाने राम के विद्यालय को जा रहा है।

It sounds improper and confusing.

(ii) Now see this one

(Same sentence can be re-written properly with the use of pronouns) :

Rām is going to his school to see his teacher and to return him his books. *(Rām apane gurujī ko milane aur un kī pustakẽ un ko lauṭāne apane vidyālay jā rahā hai)*

राम अपने शिक्षक को मिलने और उनकी पुस्तकें उनको लौटाने अपने विद्यालय जा रहा है।

It reads improper.

REMEMBER (change in pronoun forms, see Tables 23-24) **:**

I = *maĩ* मैं। He, she, that = *vah* वह। It, this = *yah* यह। They, those = *ve* वे। These = *ye* ये।

When any suffix is attached to these pronouns, they change to : *maĩ* मैं changes to → ***muz* मुझ।** ***vah* वह** changes to → ***us* उस।** ***yah* यह** changes to → ***is* इस।** ***ve* वे** changes to → ***un* उन।** ***ye* ये** changes to → ***in* इन।**

15.7 THE PERSONAL PRONOUNS

DEFINITION :

A word used in place of the name of a person is a Personal Pronoun (a thing, is Impersonal Pronoun) .

e.g.	I,	we,	you,	he, she,	they,	it, this,	these,	they and those.
	maĩ,	*ham,*	*āp*	*vah,*	*ve,*	*yah,*	*ye,*	*ve*
	मैं,	हम,	आप,	वह,	वे,	यह,	ये,	वे।

NOTES :

1. As you see in Table 23-24, by attaching the case suffixes, the pronuns (i) he, she वह (*vah*) change to him, her उस (*us*); (ii) they, and those वे (*ve*) change to them; (iii) I and we change to my मेरा (*merā*), and our हमारा (*hamārā).*

2. (i) He, she, that = वह *vah;* (ii) This, it = यह *yah;* (iii) They, those = वे *ve;* (iv) These = ये *ye.*

3. For saying : he, she, that, वह (*vah*) as well as for saying they and those वे (*ve*) - some people say वो (*vo*) .

15.8 THE INTERROGATIVE PRONOUNS

The pronoun that is employed for asking a question is an Interrogative Pronoun.

(1) कौन (*kaun?* who) :

Who sleeps here? *(yahā̃ kaun sotā hai?)* यहाँ कौन सोता है?

(2) क्यों (*kyõ?* why) :

Why do you sleep here? आप यहाँ क्यों सोते हैं?

(3) क्या (*kyā?* what) :

What are you doing here now? *(āp ab yahā̃ kyā kar rahe haĩ?)* आप अब यहाँ क्या कर रहे हैं?

What is your name? *āpkā nām kyā hai?* आप का नाम क्या है?

(4) कब (*kab?* When) :

When will you come? *(āp kab āyeṅge?)* आप कब आयेंगे?

(5) कहाँ (*kahā̃?* where) :

Where does he live? *(vah kahā̃ rahatā hai?)* वह कहाँ रहता है?

TABLE 23 : CHART FOR THE PRONOUNS

The Hindī Chart (English Chart is on the Next Page)

REMEMBER : (i) I = मैं। He, she, that = वह। It, this = यह। They, those = वे। These = ये।

(ii) When any suffix is attached to these pronouns : मैं changes to **मुझ। वह** changes to **उस। यह** changes to **इस। वे** changes to **उन। ये** changes to **इन।**

			I, we, us	**You**	**He, she, him, her, that they, them, those**	**It, these**
1st., 2nd., 3rd. Person →			मैं, हम	आप	वह, वे	यह, ये
with suffix ने		singular→	मैंने	आपने	उसने	इसने
1N◦ (Perfect, transitive)		plural→	हमने	आपने	उन्हों ने	इन्हों ने
2 A◦	to को	singular→	मुझको, मुझे	आपको	उसको, उसे	इसको, इसे
to		plural→	हमको, हमें	आपको	उनको, उन्हें	इनको, इन्हें
3 I◦	with, by से	singular→	मुझसे	आपसे	उससे	इससे
		plural→	हमसे	आपसे	उनसे	इनसे
4 D◦	for के लिये	singular→	मेरे लिये	आपके लिये	उसके लिये	इसके लिये
		plural→	हमारे लिये	आपके लिये	उनके लिये	इनके लिये
5 A◦	from से	singular→	मुझसे, मेरेसे	आपसे	उससे	इससे
		plural→	हमसे	आपसे	उनसे	इनसे
6 P◦	of का, रा –	singular→	मेरा–मेरी	आपका–की	उसका–की	इसका–की
		plural→	हमारा–री	आपका–की	उनका–की	इनका–की
7 L◦	in में	singular→	मुझमें	आपमें	उसमें	इसमें
		plural→	हममें	आपमें	उनमें	इनमें
	in पर	singular→	मुझ पर	आप पर	उस पर	इस पर
		plural→	हम पर	आप पर	उन पर	इन पर

TABLE 24 : CHART FOR THE PRONOUNS

The English Chart (Hindī Chart is on the Previous Page)

REMEMBER : (i) I = ***maĩ;*** **He, she, that =** ***vah;*** **It, this =** ***yah;*** **They, those =** ***ve;*** **These =** ***ye.***

(ii) When any suffix is attached to these pronouns : ***maĩ*** changes to ***muz; vah*** changes to ***us; yah*** changes to ***is; ve*** changes to ***un; ye*** changes to ***in.***

			I, we, us	**You**	**He, she, him, her, that they, them, those**	**It, these**
1st., 2nd., 3rd. Person →			*maĩ, ham*	*āp*	*vah, ve*	*yah, ye*
with suffix	*ne*	singular→	*maĩ ne*	*āp ne*	*us ne*	*is ne*
1N∘ (Perfect, transitive)		plural→	*ham ne*	*āp ne*	*unhõ ne*	*inhõ ne*
2 A∘	to *ko*	singular→	*mujh ko, mujhe*	*āp ko*	*us ko, use*	*isko, ise*
		plural→	*hamẽ*	*āp ko*	*un ko, unhẽ*	*inko, inhẽ*
3 I∘	with, by *se*	singular→	*mujh se*	*āp se*	*us se*	*is se*
		plural→	*ham se*	*āp se*	*un se*	*in se*
4 D∘	for *ke liye*	singular→	*mere liye*	*āpke liye*	*us ke liye*	*is ke liye*
		plural→	*hamāre liye*	*āpke liye*	*un ke liye*	*in ke liye*
5 A∘	from *se*	singular→	*mujh se*	*āp se*	*us se*	*is se*
		plural→	*ham se*	*āp se*	*un se*	*in se*
6 P∘	of *kā, rā*	singular→	*merā-meri*	*āpkā-kī*	*uskā-kī*	*iskā-kī*
		plural→	*hamārā-rī*	*āpkā-kī*	*unkā-kī*	*inkā-kī*
7 L∘	in *mẽ*	singular→	*mujh mẽ*	*āp mẽ*	*us mẽ*	*un mẽ*
		plural→	*ham mẽ*	*āp mẽ*	*un mẽ*	*in mẽ*
	on, at *par*	singular→	*mujh par*	*āp par*	*us par*	*is par*
		plural→	*ham par*	*āp par*	*un par*	*in par*

USE OF PRONOUNS AND POSSESSIVE ADJECTIVES

Review of what we learned so far, the 'cumulative learning'

EXERCISE 31 : Translate the English sentences into Hindī (Answers are provided for help)

1ST PERSON : I, We

1. I, We (*maĩ, ham*) मैं, हम।
2. I am. (*maĩ hũ*) मैं हूँ।
3. We are friends. (*ham dost haĩ*) हम दोस्त हैं।
4. Give me one thing. (*mujhe ek chīj dījiye*) मुझे एक चीज दीजिये।
5. Tell us one thing. (*hamẽ ek bāt batāiye*) हमें एक बात बताइये।
6. It will not be done by me. (*yah mujh se nahĩ hogā*) यह मुझसे नहीं होगा।
7. It will be done by us. (*yah ham se hogā*) यह हमसे होगा।
8. This is for me. (*yah mere liye hai*) यह मेरे लिये है।
9. Bring water for us. (*hamāre liye pānī lāiye*) हमारे लिये पानी लाइये।
10. He took money from me. (*us ne mujh se paisā liyā*) उसने मुझसे पैसा लिया।
11. That is far from us. (*vah ham se dūr hai*) वह हमसे दूर है।
12. He is my brother. (*vah merā bhāī hai*) वह मेरा भाई है।
13. Our books. (*hamārī kitābẽ*) हमारी किताबें।
14. Please belive in me. (*mujh par bharosā kījiye*) मुझ पर भरोसा कीजिये।
15. He depends on us. (*vah ham par nirbhar hai*) वह हम पर निर्भर है।
16. My dog. (*merā kuttā*) मेरा कुत्ता।
17. My dogs. (*mere kutte*) मेरे कुत्ते।
18. Our dog. (*hamārā kuttā*) हमारा कुत्ता।
19. Our dogs. (*hamāre kutte*) हमारे कुत्ते।
20. My car. (*merī gādī*) मेरी गाड़ी।
21. My cars. (*merī gāḍiyā̃*) मेरी गाड़ियाँ।
22. Our car. (*hamārī gāḍī*) हमारी गाड़ी।
23. Our cars. (*hamārī gāḍiyā̃*) हमारी गाड़ियाँ।

2ND PERSON : You

1. You, *āp* आप।
2. You are. *(āp haĩ)* आप हैं।
3. You are friends. *(āp dost haĩ)* आप दोस्त हैं।
4. I will give you one thing. *(maĩ āp ko ek chīj dūṅgā-dūṅgī)* मैं आपको एक चीज दूँगा/दूँगी।
5. I will tell you (all) one thing. *(maĩ āp ko ek bāt batāūṅgā-batāūṅgī)* मैं आपको (आप लोगों को) एक बात बताऊँगा/बताऊँगी।
6. It will not be done by you. *(yah āp se nahĩ hogā)* यह आपसे नहीं होगा।
7. It will be done by you all. *(yah āp logõ se hogā)* यह आप लोगों से होगा।
8. This is for you. *(yah āp ke liye hai)* यह आपके लिये है।
9. I will bring water for you all. *(maĩ āp logõ ke liye pānī lāūṅgā-lāūṅgī)* मैं आप लोगों के लिये पानी लाऊँगा/लाऊँगी।
10. He took money from you. *(us ne āp se paise liye)* उसने आपसे पैसे लिये (पैसा लिया।
11. That is far from you all. *(vah āp logõ se dūr hai)* वह आप लोगों से दूर है।
12. He is your brother. *(vah āp kā bhāī hai)* वह आपका भाई है।
13. Your books. *(āp kī kitābẽ)* आपकी किताबें।
14. I believe in you. *(maĩ āp par bharosā kartā hū̃)* मैं आप पर भरोसा करता हूँ।
15. He depends on you. *(vah āp par nirbhar hai)* वह आप पर निर्भर है।
16. Your dog. *(āp kā kuttā)* आपका कुत्ता।
17. Your dogs. *(āp ke kutte)* आपके कुत्ते।
18. Your car. *(āp kī gāḍī)* आपकी गाड़ी।
19. Your cars. *(āp kī gāḍiyā̃)* आपकी गड़ियाँ।

3RD PERSON : He, she, it, they, these, those

1. He, she, it, they, these *vah, vah, yah, ve, ye.* वह, वह, यह, वे, ये।
2. He-she is. *(vah hai)* वह है। Those are friends. *(ve dost haĩ)* वे दोस्त हैं।
3. They are friends. *(ve dost haĩ)* वे दोस्त हैं। These are friends. *(ye dost haĩ)* ये दोस्त हैं।
4. Give him-her one thing. *(us ko ek chij dījiye)* उसको एक चीज दीजिये।
5. Tell them one thing. *(un ko ek bāt batāiye)* उनको/उन्हें एक बात बताइये।
6. It will not be done by him-her. *(yah us se nahĩ hogā)* यह उससे नहीं होगा।

7. It will be done by them. *(yah un se hogā)* यह उनसे होगा।

8. This is for her-him. *(yah us ke liye hai)* यह उसके लिये है।

9. Bring water for them. *(un ke liye pānī lāiye)* उनके लिये पानी लाइये।

10. He took it from him-her. (us ne us se liyā) उसने उससे लिया।

11. That is far from them. *(vah un se dūr hai)* वह उनसे दूर है।

12. He is his-her brother. *(vah us kā bhāī hai)* वह उसका भाई है।

13. Their books. *(un kī kitābeँ)* उनकी किताबें।

14. Belive in him-her. *(us par bharosā kījiye)* उस पर भरोसा कीजिये।

15. He depends on them. *(vah un par bharosā kartā hai)* वह उन पर भरोसा करता है।

16. His dog. *(us kā kuttā)* उसका कुत्ता।

17. His dogs. *(us ke kutte)* उसके कुत्ते।

18. Her dog. *(us kā kuttā)* उसका कुत्ता।

19. Her dogs. *(us ke kutte)* उसके कुत्ते।

20. Their dog. *(un kā kuttā)* उनका कुत्ता।

21. Their dogs. *(un ke kutte)* उनके कुत्ते।

22. His car. *(us kī gāḍī)* उसकी गाड़ी।

23. Her car. *(us kī gāḍī)* उसकी गाड़ी।

24. His cars. *(us kī gāḍiyaँ)* उसकी गाड़ियाँ।

25. Her cars. *(us kī gāḍiyaँ)* उसकी गाड़ियाँ।

26. Their car. *(un kī gāḍī)* उनकी गाड़ी।

27. Their cars. *(un kī gāḍiyaँ)* उनकी गाड़ियाँ।

28. My house *(merā ghar)* मेरा घर। My houses *(mere ghar)* मेरे घर। My book *(merī kitāb)* मेरी किताब। My books *(merī kitābeँ)* मेरी किताबें। My dog *(merā kuttā)* मेरा कुत्ता। My dogs *(mere kutte)* मेरे कुत्ते। My car *(merī gāḍī)* मेरी गाड़ी। My cars *(merī gāḍiyaँ)* मेरी गाड़ियाँ।

29. Our house *(hamārā ghar)* हमारा घर। Our houses *(hamāre ghar)* हमारे घर। Our book *(hamārī kitāb)* हमारी किताब। Our books *(hamārī kitābeँ)* हमारी किताबें। Our dog *(hamārā kuttā)* हमारा कुत्ता। Our dogs *(hamāre kutte)* हमारे कुत्ते। Our car *(hamārī gāḍī)* हमारी गाड़ी। Our cars *(hamārī gāḍiyaँ)* हमारी गाड़ियाँ। These houses *(ye ghar)* ये घर। Those houses *(ve ghar)* वे घर।

30. Your house *(āp kā ghar)* आपका घर। Your houses *(āp ke ghar)* आपके घर। Your book *(āp kī kitāb)* आपकी किताब। Your books *(āp kī kitābeँ)* आपकी किताबें। Your dog *(āp kā kuttā)* आपका कुत्ता। Your dogs *(āp ke kutte)* आपके कुत्ते। Your car *(āp kī gāḍī)* आपकी गाड़ी। Your cars *(āp kī gāḍiyaँ)* आपकी गाड़ियाँ। Your cat (f॰) *(āp kī billī)* आपकी बिल्ली।

31. His-her house *(us kā ghar)* उसका घर। His-her houses *(us ke ghar)* उसके घर। His-her book *(us kī kitāb)* उसकी किताब। His-her books *(us kī kitābe͂)* उसकी किताबें। His-her dog *(us kā kuttā)* उसका कुत्ता। His-her dogs *(us ke kutte)* उसके कुत्ते। His-her car *(us kī gāḍī)* उसकी गाड़ी। His-her cars *(us kī gāḍiyā͂)* उसकी गाड़ियाँ। This car *yah gāḍī* यह गाड़ी। These cars *ye gāḍiyā͂* ये गाड़ियाँ।

32. Their house *(un kā ghar)* उनका घर। Their houses *(un ke ghar)* उनका घर। Their book *(un kī kitāb)* उनकी किताब। Their books *(un kī kitābe͂)* उनकी किताबें। Their dog *(un kā kuttā)* उनका कुत्ता। Their dogs *(un ke kutte)* उनके कुत्ते। Their car *(un kī gāḍī)* उनकी गाड़ी। Their cars *(un kī gāḍiyā͂)* उनकी गाड़ियाँ। This book *(yah kitāb)* यह किताब। That book *(vah kitāb)* वह किताब।

33. My book *(merī kitāb)* मेरी किताब। My books *(merī kitābe͂)* मेरी किताबें। Your book *(āp kī kitab)* आपकी किताब। Your books *(āp kī kitābe͂)* आपकी किताबें। His book *(us kī kitāb)* उसकी किताब। His books *(us kī kitābe͂)* उसकी किताबें। Her book *(us kī kitāb)* उसकी किताब। Her books *(us kī kitābe͂)* उसकी किताबें। Their book *(un kī kitāb)* उनकी किताब। Their books *(un kī kitābe͂)* उनकी किताबें। These books *(ye kitābe͂)* ये किताबें। Those books *(ve kitābe͂)* वे किताबें।

NEW EXPRESSIONS TO LEARN :

(1) Across = *us pār* (उस पार)
(2) After = *bād me͂* (बाद में)
(3) Again = *fir, punaḥ* (फिर, पुनः)
(4) Again and again = *bārambār* (बारंबार)
(5) Although = *yadyapi* (यद्यपि)
(6) If = *yadi* (यदि)
(7) Then = *fir, bād me͂* (फिर, बाद में)
(8) Before = *pahale* (पहले)
(9) Between = *bīch me͂* (बीच में)
(10) Beyond = *us pār* (उस पार)
(11) There = *vahā͂* (वहाँ)
(12) Here = *yahā͂* (यहाँ)
(13) On this side = *idhar* (इधर)
(14) On that side = *udhar* (उधर)
(15) Where? = *kahā͂?* (कहाँ?)
(16) On which side? = *kidhar?* (किधर?)
(17) Where = *jahā͂* (जहाँ)
(18) On which side = *jidhar* (जिधर)
(19) Near = *pās, ke pās* (पास, के पास)
(20) With = *sāth, ke sāth* (साथ, के साथ)
(21) For = *ke liye* (के लिये)
(22) Inside = *andar, bhītar* (अंदर, भीतर),
(23) Out side = *bāhar* (बाहर)
(24) On, Over = *ūpar, par* (ऊपर, पर)

TABLE 25 : SIMILARITY BETWEEN VARIOUS PRONOUNS

He	*vah*	वह
She	*vah*	वह
That	*vah*	वह
This	*yah*	यह
This	*yah*	यह
That	*vah*	वह
Who?	*kaun*	कौन?
Who	*jo*	जो
Here	*yahā̃*	यहाँ
There	*vahā̃*	वहाँ
Where?	*kahā̃*	कहाँ?
Where	*jahā̃*	जहाँ
On this side	*idhar*	इधर
On that side	*udhar*	उधर
On which side?	*kidhar*	किधर?
On which side	*jidhar*	जिधर
Now	*ab*	अब
Then	*tab*	तब
When?	*kab*	कब?
When	*jab*	जब
Like this	*aisā*	ऐसा
Like that	*vaisā*	वैसा

Like what, how?	*kaisā*	कैसा?
Like which, as	*jaisā*	जैसा
Like this	*is tarah*	इस तरह
Like that	*us tarah*	उस तरह
Like what?	*kis tarah*	किस तरह?
Like which	*jis tarah*	जिस तरह
Like these	*aise*	ऐसे
Like those	*vaise*	वैसे
Like what, how?	*kaise*	कैसे?
Like which	*jaise*	जैसे
This much	*itnā*	इतना
That much	*utanā*	उतना
How much?	*kitnā*	कितना
As much	*jitnā*	जितना
This much (f∘)	*itnī*	इतनी
That much	*utnī*	उतनी
How much?	*kitnī*	कितनी
As much	*jitnī*	जितनी
These many	*itne*	इतने
That many	*utne*	उतने
How many?	*kitne*	कितने?
As many	*jitne*	जितने

This person (did)	*is ne*	इसने
He, she (did)	*us ne*	उसने
Who (did ?)	*kis ne*	किसने
Who (did)	*jis ne*	जिसने

To this	*is ko*	इसको
To that	*us ko*	उसको
To him	*us ko*	उसको
To her	*us ko*	उसको

To these	*in ko*	इनको
To those	*un ko*	उनको
To them	*un ko*	उनको
To whom?	*kis ko*	किसको

With this	*is se*	इससे
With that	*us se*	उससे
With what?	*kis se*	किससे?
With which	*jis se*	जिससे

For this	*is liye*	इस लिये
For that	*us liye*	उस लिये
For what?	*kis liye*	किस लिये?
For which	*jis liye*	जिस लिये

From this	*is se*	इससे
From that	*us se*	उससे
From what?	*kis se*	किससे
From which	*jis se*	जिससे

Of this	*is kā*	इसका
Of that	*us kā*	उसका
Of what?	*kis kā*	किसका?
Of which	*jis kā*	जिसका

Of this	*is kī*	इसकी
Of that	*us kī*	उसकी
Of what?	*kis kī*	किसकी?
Of which	*jis kī*	जिसकी

Of this	*is ke*	इसके
Of that	*us ke*	उसके
Of what?	*kis ke*	किसके?
Of which	*jis ke*	जिसके

In this	*is mẽ*	इसमें
In that	*us mẽ*	उसमें
In what?	*kis mẽ*	किसमें?
In which	*jis mẽ*	जिसमें

On this	*is par*	इस पर
On that	*us par*	उस पर
On what?	*kis par*	किस पर
On which	*jis par*	जिस पर

Why?	*kyõ*	क्यों?
so	*yõ*	यों
thus	*tyõ*	त्यों
as	*jyõ*	ज्यों

TABLE 26 : RATNAKAR'S CHART OF VERB APPLICATIONS

Say = verb stem *kah* कह. to say = *kahnā* कहना). Only the verb stems are used in tenses.

Verb stem	say	*(kah)*	कह
Verbal noun (infinitive)	to say	*(kahanā)*	कहना
He does	He says	*(vah kahatā hai)*	वह कहता है
She does	She says	*(vah kahatī hai)*	वह कहती है
They do	They say	*(ve kahate haĩ)*	वे कहते हैं
I did (m◦ object)	I said a word	*(maĩ ne shabda kahā)*	मैंने शब्द कहा
(m◦ pl◦ object)	I said words	*(maĩ ne shabda kahe)*	मैंने शब्द कहे
(f◦ object)	I said a poem	*(maĩ ne kavitā kahī)*	मैंने कविता कही
(f◦ pl◦ object)	I said poems	*(maĩ ne kavitāẽ kahī̃)*	मैंने कविताएँ कहीं
I will (m◦ subject)	I will say	*(maĩ kahūṅgā)*	मैं कहूँगा
I will (f◦ subject)	I will say	*(maĩ kahūṅgī)*	मैं कहूँगी
He will	He will say	*(vah kahegā)*	वह कहेगा
She will	She will say	*(vah kahegī)*	वह कहेगी
They will (m◦)	They will say	*(ve kaheṅge)*	वे कहेंगे
(f◦ subject)	They will say	*(ve kaheṅgī)*	वे कहेंगी
Perfect (m◦ subject)	He has already said	*(vah kaha chukā hai)*	वह कह चुका है
Perfect (f◦ subject)	She has already said	*(vah kah chukī hai)*	वह कह चुकी है
Participle	Having said I came	*(maĩ kah kar āyā)*	मैं कहकर आया
Gerund	While saying	*(kahate hue)*	कहते हुए
Adjective, doer (m◦)	He is a speaker	*(vah kahane wālā hai)*	वह कहनेवाला है
Adjective, doer (f◦)	She is a speaker	*(vah kahane wālī hai)*	वह कहनेवाली है
for	FOR saying,	*(kahane ke liye)*	कहने के लिये
in	IN saying	*(kahane mẽ)*	कहने में
Interrogative	May I say?	*(kyā maĩ kahū̃?)*	क्या मैं कहूँ?
Imperative (respect)	Please say!	*(kṛpayā kahiye!)*	कहिए! कृपया कहिए!
(Imperative *tū-tum*)	Say!	*(kah! kaho!)*	कह! कहो!

15.9 VERB APPLICATIONS

What we have learned so far, the cumulative learning

e.g. verb stem *gir (√गिर)* - fall, verb stem *likh* (लिख) - write

(A) INTRANSITIVE verb, to fall = *gir* गिर, verbal noun = falling *(giranā)* गिरना।

(B) TRANSITIVE verb, to write = *likh* लिख, verbal noun = writing *(likhnā)* लिखना।

(1) **SIMPLE PRESENT** ACTIONS : (all Even Numbered sentences are Transitive)

1. I fall, I do fall (m◦ and f◦ subject). *(m◦ maĩ girtā hū̃, f◦ maĩ girtī hū̃)* m◦ मैं गिरता हूँ, f◦ मैं गिरती हूँ।
2. I write, I do write (m◦ and f◦ subject). *(maĩ likhtā hū̃, maĩ likhtī hū̃)* मैं लिखता हूँ, मैं लिखती हूँ।
3. We fall (m◦ and f◦ subject). *(ham girte haĩ, ham girtī̃ haĩ)* हम गिरते हैं, हम गिरतीं हैं।
4. We write (m◦ and f◦ subject). *(ham likhte haĩ, ham likhtī̃ haĩ)* हम लिखते हैं, हम लिखतीं हैं।
5. You fall (m◦ and f◦ subject). *(āp girte haĩ, āp girtī̃ haĩ)* आप गिरते हैं, आप गिरतीं हैं।
6. You write (m◦ and f◦ subject). *(āp likhte haĩ, āp likhtī̃ haĩ)* आप लिखते हैं, आप लिखतीं हैं।
7. He falls. *(vah girtā hai)* वह गिरता है। 8. He writes. *(vah likhtā hai)* वह लिखता है।
9. She falls. *(vah girtī hai)* वह गिरती है। 10. She writes. *(vah likhtī hai)* वह लिखती है।
11. They fall (m◦ and f◦ subject). *(ve girte haĩ, ve girtī̃ haĩ)* वे गिरते हैं, वे गिरतीं हैं।
12. They write (m◦ and f◦ subject). *(ve likhte haĩ, ve likhtī̃ haĩ)* वे लिखते हैं, वे लिखतीं हैं।

(2) **PRESENT CONTINUOUS** ACTIONS : (all Even Numbered sentences are Transitive)

1. I am falling (m◦ and f◦). *(maĩ gir rahā hū̃, maĩ gir rahī hū̃)* मैं गिर रहा हूँ, मैं गिर रही हूँ।
2. I am writing (m◦ and f◦). (*maĩ likh rahā hū̃, maĩ likh rahī hū̃)* मैं लिख रहा हूँ, मैं लिख रही हूँ।
3. We are falling (m◦ and f◦). *(ham gir rahe haĩ, ham gir rahī̃ haĩ)* हम गिर रहे हैं, हम गिर रहीं हैं।
4. We are writing (m◦ f◦). *(ham likh rahe haĩ, ham likh rahī̃ haĩ)* हम लिख रहे हैं, हम लिख रहीं हैं।
5. You are falling (m◦ f◦). *(āp gir rahe haĩ, āp gir rahī̃ haĩ)* आप गिर रहे हैं, आप गिर रहीं हैं।
6. You are writing (m◦ f◦). (*āp likh rahe haĩ, āp likh rahī̃ haĩ)* आप लिख रहे हैं, आप लिख रहीं हैं।
7. He is falling. *(vah gir rahā hai)* वह गिर रहा है।
8. He is writing. (*vah likh rahā hai*) वह लिख रहा है।
9. She is falling. *(vah gir rahī hai*) वह गिर रही है।
10. She is writing. (*vah likh rahī hai*) वह लिख रही है।

11. They are falling (m○ f○). (*ve gir rahe haĩ, ve gir rahī haĩ*) वे गिर रहे हैं, वे गिर रहीं हैं।

12. They are writing (m○ f○). (*ve likh rahe haĩ, ve likh rahī haĩ*) वे लिख रहे हैं, वे लिख रहीं हैं।

(3) **PRESENT PERFECT** ACTIONS : (all Even Numbered sentences are Transitive)

1. I have fallen (m○ f○). (*maĩ girā hū̃, maĩ girī hū̃*) मैं गिरा हूँ, मैं गिरी हूँ।

2. I have written (m○ f○). (*maĩ ne likhā hai, maĩ ne likhe haĩ, maĩ ne likhī hai, maĩ ne likhī̃ haĩ*) मैंने लिखा है, मैंने लिखे हैं, मैंने लिखी है, मैंने लिखीं हैं।

3. We have fallen (m○ f○). (*ham gire haĩ, ham girī̃ haĩ*) हम गिरे हैं, हम गिरीं हैं।

4. We have written (m○ f○). (*ham ne likhā hai, ham ne likhe haĩ, ham ne likhī hai, ham ne likhī̃ hai*) हमने लिखा हैं, हमने लिखे हैं, हमने लिखी है, हमने लिखीं हैं।

5. You have fallen (m○ f○). (*āp gire haĩ, āp girī̃ haĩ*) आप गिरे हैं, आप गिरीं हैं।

6. You have written (m○ f○). (*āp ne likhā hai, āp ne likhe hai, āp ne likhī hai, āp ne likhī̃ haĩ*) आपने लिखा हैं, आपने लिखे है, आपने लिखी है, आपने लिखीं हैं।

7. He has fallen. (*vah girā hai*), वह गिरा है।

8. He has written. (*us ne likhā hai, us ne likhe hai, us ne likhī hai, us ne likhī̃ haĩ*) उसने लिखा है, उसने लिखे हैं, उसने लिखी है, उसने लिखीं हैं।

9. She has fallen. (*vah girī hai*) वह गिरी है।

10. She has written. (*us ne likhā hai, us ne likhe hai, us ne likhī hai, us ne likhī̃ haĩ*) उसने लिखा है, उसने लिखे हैं, उसने लिखी है, उसने लिखीं हैं।

11. They have fallen (m○ f○). (*ve gire haĩ, ve girī̃ haĩ*) वे गिरे हैं, वे गिरीं हैं।

12. They have written (m○ f○). (*unhõ ne likhā hai, unhõ ne likhe hai, unhõ ne likhī hai, unhõ ne likhī̃ hai*) उन्होंने लिखा है, उन्होंने लिखे हैं, उन्होंने लिखी है, उन्होंने लिखीं हैं।

(4) SIMPLE PAST or PAST INDEFINITE PERFECT ACTIONS : (all Even ones are Transitive)

1. I fell, I did fall (m○ f○). (*maĩ girā, maĩ girī*) मैं गिरा, मैं गिरी।

2. I wrote, I did write (m○ f○). (*maĩ ne likhā, maĩ ne likhe, maĩ ne likhī, maĩ ne likhī̃*) मैंने लिखा, मैंने लिखे, मैंने लिखी, मैंने लिखीं।

3. We fell (m○ f○). (*ham gire, ham girī̃*) हम गिरे, हम गिरीं।

4. We wrote (m○ f○). (*ham ne likhā, ham ne likhe, ham ne likhī, ham ne likhī̃*) हमने लिखा, हमने लिखे, हमने लिखी, हमने लिखीं।

5. You fell (m◦ f◦). *(āp gire, āp girī̃)* आप गिरे, आप गिरीं।

6. You wrote (m◦ f◦). *(āp ne likhā, āp ne likhe, āp ne likhī, āp ne likhī̃)* आप ने लिखा, आपने लिखे, आपने लिखी, आपने लिखीं।

7. He fell. *(vah girā)* वह गिरा।

8. He wrote. *(us ne likhā, us ne likhe, us ne likhī, us ne likhī̃)* उसने लिखा, उसने लिखे, उसने लिखी, उसने लिखीं।

9. She fell. *(vah girī)* वह गिरी।

10. She wrote. *(us ne likhā, us ne likhe, us ne likhī, us ne likhī̃)* उसने लिखा, उसने लिखे, उसने लिखी, उसने लिखीं।

11. They fell (m◦ f◦). *(ve gire, ve girī̃)* वे गिरे, वे गिरीं।

12. They wrote (m◦ f◦). *(unhõ ne likhā, unhõ ne likhe, unhõ ne likhī, unhõ ne likhī̃)* उन्होंने लिखा, उन्होंने लिखे, उन्होंने लिखी, उन्होंने लिखीं।

(5) **PAST CONTINUOUS** ACTIONS : (all Even Numbered sentences are Transitive)

1. I was falling (m◦ f◦). *(maĩ gir rahā thā, maĩ gir rahī thī)* मैं गिर रहा था, मैं गिर रही थी।
2. I was writing (m◦ f◦). *(maĩ likh rahā thā, maĩ likh rahī thī)* मैं लिख रहा था, मैं लिख रही थी।
3. We were falling (m◦ f◦). *(ham gir rahe the, ham gir rahī̃ thī̃)* हम गिर रहे थे, हम गिर रहीं थीं।
4. We were writing (m◦ f◦). *(ham likh rahe the, ham likh rahī̃ thī̃)* हम लिख रहे थे, हम लिख रहीं थीं।
5. You were falling (m◦ f◦). *(āp gir rahe the, āp gir rahī̃ thī̃)* आप गिर रहे थे, आप गिर रहीं थीं।
6. You were writing (m◦ f◦). *(āp likh rahe the, āp likh rahī̃ thī̃)* आप लिख रहे थे, आप लिख रहीं थीं।
7. He was falling. *(vah gir rahā thā)* वह गिर रहा था।
8. He was writing. *(vah likh rahā thā)* वह लिख रहा था।
9. She was falling. *(vah gir rahī thī)* वह गिर रही थी।
10. She was writing. *(vah likh rahī thī)* वह लिख रही थी।
11. They were falling (m◦ f◦). *(ve gir rahe the, ve gir rahī̃ thī̃)* वे गिर रहे थे, वे गिर रहीं थीं।
12. They were writing (m◦ f◦). *(ve likh rahe the, ve likh rahī̃ thī̃)* वे लिख रहे थे, वे लिख रहीं थीं।

(6) PAST PERFECT ACTIONS : (all Even Numbered sentences are Transitive)

1. I had fallen (m◦ f◦). *(maĩ girā thā, maĩ girī thī)* मैं गिरा था, मैं गिरी थी।
2. I had written (m◦ f◦). *(maĩ ne likhā thā, maĩ ne likhe the, maĩ ne likhī thī, maĩ ne likhī̃ thī̃)* मैंने

लिखा था, मैंने लिखे थे, मैंने लिखी थी, मैंने लिखीं थीं।

3. We had fallen (m◦ f◦). *(ham gire the, ham girī̐ thī̐)* हम गिरे थे, हम गिरीं थीं।

4. We had written (m◦ f◦). *(ham ne likhā thā, ham ne likhe the, ham ne likhī thī, ham ne likhī̐ thī̐)* हमने लिखा था, हमने लिखे थे, हमने लिखी थी, हमने लिखीं थीं।

5. You had fallen (m◦ f◦). *(āp gire the, āp girī̐ thī̐)* आप गिरे थे, आप गिरीं थीं।

6. You had written (m◦ f◦). *(āp ne likhā thā, āp ne likhe the, āp ne likhī thī, āp ne likhī̐ thī̐)* आप ने लिखा था, आपने लिखे थे, आपने लिखी थी, आपने लिखीं थीं।

7. He had fallen. *(vah girā thā)* वह गिरा था।

8. He had written. *(us ne likhā thā, us ne likhe the, us ne likhī thī, us ne likhī̐ thī̐)* उसने लिखा था, उसने लिखे थे, उसने लिखी थी, उसने लिखीं थीं।

9. She had fallen. *(vah girī thī)* वह गिरी थी।

10. She had written. *(us ne likhā thā, us ne likhe the, us ne likhī thī, us ne likhī̐ thī̐)* उसने लिखा था, उसने लिखे थे, उसने लिखी थी, उसने लिखीं थीं।

11. They had fallen (m◦ f◦). *(ve gire the, ve girī̐ thī̐)* वे गिरे थे, वे गिरीं थीं।

12. They had written (m◦ f◦). *(unho̐ne likhā thā, unho̐ne likhe the, unho̐ne likhī thī, unho̐ne likhī̐ thī̐)* उन्होंने लिखा था, उन्होंने लिखे थे, उन्होंने लिखी थी, उन्होंने लिखीं थीं।

(7) **SIMPLE FUTURE** ACTIONS : (all Even Numbered sentences are Transitive)

1. I will fall (m◦ f◦). *(maı̐ girū̐ngā, maı̐ girū̐ngī)* मैं गिरूँगा, मैं गिरूँगी।

2. I will write (m◦ f◦). *(maı̐ likhū̇ngā, maı̐ likhū̇ngī)* मैं लिखूँगा, मैं लिखूँगी।

3. We will fall (m◦ f◦). *(ham gireṅge, ham gireṅgī)* हम गिरेंगे, हम गिरेंगी।

4. We will write (m◦ f◦). *(ham likheṅge, ham likheṅgī)* हम लिखेंगे, हम लिखेंगी।

5. You will fall (m◦ f◦). *(āp gireṅge, āp gireṅgī)* आप गिरेंगे, आप गिरेंगी।

6. You will write (m◦ f◦). *(āp likheṅge, āp likheṅgī)* आप लिखेंगे, आप लिखेंगी।

7. He will fall. *(vah giregā)* वह गिरेगा।

8. He will write. *(vah likhegā)* वह लिखेगा।

9. She will fall. *(vah giregī)* वह गिरेगी।

10. She will write. *(vah likhegī)* वह लिखेगी।

11. They will fall (m◦ f◦). *(ve gireṅge, ve gireṅgī)* वे गिरेंगे, वे गिरेंगी।

12. They will write (m◦ f◦). *(ve likheṅge, ve likheṅgī)* वे लिखेंगे, वे लिखेंगी।

(8) **POTENTIAL** MOOD (may, should) : (all Even Numbered sentences are Transitive)

1. I may fall (m◦ f◦). *(maiṅ giruṅ, maiṅ shāyad giruṅ)* मैं गिरूँ। मैं शायद गिरूँ।

2. I may write (m◦ f◦). *(maiṅ likhuṅ)* मैं लिखूँ।

3. We may fall (m◦ f◦). *(ham gireṅ)* हम गिरें।

4. We may write (m◦ f◦). *(ham likheṅ)* हम लिखें।

5. You may fall (m◦ f◦). *(āp gireṅ)* आप गिरें।

6. You may write (m◦ f◦). *(āp likheṅ)* आप लिखें।

7. He may fall. *(vah gire)* वह गिरे।

8. He may write. *(vah likhe)* वह लिखे।

9. She may fall. *(vah gire)* वह गिरे।

10. She may write. *(vah likhe)* वह लिखे।

11. They may fall (m◦ f◦). *(ve gireṅ)* वे गिरें।

12. They may write (m◦ f◦). *(ve likheṅ)* वे लिखें।

(9) **INTERROGATIVE** MOOD

1. May I fall (m◦ f◦)? *(kyā maiṅ giruṅ? maiṅ giruṅ kyā?)* क्या मैं गिरूँ? मैं गिरूँ क्या?
2. May I write (m◦ f◦)? *(kyā maiṅ likhuṅ?)* क्या मैं लिखूँ? मैं लिखूँ क्या ?
3. May we fall (m◦ f◦)? *(kyā ham gireṅ?)* क्या हम गिरें?
4. May we write (m◦ f◦)? *(kyā ham likheṅ?)* क्या हम लिखें?
5. May he fall? *(kyā vah gire?)* क्या वह गिरे?
6. May he write? *(kyā vah likhe?)* क्या वह लिखे?
7. May she fall? *(kyā vah gire?)* क्या वह गिरे?
8. May she write? *(kyā vah likhe?)* क्या वह लिखे?
9. May they fall (m◦ f◦)? *(kyā ve gireṅ?)* क्या वे गिरें?
10. May they write (m◦ f◦)? *(kyā ve likheṅ?)* क्या वे लिखें? वे लिखें क्या?

(10) **CAUSATIVE** PRESENT ACTIONS : (all Even Numbered sentences are Transitive)

(to fall = *gir;* to cause to fall = to write *likh;* to cause to write = *likhā*)

1. I have caused to fall = I have dropped (m◦ and f◦ object-objects). *(maiṅ ne girāy hai, maiṅ ne girāye haiṅ, maiṅ ne girāyī hai, maiṅ ne girāyīṅ haiṅ)* मैंने गिराया है, मैंने गिराये हैं, मैंने गिरायी है, मैंने गिरायीं हैं।
2. I have caused to write (m◦ and f◦ object-objects). *(maiṅ ne likhāyā hai, maiṅ ne likhāye haiṅ, maiṅ ne likhāyīṅ haiṅ, maiṅ ne likhāyīṅ haiṅ)* मैंने लिखाया है, मैंने लिखाए हैं, मैंने लिखाई है, मैंने लिखाईं हैं।
3. We have caused to fall (m◦ and f◦ object-objects). *(ham ne girāyā hai, ham ne girāye haiṅ, ham ne girāyī hai, ham ne girāyīṅ haiṅ)* हमने गिराया है, हमने गिराये हैं, हमने गिरायी है, हमने गिरायीं हैं।

4. We have caused to write (m∘ and f∘ object-objects). *(ham ne likhāyā hai, ham ne likhāye haĩ, ham ne likhāyī hai, ham ne likhāyī̃ haĩ)* हमने लिखाया है, हमने लिखाए हैं, हमने लिखाई है, हमने लिखाईं हैं।

5. You have caused to fall (m∘ and f∘ object-objects). *(āp ne girāyā hai, āp ne girāye haĩ, āp ne girāyī hai, āp ne likhāyī̃ haĩ)* आपने गिराया है, आपने गिराये हैं, आपने गिरायी है, आपने गिरायीं हैं।

6. You have caused to write (m∘ and f∘ object-objects). *(āp ne likhāyā hai, āp ne likhāye haĩ, āp ne likhāyī hai, āp ne likhāyī̃ haĩ.* आपने लिखाया है, आपने लिखाए हैं, आपने लिखाई है, आपने लिखाईं हैं।

7. He has caused to fall (m∘ and f∘ object-objects). *(us ne girāyā hai, us ne girāye haĩ, us ne girāyī hai, us ne girāyī̃ haĩ)* उसने गिराया है, उसने गिराये हैं, उसने गिरायी है, उसने गिरायीं हैं।

8. He has caused to write (m∘ and f∘ object-objects). *(us ne likhāyā hai, us ne likhāye haĩ, us ne likhāyī hai, us ne likhāī̃ haĩ)* उसने लिखाया है, उसने लिखाए हैं, उसने लिखाई है, उसने लिखाईं हैं।

9. She has caused to fall (m∘ and f∘ object-objects). *(us ne girāyā hai, us ne girāye haĩ, us ne girāyī hai, us ne girāyī̃ haĩ)* उसने गिराया है, उसने गिराये हैं, उसने गिरायी है, उसने गिरायीं हैं।

10. She has caused to write (m∘ and f∘ object-objects). *(us ne likhāyā hai, us ne likhāye haĩ, us ne likhāyī hai, us ne likhāyī̃ haĩ)* उसने लिखाया है, उसने लिखाए हैं, उसने लिखाई है, उसने लिखाईं हैं।

11. They have caused to fall (m∘ f∘ object-objects). *(unhõ ne girāyā hai, unhõ ne girāye haĩ, unhõ ne girāyī hai, unhõ ne girāyī̃ haĩ)* उन्हों ने गिराया है, उन्हों ने गिराये हैं, उन्हों ने गिरायी है, उन्हों ने गिरायीं हैं।

12. They have caused to write (m∘ and f∘ object-objects). *(unhõ ne likhāyā hai, unhõ ne likhāye haĩ, unhõ ne likhāyī hai, unhõ ne likhāyī̃ haĩ)* उन्हों ने लिखाया है, उन्हों ने लिखाए हैं, उन्हों ने लिखाई है, उन्हों ने लिखाईं हैं।

(11) **ASSERTIVE** PRESENT ACTIONS : (all Even Numbered sentences are Transitive)

1. I can fall (m∘ f∘ subject). *(maĩ gir sakatā hũ, maĩ gir sakatī hũ)* मैं गिर सकता हूँ, मैं गिर सकती हूँ।
2. I can write (m∘ f∘). *(maĩ likh sakatā hũ, maĩ likh sakatī hũ)* मैं लिख सकता हूँ, मैं लिख सकती हूँ।
3. We can fall (m∘ f∘). *(ham gir sakate haĩ, ham gir sakatī̃ haĩ)* हम गिर सकते हैं, हम गिर सकतीं हैं।
4. We can write (m∘ f∘). *(ham likh sakate haĩ, ham likh sakatī̃ haĩ)* हम लिख सकते हैं, हम लिख सकतीं हैं।
5. You can fall (m∘ f∘). *(āp gir sakate haĩ, āp gir sakatī̃ haĩ)* आप गिर सकते हैं, आप गिर सकतीं हैं।
6. You can write (m∘ f∘). *(āp likh sakate haĩ, āp likh sakatī̃ haĩ)* आप लिख सकते हैं, आप लिख सकतीं हैं।
7. He can fall. *(vah gir sakatā hai)* वह गिर सकता है।
8. He can write. *(vah likh sakatā hai)* वह लिख सकता है।
9. She can fall. *(vah gir sakatī hai)* वह गिर सकती है।

10. She can write subject. *(vah likh sakatī hai)* वह लिख सकती है।

11. They can fall (m◦ f◦). *(ve gir sakate haĩ, ve gir sakatī̃ haĩ)* वे गिर सकते हैं, वे गिर सकतीं हैं।

12. They can write (m◦ f◦). *(ve likh sakate haĩ, ve likh sakatī̃ haĩ)* वे लिख सकते हैं, वे लिख सकतीं हैं।

13. Someone can fall (m◦ f◦). *(koī gir sakatā hai, koī gir sakatī hai)* कोई गिर सकता है, कोई गिर सकती है।

14. Someone can write (m◦ f◦ subject). *(koī likh sakatā hai)* कोई लिख सकता है।

15. Anybody can fall (m◦ f◦ subject). *(koī bhī gir sakatā hai)* कोई भी गिर सकता है।

16. Anybody can write (m◦ f◦ subject). *(koī bhī likh sakatā hai)* कोई भी लिख सकता है।)

17. Anything can fall (m◦ f◦ subject). *(kuchh bhī gir sakatā hai, koī bhī chīj gir sakatī hai)* कुछ भी गिर सकता है, कोई भी चीज गिर सकती है।)

18. Nothing can fall (m◦ f◦). *(kuchh bhī nahī̃ gir sakatā)* कुछ भी नहीं गिर सकता।

(12) **DESIDERATIVE** MOOD (expressing a desire or wish to do)

1. I want to fall. *maĩ giranā chāhatā hū̃, maĩ giranā chāhatī hū̃.* मैं गिरना चाहता हूँ, मैं गिरना चाहती हूँ।

2. I want to write (m◦ f◦). *(maĩ likhnā chāhatā hū̃, maĩ likhnā chāhattī hū̃)* मैं लिखना चाहता हूँ, मैं लिखना चाहती हूँ।

3. We want to fall (m◦ f◦). *(ham giranā chāhate haĩ, ham giranā chāhatī̃ haĩ)* हम गिरना चाहते हैं, हम गिरना चाहतीं हैं।

4. We want to write (m◦ f◦). *(ham likhnā chāhate haĩ, ham likhnā chāhatī̃ haĩ)* हम लिखना चाहते हैं, हम लिखना चाहतीं हैं।

5. You want to fall (m◦ f◦). *(āp giranā chāhate haĩ, āp giranā chāhatī̃ haĩ)* आप गिरना चाहते हैं, आप गिरना चाहतीं हैं।

6. You want to write (m◦ f◦). *(āp likhnā chāhate haĩ, āp likhnā chāhatī̃ haĩ)* आप लिखना चाहते हैं, आप लिखना चाहतीं हैं।

7. He wants to fall. *(vah giranā chāhatā hai)* वह गिरना चाहता है।

8. He wants to write. *(vah likhnā chāhatā hai)* वह लिखना चाहता है।

9. She wants to fall. *(vah giranā chāhatī hai)* वह गिरना चाहती है।

10. She wants to write. *(vah likhnā chāhatī hai)* वह लिखना चाहती है।

11. They want to fall (m◦ f◦). *ve giranā chāhate-chāhatī̃ haĩ.* वे गिरना चाहते-चाहतीं हैं।

12. They want to write (m◦ f◦). *(ve likhnā chāhate haĩ, ve likhnā chāhatī̃ haĩ)* वे लिखना चाहते हैं, वे लिखना चाहतीं हैं। ... and so on.

LESSON 16

तेरहवाँ पाठ

THE ADJECTIVES and ADVERBS

The word that describes, qualifies or adds something to a noun is an ADJECTIVE.

1. Good boy *(achchhā laḍkā)* अच्छा लड़का
2. Good boys *(achchhe laḍke)* अच्छे लड़के
3. Good girl *(achchhī laḍkī)* अच्छी लड़की
4. Good girls *(achchhī laḍkiyā̃)* अच्छी लड़कियाँ

The word that qualifies a verb or an adjective, is an ADVERB.

1. Eat slowly. *(dhīre khāiye)* धीरे खाइये।
2. Walk fast. *(tej chaliye)* तेज चलिये।
3. Very good. *(bahut achchhā)* बहुत अच्छा।
4. It is heavy. *(yah bhārī hai)* यह भारी है।

16.1 THE ADJECTIVES

RULE : In Hindī, the adjectives have same gender and number as the nouns they qualify.

	Singular	Plural
MASCULINE	*maĩ achchhā laḍkā hū̃*	*ham achchhe laḍke haĩ*
	āp achchhe laḍke haĩ	*āp achchhe laḍke haĩ*
	vah achchhā laḍkā hai	*ve achchhe laḍke haĩ*
FEMININE	*maĩ achchhī laḍkī hū̃*	*ham achchhī laḍkiyā̃ haĩ*
	āp achchhī laḍkī haĩ	*āp achchhī laḍkiyā̃ haĩ*
	vah achchhī laḍkī hai	*ve achchhī laḍkiyā̃ haĩ*
MASCULINE	मैं अच्छा लड़का हूँ।	हम अच्छे लड़के हैं।
	आप अच्छे लड़के हैं।	आप अच्छे लड़के हैं।
	वह अच्छा लड़का है।	वे अच्छे लड़के हैं।
FEMININE	मैं अच्छी लड़की हूँ।	हम अच्छी लड़कियाँ हैं।
	आप अच्छी लड़की हैं।	आप अच्छी लड़कियाँ हैं।
	वह अच्छी लड़की है।	वे अच्छी लड़कियाँ हैं।

EXERCISE 32 : Translate the English sentences into Hindī (Answers are given for help)

1. Rānī does good work. *(Rānī achchhā kām kartī hai)* रानी अच्छा काम करती है।
2. The oranges are sweet. *(santare mīṭhe haĩ)* संतरे मीठे हैं। (Sweet = m◦ *mīṭhā*)

3. We saw a yellow rose. *(ham ne pīlā gulāb dekhā)* हमने पीला गुलाब देखा। (Yellow = m◦ *pīlā*)

4. Eat with right hand. *(dāhine hāth se khāiye)* दाहिने हाथ से खाइये। (Right = m◦ *dāhinā*)

5. He has one Dollar-Rupee. *(us ke pāsa ek Dollar-rupayā hai)* उसके पास एक डालर/रुपया है।

6. Sunīl is tall boy. *(Sunīl lambā laḍkā hai)* सुनील लंबा लड़का है। (Tall, long = m◦ *lambā*)

7. The clothes are wet. *(kapaḍe gīle haiँ)* कपड़े गीले हैं। (Wet = m◦ *gīlā*)

8. My shirt is blue. *(merī kamīj nīlī hai)* मेरी कमीज नीली है। (Blue = m◦ *nīlā*)

9. You are tired. *āp thake haiँ.* *(√thak)* आप थके हैं। (Tired = m◦ *thakā*)

10. Here the water is deep. *(yahāँ pānī gaharā hai)* यहाँ पानी गहरा है। (deep = m◦ *gaharā*)

11. It is true. *(yah sach hai)* यह सच है। (True = *sach*)

12. The window is open. *(khiḍakī khulī hai -(√khul)* खिड़की खुली है। (Open = m◦ *khulā*)

13. This job is small. *(yah kām chhoṭā hai)* यह काम छोटा है। (Small = m◦ *choṭā*)

14. I brought fresh fruits. *(maiँ tāje fal lāyā)* मैं ताजे फल लाया। (Fresh = m◦ *tājā*)

15. He took a longer route. *(us ne lambā rāstā liyā)* उसने लंबा रास्ता लिया। (long = m◦ *lambā*)

NEW ADJECTIVES TO LEARN

(1) Good *achchhā* (अच्छा)	(2) Bad *burā* (बुरा)	(3) Sweet *mīṭhā* (मीठा)
(4) Sour *khaṭṭā* (खट्टा)	(5) Hot *garam* (गरम)	(6) Cold *ṭhaṇḍā* (ठंडा)
(7) Heavy *bhārī* (भारी)	(8) Light *halakā* (हलका)	(9) Fat *moṭa* (मोटा)
(10) Thin *patalā* (पतला)	(11) Beautiful *sundar* (सुंदर)	(12) Dirty *gandā* (गंदा)
(13) Young *jawān* (जवान)	(14) Old *būḍhā* (बूढ़ा)	(15) Open *khulā* (खुला)
(16) Closed *band* (बंद)	(17) Smart *hoshiyār* (होशियार)	(18) Lazy *ālasī* (आलसी)
(19) Easy *āsān* (आसान)	(20) Hard *kaṭhin* (कठिन)	(21) Little *chhoṭā* (छोटा)
(22) More *jyādā* (ज्यादा)	(23) Large, big *baḍā* (बड़ा)	(24) Less *kam* (कम) (adv◦)
(25) True *sachchā* (सच्चा)	(26) Tall, long *lambā* (लंबा)	(27) False *jhūṭhā* (झूठा)
(28) All *sab* (सब)	(29) Happy *khush* (खुश)	(30) Sad *dukhī* (दु:खी)
(31) Hard *kaḍā* (कड़ा)	(32) Soft *komal* (कोमल)	(33) Wise *gyānī* (ज्ञानी)
(34) Poor *garīb* (गरीब)	(35) Foolish *mūrkha* (मूर्ख)	(36) Rich *amīr* (अमीर)
(37) Short *chhoṭā* (छोटा)	(38) Quick, *chañchal* (चंचल)	(39) Slow *mand* (मंद)
(40) Strong *balavān* (बलवान्)	(41) Weak *kamjor* (कमजोर)	(42) Dishonest *beīmān* (बेईमान)

NOTE : See next page for more adjectives.

All names of Numerals and Colours are adjectives.

For numerals, please see Lesson 10, *Introduction to Numerals.*

COLOURS : (m∘)

Red (*lāl*) लाल	Green (*harā*) हरा	Blue (*nīlā*) नीला	Yellow (*pīlā*) पीला
Black (*kālā*) काला	White (*safed*) सफेद	Purple (*Jamunī*) जामुनी	Orange (*nārangī*) नारंगी
Dark (*gaḍhā*) गाढ़ा	Light (*phīkā*) फीका		

EXERCISE 33 : Translate the English sentences into Hindī (Answers are given for help)

(1) Two red flowers. *(do lāl phūl)* दो लाल फूल।

(2) This car is blue. *(yah gāḍī nīlī hai)* यह गाड़ी नीली है।

(3) There are yellow flowers on this tree. *(is peḍ par pīle phūl haĩ)* इस पेड़ पर पीले फूल हैं।

(4) Please give me ten Rupees. *(mujhe das rupaye dījiye)* मुझे दस रुपये दीजिये।

(5) One sari is dark black and other sari is light green. *(ek sāḍī gāḍhī kālī hai aur dūsarī sāḍī phīkī harī hai)* एक साड़ी गाढ़ी काली है और दूसरी साड़ी फीकी हरी है।

16.2 THE ADVERBS

DEFINITION : The word that qualifies a verb or an adjective is an Adverb.

RULE : Adverbs do not have any gender, number, person, tense or case. They do not change with the verb or adjective they qualify, therefore, they are called INDECLINABLES.

EXERCISE 34 : Translate the English sentences into Hindī (Answers are given for help)

1. Rānī walks fast. *(Rānī tej chaltī hai)* रानी तेज चलती है।
2. He always helps. *(vah hameshā madad kartā hai)* वह हमेशा मदद करता है।
3. Please move backward. *(kṛpayā pīchhe haṭiye)* कृपया पीछे हटिये।
4. I came before he did. *(maĩ us se pahale āyā)* मैं उससे पहले आया।
5. He wants money right now. *(us ko paise abhī chāhiye)* उसको पैसे अभी चाहिये।
6. Sunīl came here twice. *(Sunīl yahā̃ do bār āyā)* सुनील यहाँ दो बार आया।

7. She knows me well. *(vah mujhe achchhī tarah se jānatī hai)* वह मुझे अच्छी तरह से जानती है।

8. This is better than that one. *(yah us se behatar hai)* यह उससे बेहतर है।

9. Kindly give me ten dollars. *(kṛpayā mujhe das dālar dījiye)* कृपया मुझे दस डॉलर दीजिये।

10. Otherwise I will go. *(varanā maĩ chal jāū̃gā)* वरना मैं चला जाऊँगा।

11. Where is your friend? *(āp kā dost kahā̃ hai?)* आपका दोस्त कहाँ है?

12. When did you hear this? *(āp ne yah kab sunā?)* आपने यह कब सुना?

13. Why are you sad? *(āp udās kyõ haĩ)* आप उदास क्यों हैं?

14. How was this written? *(yah kaise likhā thā?)* यह कैसे लिखा था?

15. Please speak slowly *(kṛpayā dhīre boliye)* कृपया धीरे बोलिये।

16. Tell me again. *(mujhe fir se kahiye)* मुझे फिर से कहिये।

17. Sunil will not come now. *(Sunīl ab nahī̃ āyegā)* सुनील अब नहीं आएगा।

18. I like it very much. *(maĩ ise bahut chāhatā hū̃, mujhe yah bahut achchhā lagatā hai)* मैं इसे बहुत चाहता हूँ, मुझे यह बहुत अच्छा लगता है।

19. It is not very bad. *(yah bahut burā nahī̃ hai)* यह बहुत बुरा नहीं है।

20. He stood at once. *(vah ekadam khaḍā huā)* वह एकदम खड़ा हुआ।

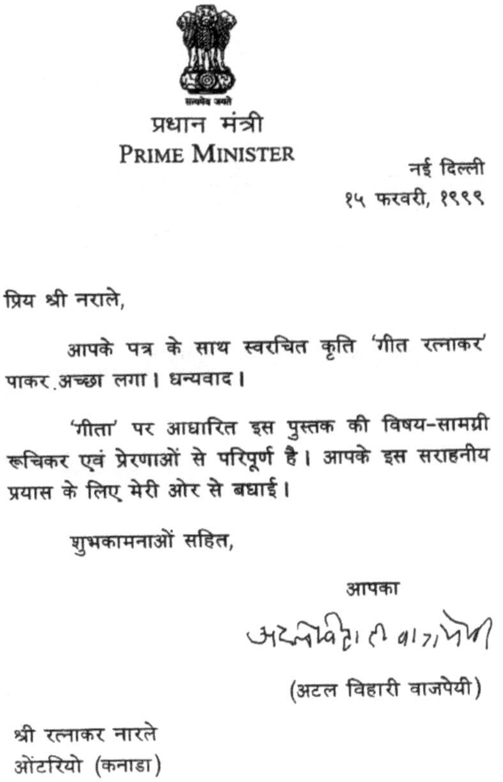

प्रधान मंत्री
PRIME MINISTER

नई दिल्ली
१५ फरवरी, १९९९

प्रिय श्री नराले,

आपके पत्र के साथ स्वरचित कृति 'गीत रत्नाकर' पाकर अच्छा लगा। धन्यवाद।

'गीता' पर आधारित इस पुस्तक की विषय-सामग्री रूचिकर एवं प्रेरणाओं से परिपूर्ण है। आपके इस सराहनीय प्रयास के लिए मेरी ओर से बधाई।

शुभकामनाओं सहित,

आपका

अटल बिहारी वाजपेयी

(अटल बिहारी वाजपेयी)

श्री रत्नाकर नारले
ओंटरियो (कनाडा)

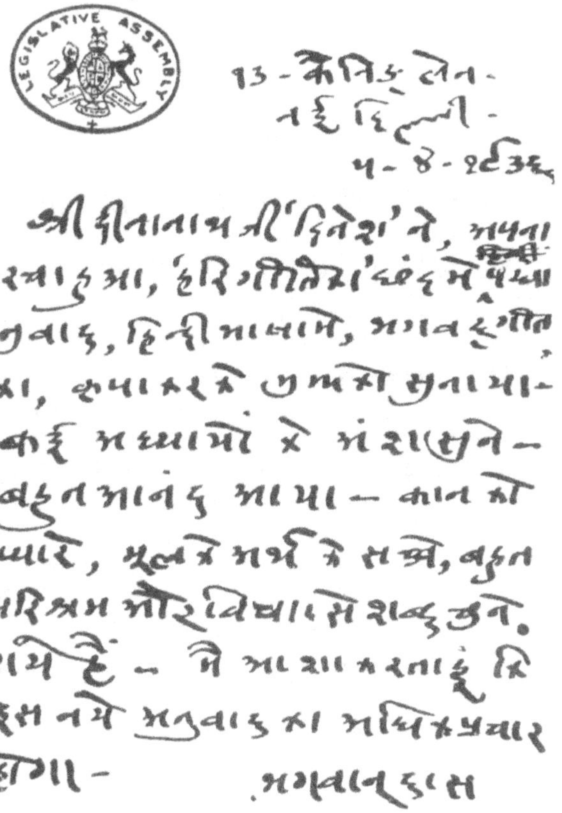

13-कैनिङ्ग लेन-
नई दिल्ली-
५-४-१९३८

श्री दीनानाथ जी 'दिनेश' ने, अपना रचा हुआ, 'हरिगीतिका' छंद में हिन्दी पद्यानुवाद, हिन्दी भाषा में, भगवद्गीता का, कृपा करके मुझको सुनाया- कई अध्यायों के अंश सुने- बहुत आनंद आया- कान को प्यारे, मूल के अर्थ के सच्चे, बहुत परिश्रम और विद्या से शब्द चुने गये हैं- मैं आशा करता हूं कि इस नये अनुवाद का अधिक प्रचार होगा-

भगवान दास

LESSON 17

THE CONJUNCTIONS, INTERJECTIONS AND OTHER EXPRESSIONS

17.1 THE CONJUNCTIONS

DEFINITONN :

Conjunctions are the words like : and, or, but, for, if, that, where, either, neither, nor, still, till, only, else, after, before, etc. which make a connection between two parts of a sentence.

EXERCISE 35 : First study the following sentences and then, as an exercise, translate the English sentences into Hindī (Answers are given for your help)

1. Rāmū AND Sunīl are friends. *(Rāmū aur Sunīl dost haĩ)* रामू और सुनील दोस्त हैं।
2. Bring mango AND a knife. *(ām aur chākū lāiye)* आम और चाकू लाइये।
3. He eats rice AND dāl. *(vah dāl va dāl khātā hai)* वह दाल व रोटी खाता है।
4. I can read AND write Hindī. *(maĩ Hindī paḍh evam likh sakatā hū̃)* मैं हिंदी पढ़ एवं लिख सकता हूँ।
5. He can speak AS WELL AS write Sanskrit. *(vah sanskṛt bol tathā likh sakatā hai)* वह संस्कृत बोल तथा लिख सकता है।
6. Give me an apple OR a banana. *(mujhe seb yā kelā dījiye)* मुझे सेब या केला दीजिये।
7. Speak in Hindī OR in English language. *(Hindī athavā aṅgrezī bhāṣā mẽ boliye)* हिंदी अथवा अंग्रेजी भाषा में बोलिये।
8. EITHER pay me money OR give me the books. *(mujhe yā to paise dījiye athavā kitābẽ dījiye)* मुझे या तो पैसे दीजिये अथवा किताबें दीजिये।
9. It is NEITHER good, NOR beautiful. *(na to yah achchhā hai na hī sundar hai)* न तो यह अच्छा है न ही सुंदर है।
10. WHETHER you like it OR NOT, it will happen. *(āp kī ichhā ho yā nahĩ ho, yah hogā hī)* आपकी इच्छा हो या नहीं हो, यह होगा ही।
11. I had no idea THAT he was in America. *(maĩ nahĩ jānatā thā ki vah amerikā mẽ thā)* मैं नहीं जानता था कि वह अमेरिका में था।
12. He told me THAT it is not right. *(us ne mujh se kahā, ki yah ṭhīk nahĩ hai)* उसने मुझसे कहा,

कि यह ठीक नहीं है।

13. He said that he would not go. *(us ne kahā ki vah nahīn jāyegā)* उसने कहा कि वह नहीं जाएगा।

14. He said, 'I will not go.' *(us ne kahā, 'maĩ nahī̃ jāū̃ngā')* उसने कहा, 'मैं नहीं जाऊँगा।'

15. Sit down OR ELSE go. *(nīche baiṭhiye anyathā jāiye)* नीचे बैठिए अन्यथा जाइये।

16. Give me money, OTHERWISE I am going. *(mujhe paise dījiye varanā maĩ jā rahā-rahī hū̃)* मुझे पैसे दीजिये वरना मैं जा रहा/रही हूँ।

17. We are not rich BUT our heart is big. *(ham amīr nahī̃ haĩ magar hamārā dil baḍā hai)* हम अमीर नहीं हैं, मगर हमारा दिल बड़ा है।

18. I told him, BUT he did not stop. *(maĩ ne us se kahā, lekin vah nahī̃ rukā)* मैंने उससे कहा, लेकिन वह नहीं रुका। (*ruk* रुक = stop)

19. He is uneducated, BUT intelligent. *(vah anapaḍha hai, par buddhimān hai)* वह अनपढ़ है, पर बुद्धिमान् है।

20. She is trailing, BUT will win. *(vah pīchhe hai, lekin jītegī)* वह पीछे है, लेकिन जीतेगी।

21. I have eaten, BUT I am still hungry. *(maĩ ne khānā khāyā hai, kintu maĩ abhī bhī bhūkhā hū̃)* मैंने खाना खाया है, किंतु मैं अभी भी भूखा हूँ।

22. He has severe pain, YET he is quiet. *(us ko kāfī dukh hai, magar vah shānt hai)* उसको काफी दुःख है, मगर वह शांत है।

23. ALTHOUGH he did not ask, I gave him money. *(yadyapi us ne nahī̃ mānge, tathāpi maĩ ne us ko paise diye)* यद्यपि उसने नहीं माँगे, तथापि मैंने उसको पैसे दिये।

24. THOUGH he wanted to, he could not go out. *(hālānki vah chāhatā thā, par vah bāhar nahī̃ jā sakā)* हालाँकि वहं चाहता था, पर वह बाहर नहीं जा सका।

25. He slept enough, STILL he is tired. *(vah kāfī soyā fir bhī thakā hai)* वह काफी सोया फिर भी थका है।

26. Notice was given IN ORDER THAT everyone may be aware. *(notice diyā gayā thā, tā ki sab ko patā ho)* नोटिस दिया गया था, ताकि सबको पता हो।

27. AS SOON AS the bell rang, I went inside. *(jyõ hī ghanṭī bajī, maĩ andar gayā-gayī)* ज्योंही घंटी बजी, मैं अंदर गया/गयी।

28. He is walking AS THOUGH he is lame. *(vah aise chal rahā hai jaise lañgaḍā ho)* वह ऐसे चल रहा जैसे लँगड़ा हो।

29. I need ONLY five Rupees. *(mujhu kewal pāñch rupaye chāhiye)* मुझे केवल पाँच रुपये चाहिये।

30. I do not need ONLY money. *(mujhe sirf paise hī nahī̃ chāhiye)* मुझे सिर्फ पैसे ही नहीं चाहिये।

31. Something certainly fell down, FOR I heard the noise. *(kuchh to avashya nīche girā, kyo̐ ki mai̐ ne āwāj sunī)* कुछ तो अवश्य नीचे गिरा, क्योंकि मैंने आवाज सुनी।

32. He sat down BECAUSE he was tired. *(vah nīche baiṭhā kyo̐ ki vah thakā thā)* वह नीचे बैठा क्योंकि वह थका था।

33. AFTER rain, the sun shone again. *(varṣā ke bād sūraj fir nikalā)* वर्षा के बाद सूरज फिर निकला।

34. WHEN I was young, I used to work very hard. *(jab mai̐ jawān thā-thī, (tab) bahut kām kartā thā, kartī thī)* जब मैं जवान था/थी (तब) बहुत काम करता था (करती थी)।

35. His watch is WHERE he kept it. *(us kī ghaḍī vahī̐ hai jahā̐ us ne rakhī thī)* उसकी घड़ी वहीं है जहाँ उसने रखी थी।

36. Let us give charity, WHILE we have money. *(jab tak apane pās paisā hai, ham dān de̐)* जब तक अपने पास पैसा है, हम दान दें।

37. WHENEVER I see him, he is happy. *(jab bhī mai̐ us ko dekhatā hū̐, vah khush hotā hai)* जब भी मैं उसको देखता हूँ, वह खुश होता है।

38. WHEREVER the rain falls, the water goes to the ocean only. *(jahā̐ kahī̐ bhī varṣā hotī hai, pānī sāgar kī or hī jātā hai)* जहाँ कहीं भी वर्षा होती है, पानी सागर की ओर ही जाता है।

39. He said yes, THEREFORE, I went there. *(us ne hā̐ kahā, is liye mai̐ vahā̐ gayā-gayī)* उसने हाँ कहा, इसलिये मैं वहाँ गया/गई।

17.2 USE OF THE SUFFIX - **कर** *kar*

Attachment of the powerful suffix ***kar* कर** (-ing) gives a meaning of (a gerund) 'having done,' 'did and then,' 'after doing' ...etc.

e.g. I eat *(mai̐ khātā hū̐)* मैं खाता हूँ। I eat after taking a bath (having taken a bath, I take bath and then) *(mai̐ nahā kar khātā hū̐)* मैं नहा **कर** खाता हूँ।

EXERCISE 36 : Translate the English sentences into Hindī (Answers are given for your help)

1. Go and give him the money. *(jā kar us ko paise dījiye)* जा **कर** उसको पैसे दीजिये।
2. Do not drive drunk (after drinking). *(pī kar gāḍī mat chalāiye)* पी **कर** गाड़ी मत चलाइये।

3. Seeing the tiger, I got scared. *(sher ko dekh kar maĩ dar gayā)* शेर को देख **कर** मैं डर गया।

4. I pray Sarasvatī and then I study. *(sarasvatī ko pūj kar maĩ paḍhatā hū̃)* सरस्वती को पूज **कर** मै पढ़ता हूँ।

5. Sit and then drink the milk. *(baiṭh kar dūdh pījiye).* बैठ **कर** दूध पीजिये।

17.2 USE OF THE SUFFIX - चाहिये *chāhiye*

चाहिये *(chāhiye)* is used for expressing a need, want or a desire. चाहिये is always attached to an object noun that is in the Dative (4th) case.

To impart a meaning of 'ought to,' the verb stem (eg. जा) must be first converted into a verbal noun *(jānā)* जाना by attaching the suffix *nā* (ना). Then add *chāhiye* (चाहिये) to it. e.g. (i) verb stem जा = go. (ii) verb stem √जा + suffix ना = verbal noun जाना to go (iii) verbal noun जाना + suffix चाहिये = adjective॰ 'ought to go,' मुझे जाना चाहिये = I ought to go.

1. I want. *(mujhe chāhiye)* मुझे चाहिये।
2. I want tea. *(mujhe chāy chāhiye)* मुझे चाय चाहिये।
3. Do you want tea? *(kyā āpako chāy chāhiye?)* क्या आपको चाय चाहिये?
4. She would want tea. *(use chāy chāhiye hogī)* उसे चाय चाहिये होगी।
5. What does she want. *(use kyā chāhiye?)* उसे क्या चाहिये?
6. I should go. *(mujhe jānā chāhiye)* मुझे जाना चाहिये।
7. I should sleep now. *(mujhe ab sonā chāhiye)* मुझे अब सोना चाहिये।
8. She should not go. *(use nahĩ jānā chāhiye)* उसे नहीं जाना चाहिये।
9. They should work. *(unhẽ kam karnā chāhiye)* उन्हें काम करना चाहिये।
10. You should come too. *(āp kop bhī ānā chāhiye)* आपको भी आना चाहिये।

GOOD NEWS

Even if you JUST READ **each and every** word of this book, patiently and thoughtfully, you will be able to understand Hindī.

LESSON 18

GENERAL KNOWLEDGE

15.1 NAMES OF THE SEVEN DAYS OF THE WEEK

(1) Sunday	*ravivār*	रविवार	(2) Monday	*somavār*	सोमवार
(3) Tuesday	*mangalavār*	मंगलवार	(4) Wednesday	*budhavār*	बुधवार
(5) Thursday	*guruvār*	गुरुवार	(6) Friday	*shukravār*	शुक्रवार
(7) Saturday	*shanivār*	शनिवार			

15.2 NAMES OF THE TWELVE MONTHS OF THE YEAR

(1) March-April	*chaitra*	चैत्र	(2) April-May	*vaishākh*	वैशाख
(3) May-June	*jyeṣṭha*	ज्येष्ठ	(4) June-july	*āṣāḍh*	आषाढ़
(5) July-August	*shrāvaṇ*	श्रावण	(6) August-September	*bhādrapad*	भाद्रपद
(7) September-October	*āshvin*	आश्विन	(8) October-November	*kārtik*	कार्तिक
(9) November-December	*mārgashirṣ*	मार्गशीर्ष	(10) December-January	*pauṣ*	पौष
(11) January-February	*māgh*	माघ	(12) February-March	*phālgun*	फाल्गुन

15.3 NAMES OF THE SIX SEASONS OF THE YEAR

(1) Spring	*vasant*	वसंत	(2) Summer	*griṣma*	ग्रीष्म
(3) Rainy season	*varṣā*	वर्षा	(4) Autumn	*sharad*	शरद्
(5) Winter(Nov-Jan)	*hemant*	हेमंत	(6) Winter(Jan-Mar)	*shishir*	शिशिर

15.4 NAMES OF THE DIRECTIONS

East	*pūrab, pūrva*	पूरब, पूर्व	West	*pashchim*	पश्चिम
North	*uttar*	उत्तर	South	*dakṣiṇ*	दक्षिण
North east	*īshān*	ईशान	South east	*vāyavya*	वायव्य
South west	*āgney*	आग्नेय	North west	*nairṛtya*	नैऋत्य

15.5 THE RELATIONSHIPS

Bride	*vadhū, dūlhan*	वधू , दूल्हन	Brother	*bhāī, bhaiyā*	भाई, भैया
Brother elder	*agraj*	अग्रज	Brother younger	*anuj*	अनुज
Brother' son	*bhatījā*	भतीजा	Brother's daughter	*bhatījī*	भतीजी
Brother's wife	bhābhī	भाभी	Child	*bachchā*	बच्चा
Daughter	*beṭī*	बेटी	Daughter-in-law	*bahū*	बहू
Family	*parivār*	परिवार	Father-in-law	*shvashura*	श्वशुर
Father's elder brother	*tāyā*	ताया	Father's younger brother	chāchā	चाचा
Father's father	*dādā*	दादा	Father's mother	*dādī*	दादी
Father's sister	*būā*	बूआ	Friend	*mitra, dost*	मित्र, दोस्त
Husband	*pati*	पति	Husband's brother	*devar*	देवर
Husband's sister	*nanand*	ननन्द	Lover	*premī, premikā*	प्रेमी, प्रेमिका
Mother	*mā̐*	माँ	Mother-in-law	*sās*	सास
Mother's brother	*māmā*	मामा	Mother's brother's wife	*māmī*	मामी
Mother's father	*nānā*	नाना	Mother's mother	*nānī*	नानी
Mother's sister	*mausī*	मौसी	Neighbor	*paḍosī*	पड़ोसी
Parents	*mātā-pitā*	माता–पिता	Relative	*bandhu*	बंधु
Sister	*bahin*	बहिन	Sister, elder	*dīdī*	दीदी
Sister, younger	*anujā*	अनुजा	Sister's daughter	*bhā̐ñjī*	भाँजी
Sister's husband	*jījā*	जीजा	Sister's son	*bhā̐ñjā*	भाँजा
Son	*beṭā*	बेटा	Son-in-law	*dāmād*	दामाद
Son's daughter	*potī*	पोती	Son's son	*pautra*	पौत्र
Stranger	*paradeshī*	परदेशी	Step xx	*sautelā-*	सौतेला–
Wife	*patnī*	पत्नी	Wife's brother	*sālā*	साला
Wife's sister	*sālī*	साली	Girl friend	*premika*	प्रेमिका
			Boy friend	*premī*	प्रेमी

LESSON 19

19.1 GENERAL DIALOGUES : **Common Pre-made 'Pet-Sentences'**

Having learned previous 18 lessons, now you can make these and similar sentence. For you, these are not pet-sentences anymore. If you have done prevoius lessons, treat this lesson as an Exercise where the answers are provided. If this is where you are starting the book, then memorize the sentences and hope you will be able to speak Hiondī.

(1) Hello! *(namaste!)* नमस्ते। What is your name? *(āpakā nām kyā hai?)* आपका नाम क्या है?

(2) My name is *(merā nām -------------------- hai)* मेरा नाम -------------------- है।

(3) How are you. How do you do? *(āp kaise haĩ? kyā hāl hai?)* आप कैसे हैं? क्या हाल है?

(4) I am fine. I am alright. *(maĩ ṭhīk hū̃)* मैं ठीक हूँ। Thank you. *dhanyavād!* धन्यवाद! You are welcome. *āp kā svāgat hai.* आपका स्वागत है।

(5) Where do you live? *(āp kahā̃ rahate haĩ?)* आप कहाँ रहते हैं?

(6) I live in Kanpur. *(maĩ Kānpur mẽ rahatā hū̃)* मैं कानपुर में रहता हूँ।

(7) Where is your house? *(āpa kā ghar kahā̃ hai?)* आपका घर कहाँ है?

(8) What is your address? *(āp kā patā kyā hai?)* आपका पता क्या है?

(9) Who is he-she? *(yah kaun hai?)* यह कौन है?

(10) What is his-her name? *(in kā nām kyā hai?)* इनका क्या नाम है?

(11) He-She is my friend *(yah merā dost, merī sahelī hai)* यह मेरा दोस्त (मेरी सहेली) है।

(12) His-her name is *(is kā nām -------------------- hai)* इसका नाम -------------------- है।

(13) Will you take tea? *(kyā āp chāy leṅge?)* क्या आप चाय लेंगे?

(14) No, thanks! *(ji nahī̃, dhanyavād! shukriyā!)* जी नहीं, धन्यवाद! जी नहीं शुक्रिया!

(15) I do not drink tea. *(maĩ chāy nahī̃ pītā-pītī)* मैं चाय नहीं पीता/पीती।

(16) Do you smoke? *(kyā āp dhūmrapān karte haĩ? kyā āp sigareṭ pīte haĩ?)* क्या आप धूम्रपान करते हैं? क्या आप सिगरेट पीते हैं?

(17) I do not smoke. *(maĩ sigareṭ nahī̃ pītā)* मैं सिगरेट नहीं पीता।

(18) Are you a vegetarian? *(kyā āp shākāhārī haĩ?)* क्या आप शाकाहारी हैं?

(19) I have heard that he is sick. *(maĩ ne sunā hai ki vah bīmār hai)* मैंने सुना है कि वह बीमार है।

(20) Is it true? *(kyā yah sacha hai?)* क्या यह सच है?

(21) You are right. *(āp ṭhīk kah rahe haĩ)* आप ठीक कह रहे हैं। आपने ठीक कहा।

(22) I know it. *(maĩ yah jānatā hū̃)* मैं यह जनता हूँ।

(23) Do not tell this to anyone. *(yah bāt kisī ko mat batāiye)* यह बात किसी को मत बताइये।

(24) I promise you. *(mai̐ āp se vādā kartā hū̐)* मैं आप से वादा करता हूँ।

(25) Your poem is very nice. *(āp ki kavitā bahut achchhī hai)* आपकी कविता बहुत अच्छी है।

(26) You are making noise. *(āp shor kar rahe hai̐)* आप शोर कर रहे हैं।

(27) Excuse me. Pardon me. *(mujhe māf-kṣamā kījiye)* मुझे माफ कीजिये। मुझे क्षमा कीजिये।

(28) She refused it. *(us ne asvīkār kiyā)* उसने अस्वीकार किया।

(29) I said no. I refused it. *(mai̐ ne inkār kiyā)* मैंने इन्कार किया।

(30) I am sorry. *(mujhe afsos hai)* मुझे अफसोस है।

(31) That was my mistake. *(vah merī galatī thī)* वह मेरी गलती थी।

(32) Who was that person? *(vah kaun thā)* वह कौन था?

(33) What are you doing? *(āp kyā kar rahe hai̐?)* आप क्या कर रहे हैं?

(34) What is the matter? *(kyā bāt hai?)* क्या बात है?

(35) What do you have? *(āp ke pās kyā hai?)* आपके पास क्या है?

(36) What do you mean? *(āp kā matalab kyā hai?)* आपका मतलब क्या है?

(37) Do you like it? *(kyā āp ko yah pasand hai? kyā āp ko yah achchchā lagatā hai?)* क्या आपको यह पसंद है? क्या आपको यह अच्छा लगता है?

(38) Have you finished it? *(kyā āp ne yah khatma kiyā?)* क्या आपने यह खत्म किया?

(39) It is ready? *(kyā yah taiyār hai?)* क्या यह तैयार है?

(40) Is it edible? *(kyā yah khāne lāyak hai?)* क्या यह खाने लायक है?

(41) Are you coming with us? *(kyā āp hamāre sāth ā rahe hai̐?)* क्या आप हमारे साथ आ रहे हैं?

(42) It is very nice. *(yah bahut baḍhiyā hai, yah bahut achchhā hai)* यह बहुत बढ़िया है, यह बहुत अच्छा है। What a coincidence! *(kyā ittafāk hai!)* क्या इत्तफाक है!

(43) Should I close it? Should I open it? *(kyā mai̐ yah band karū̐? kyā mai̐ yah kholū̐?)* क्या मैं यह बंद करूँ? क्या मैं यह खोलूँ? Please warn me. *mujhe chetāvanī dījiye.* मुझे चेतावनी दीजिये।

(44) Wait for me. *(mere liye rukiye, merā intajār kījiye)* मेरे लिये रुकिए, मेरा इंतजार कीजिये।

(45) Do you trust him? I trust him fully *(kyā āp us par bharosā karte hai̐? merā us par pūrā bharosā hai)* क्या आप उस पर भरोसा करते हैं? मेरा उस पर पूरा भरोसा है।)

(46) That is completely wrong. This is very correct. *(vah pūrī tarah se galat hai. Yah bilkul ṭhīk hai)* वह पूरी तरह से गलत है। यह बिल्कुल ठीक है।)

(47) I think so too. *(mai̐ bhī yahī sochatā hūn)* मैं भी यही सोचता हूँ।

(48) Is it possible. *(kyā yah sambhav hai)* क्या यह संभव है? क्या यह हो सकता है?

(49) He is not well. *(us kī tabīyat ṭhīk nahĩ hai)* उसकी तबीयत ठीक नहीं है।

(50) Let him go. *(use jāne dījiye)* उसे जाने दीजिये।

(51) I must go now. *(mujhe ab jānā chāhiye)* मुझे अब जाना चाहिये।

(52) I am in a rush. *(maĩ jaldī mẽ hũ)*मैं जल्दी में हूँ।

(53) You are lucky. *(āp bhāgyavān haĩ)* आप भाग्यवान् हैं।

(54) He surprised me. *(us ne mujhe acharaj mẽ dālā)* उसने मुझे अचरज में डाला।

(55) He fooled me. *(us ne mujhe bevakūf banāyā)* उसने मुझे बेवकूफ बनाया।

(56) What a shame? *(kitanī sharma kī bāt hai)* कितनी शर्म की बात है!

(57) I am angry. *(maĩ nārāj hũ)* मैं नाराज हूँ।

(58) What could be the reason? *(kyā kāraṇ ho sakatā hai?)* क्या कारण हो सकता है?

(59) Please, be patient. *(kṛpayā dhīraj rakhiye)* कृपया धीरज रखिये।

(60) Please do not do it again. *(kṛpayā yah fir se mat kījiye)* कृपया यह फिर से मत कीजिये।

(61) Try to improve it. *(ise sudhārane kī koshisha kījiye)* इसे सुधारने की कोशिश कीजिये।

(62) It is very hard for me. *(yah mere liye bahut mushkil hai)* यह मेरे लिये बहुत मुश्किल है।

(63) Don't try to be more smart. *(jyādā hoshiyār banane kī koshish mat kījiye)* ज्यादा होशियार बनने की कोशिश मत कीजिये। I remember. *(muze yād hai)* मुझे याद है।

(64) Let us go for a walk. *(chaliye ṭahalane ke liye chalte haĩ, chaliye sair ke liye chalte haĩ)* चलिये टहलने के लिये चलते हैं, चलिये सैर के लिये चलते हैं।

(65) Please, walk a bit faster. *(kṛpayā jarā tej chaliye)* जरा तेज चलिये।

(66) It is thundering, let us go back. *(bijalī chamak rahī hai, chaliye vāpas chalte haĩ)* बिजली चमक रही है, चलिये वापस चलते हैं।

(67) May be a storm is coming. *(shāyad tūfān āne wālā hai)* शायद तूफान आनेवाला है?

(68) How does it work? *(yah kaise kām kartā hai?)* यह कैसे काम करता है?

(69) We should be careful. *(hamẽ sāvadhān rahanā chahiye)* हमें सावधान रहना चाहिये।

(70) I forgot to tell you one thing. *(maĩ āp se ek bāt kahanā bhūl gayā)* मैं आपसे एक बात कहना भूल गया। I forgot to bring one thing. *(maĩ ek chīj lānā bhūl gayā)* मैं एक चीज लाना भूल गया।

(71) What is the use of waiting here? *(yahā̃ intajār karne se kyā lābh?)* यहाँ इंतजार करने से क्या लाभ? The child is crying constantly. *bachchā roe jā rahā hai.* बच्चा रोए जा रहा है।

(72) Do not worry, I will take care of that. *(chintā mat kījiye, maĩ vah dekh lūṅgā)* चिंता मत

कीजिये, मैं वह देख लूँगा। Have a nice journey! *(yātrā sukhamaya ho!)* यात्रा सुखमय हो।

(73) What is the news? *(kyā khabar hai? kyā samaāchār hai?)* क्या खबर है? क्या समाचार है?

(74) Everything is OK. *(sab kuchh ṭhīk hai)* सब कुछ ठीक है।

(75) We will wait for you. *(ham āp kī rāha dekheṅge)* हम आपकी राह देखेंगे।

(76) Why are you late? *(āp ko der kyõ huī?)* आपको देर क्यों हुई?

(77) Did you get my letter? *(kyā āp ko merā patra milā? āp ko merī chiṭṭhī milī kyā?)* क्या आपको मेरा पत्र मिला? आपको मेरी चिट्ठी मिली क्या? Be happy! *(khush rahiye!)* खुश रहिये!

(78) Why did you trust him? *(āp ne us par bharosā kyõ kiyā?)* आपने उस पर भरोसा क्यों किया?

(79) I was impressed by his talk. *(maĩ us ke bolane se prabhāvit huā thā)* मैं उसके बोलने से प्रभावित हुआ था। It is true. *(yah sach hai)* यह सच है।

(80) How quickly time passes! *(samay kitnā jaldī bītatā hai!)* समय कितना जल्दी बीतता है!

(81) I will return quickly. *(maĩ jaldī lauṭūṅgā)* मैं जल्दी लौटूँगा।

(82) Brother! Move a bit forward. *(Bhaī sāhab! jarā āge baḍhīye)* भाई साहब! जरा आगे बढ़िये।

(83) Could you help me? *(kyā āp merī madad kar sakate haĩ?)* क्या आप मेरी मदद कर सकते हैं? Please do me a favour. *(merā ek kām kījiye)* मेरा एक काम कीजिये।

(84) How is your health? *(āp ka svāsthya kaisā hai? āp kī tabaīyat kaisī hai?)* आपका स्वास्थ्य कैसा है? आपकी तबीयत कैसी है?

(85) How did your bone break? *(āp kī haḍḍī kaise ṭūṭī?)* आपकी हड्डी कैसे टूटी?

(86) Come in. *(andar āiye)* अंदर आइये। Welcome. *susvāgatam.* सुस्वागतम्.

(87) Wish you a happy Diwālī. *(diwālī kī shubh kāmanāẽ)* दिवाली/दीपावली की शुभ कामनाएँ।

(88) OK! We will meet again. *(achchhā ji! ham fir mileṅge)* अच्छा जी! हम फिर मिलेंगे।

(89) Say our hello to everyone. *(sab ko hamārī namaste kahanā)* सबको हमारी नमस्ते कहना।

(90) OK! Sir (Madam). *(ṭhīk hai shrīmān! ṭhīk hai shrīmatī jī!)* ठीक है श्रीमान्! ठीक है श्रीमतीजी!

(91) Hi *(namaste ji!)* नमस्ते जी। Happy Birthday! *(janmadin mubārak!)* जन्मदिन मुबारक!

(92) Good morning. *(suprabhāt)* सुप्रभात। Good night *(shubha rātri)* शुभ रात्रि।

(93) How is your father? *(āpke pitājī kaise haĩ)* आपके पिताजी कैसे हैं?

(94) He is fine. *(ve kushal haĩ)* वे कुशल हैं।

(95) Is everything well at home? *(kyā ghar par sab ṭhīk-ṭhāk hai?)* क्या घर पर सब ठीक ठाक है? Everything is fine. *(sab kushal hai)* सब कुशल है।

(96) Where are you coming from? *(āp kahā̃ se ā rahe haĩ?)* आप कहाँ से आ रहे हैं?

(97) I am coming from office. *(maiँ daftar se ā rahā hūँ)* मैं दफ्तर से आ रहा हूँ।

(98) Please come in and have a seat. *(kṛpayā andar ā kar baiṭhiye)* कृपया अंदर आकर बैठिये।

(99) What was he saying? *(vah kyā kah rahā thā?)* वह क्या कह रहा था?

(100) He said that I do not want anything. *(vah kah rahā thā ki mujhe kuchh nahīँ chāhiye)* वह कह रहा था कि मुझे कुछ नहीं चाहिये।

(101) What is your opinion? *(āp kī kyā rāy hai?)* आप की क्या राय है?

(102) Let us see what happens. *(dekhate haiँ kyā hotā hai)* देखते हैं क्या होता है।

(103) I will try my best. *(maiँ pūrī koshīsh karūँgā, karūँgī)* मैं पूरी कोशिश करूँगा, करूँगी।

(104) It will never happen. *(yah kabhī nahīँ hogā).* यह कभी नहीं होगा। It can not happen. *(yah nahīँ ho sakatā)* यह नहीं हो सकता।

(105) It is not possible. *(yah sambhav nahīँ hai)* यह संभव नहीं है। यह असंभव है।

(106) There is no doubt about it. *(is meँ koī sandeh nahīँ hai)* इसमें कोई संदेह नहीं है।

(107) I did not know it. *(maiँ yah nahīँ jānatā thā)* मैं यह नहीं जानता था।

(108) How should I say it to you? *(maiँ āp se yah kaise kahūँ?)* मैं आपसे यह कैसे कहूँ?

(109) Do you have time? *(kyā āp ke pās samay hai?)* क्या आपके पास समय है?

(110) What is your program tomorrow? *(kal āp kā kyā kāryakram hai?)* कल आपका क्या कार्यक्रम है? I am not sure. *(muze pakkā patā nahīँ hai)* मुझे पक्का पता नहीं है।

(111) I will go once again. *(maiँ ek bār fir jaūँgā-jāūँgī)* मैं एक बार फिर जाऊँगा, जाऊँगी।

(112) It happens sometimes. *(kabhī-kabhī aisā hotā hai)* कभी-कभी ऐसा होता है।

(113) Who does not want it? *(yah kaun nahīँ chāhatā hai?)* यह कौन नहीं चाहता है?

(114) I have no objection. *(mujhe āpatti nahīँ hai)* मुझे आपत्ति नहीं है।

(115) I will do it, even if it is difficult. *(yah mushkil hai fir bhī maiँ karūँgā)* यह मुश्किल है फिर भी मैं करूँगा। It does not matter. *(koī bāt nahīँ)* कोई बात नहीं।

(116) Please do not worry. *(kṛpayā āp chintā mat kījiye.* कृपया आप चिंता मत कीजिये।

(117) Please listen to me. *(kṛpayā merī bāt suniye)* कृपया मेरी बात सुनिये।

(118) What does it mean? *(is kā matalab kyā hai)* इसका मतलब क्या है?

(119) What is the reason for this? *(is kā kāraṇ kyā hai?)* इसका कारण क्या है?

(120) Why did it happen? *(yah kyoँ huā?)* यह क्यों हुआ? How did it happen? *(yah kaise huā?)* यह कैसे हुआ? You have no right. *āp ko koī hak nahīँ hai.* आपको कोई हक नहीं है।

(121) Is it true? *(yah sach hai yā nahīँ?)* क्या यह सच है? यह सच है या नहीं?

(122) That I also know. *(vah to maĩ bhī jānatā hũ)* वह तो मैं भी जानता हूँ।

(123) Why did you not say so before? *(yah āp ne pahale kyõ nahĩ kahā?)* यह आपने पहले क्यों नहीं कहा? Say it again. *(fir se kahiye)* फिर से कहिये।

(124) Where were you that time? *(tab āp kahã the?)* तब आप कहाँ थे?

(125) It is not my fault. *(yah merā doṣ nahĩ hai)* यह मेरा दोष नहीं है। It is my mistake. *(yah merī galatī hai)* यह मेरी गलती है।

(126) I have no idea. *(mujhe patā nahĩ)* मुझे पता नहीं।

(127) Please do not get serious like this. *(aise gambhīr mat hoīye)* ऐसे गंभीर मत होइये।

(128) It is only a rumour. *(yah kewal afwāh, uḍatī khabar hai)* यह तो केवल अफवाह (उड़ती खबर) है। I think so. *(merā yah khyāl hai)* मेरा यह ख्याल है।

(129) You are right. *(āp kī bāt sahī hai)* आपकी बात सही है।

(130) At that time I could not think of anything. *(us samay maĩ kuchh soch nahĩ sakā-sakī)* उस समय मैं कुछ सोच नहीं सका/सकी।

(131) It should not have happened. *(yah nahĩ honā chāhiye thā)* यह नहीं होना चाहिये था।

(132) I do not have your address. *(mere pās āp kā patā nahĩ hai)* मेरे पास आपका पता नहीं है।

(133) I was thinking of you yesterday. *(kal maĩ āp ko yād kar rahā thā)* कल मैं आपको याद कर रहा था। I am alone. *(maĩ akelā hũ)* मैं अकेला हूँ।

(134) There was an accident on the way, that is why I became late. *(rāste mẽ durghaṭanā huī thī, is liye muze āne mẽ derī huī)* रास्ते में एक दुर्घटना हुई थी, इसलिये मुझे आने में देरी हुई।

(135) Have you finished your housework? *(kyā āp ne ghar kā kām kiyā hai?)* क्या आपने घर का काम किया है?

(136) I have to work too. *(mujhe bhī kām karanā hai)* मुझे भी काम करना है।

(137) I have to go to the office too. *(mujhe kāryālay bhī jānā hai)* मुझे दफ्तर भी जाना है।

(138) I will talk to you about this. *(maĩ āp se is bāre mẽ fir bāt karū̃gā)* मैं आपसे इस बारे में बात करूँगा। Still there is plenty of time. *(abhī bhī kāfī samaya hai)* अभी भी काफी समय है।

(139) Did you call me yesterday? *(kyā āp ne mujhe kal bulāya?* क्या आपने मुझे कल बुलाया?

(140) Were there any calls for me. *(kyā mere liye koī phon āyā thā?)* क्या मेरे लिये कोई फोन आया था? My sympothy! *(merī sahānubhuti!)* मेरी सहानुभुति।

(141) See me next week. *(mujh se agale hafte miliye)* मुझसे अगले हफ्ते मिलिये।

(142) We should sit and think about it. *(hamẽ baiṭh kar is bāre mẽ sochnā chāhiye)* हमें बैठकर

इस बारे में सोचना चाहिये। He will not refrain. *vaha bāz nahī̃ āegā.* वह बाज नहीं आएगा।

(143) Today I am not feeling well. *(āj maĩ ṭhīk mahasūs nahī̃ kar rahā hū̃)* आज मैं ठीक महसूस नहीं कर रहा हूँ।

(144) I am sick. *(maĩ bīmār hū̃)* मैं बीमार हूँ।

(145) Yesterday it snowed all night. *(kal rāt bhar barf girī)* कल रात भर बर्फ गिरी।

(146) And today it is very foggy. *(aur āj bahut dhũdhalā hai)* और आज बहुत धुँधला है।

(147) Drive carefully. *(sāvadhānī se gāḍī chalāiye)* सावधानी से गाड़ी चलाइये।

(148) It is slippery outside. *(bāhar fisalan hai)* बाहर फिसलन है।

(149) It snowed almost four inches. *(lagabhag chār inch barf girī)* लगभग चार इंच बर्फ गिरी।

(150) Many roads are not cleared yet. *(kaī saḍakẽ abhī tak sāf nahī̃ huī hai̐)* कई सड़कें अभी तक साफ नहीं हुई हैं।

(151) Tomorrow it is going to be warm. *(kal garam hone wālā hai)* कल गरम होनेवाला है।

(152) Tomorrow we will wash our car. *(kal ham apanī gāḍī dhoenge)* कल हम अपनी गाड़ी धोएँगे। He is a government servant. *vah sarakārī naukar hai.* वह सरकारी नौकर है।

(153) I organized my room. *(maĩ ne apanā kamrā ṭhīk kiyā)* मैंने अपना कमरा ठीक किया।

(154) I sleep near the window. *(maĩ khiḍakī ke pās sotā hū̃)* मैं खिड़की के पास सोता हूँ।

(155) I will keep the door open. *(maĩ daravājā khulā rakhū̃gā)* मैं दरवाजा खुला रखूँगा।

(156) I read Hindī everyday. *(maĩ roj Hindī paḍhatā hū̃)* मैं रोज हिंदी पढ़ता हूँ।

(157) Our neighbor is a good person. *(hamārā paḍosī achchhā hai)* हमारा पड़ोसी अच्छा है।

(158) They know Hindī, they can speak Hindi. *(ve Hindī jānate hai̐, ve Hindī bol sakate hai̐)* वे हिंदी जानते हैं, वे हिंदी बोल सकते हैं।

(159) They have learned Hindī. *(unhõ ne Hindī sīkhī hai)* उन्हों ने हिंदी सीखी है।

(160) They want to learn Hindī. *(ve Hindī sīkhanā chāhate hai̐)* वे हिंदी सीखना चाहते हैं।

(161) Do you want to learn Hindī? *(kyā āp Hindī sīkhanā chāhate hai̐?)* क्या आप हिंदी सीखना चाहते हैं? Congratulations! *(badhāī! badhāī ho!)* बधाई! बधाई हो। बधाइयाँ हों।

(162) We can most certainly learn Hindī with this book. *(ham is kitāb-pustak se Hindī avashya sīkh sakate hai̐)* हम इस किताब/पुस्तक से हिंदी अवश्य सीख सकते हैं।

(163) How do we go from here to there? *(yahā̃ se vahā̃ kaise jāte hai̐?)* यहाँ से वहाँ कैसे जाते हैं?

(164) How will I come to your house from my home? *(maĩ apne ghar se āpke ghar kaise āū̃gā?)* मैं अपने घर से आपके घर कैसे आऊंगा?

EATING OUT

बाहर खाना। *bāhar khānā*

1. Can you recommend us a good restaurant? *(kyā āp hamẽ koī accha sā restarā̃-bhojanālaya batā sakate haĩ?)* क्या आप हमें कोई अच्छा सा रेस्तराँ (भोजनालय) बता सकते हैं?
2. Is there any vegetarian (or non-vegetarian, Chinese, Italian) restaurant near here? *(yahā̃ najadīk koī śākāhārī-māṁsāhārī-cīnī-italian- restarā̃ hai?)* यहाँ नजदीक में कोई शाकाहारी (मांसाहारी, चीनी, इटालियन) रेस्तराँ है?
3. How do we get there? *(vahā̃ kaise pahuñcate haĩ?)* वहाँ कैसे पहुँचते हैं?
5. Hello, I would like to reserve a table for tomorrow 7pm for four please *(Hello! maĩ kal śām sāt baje ke liye, cār logõ ke liye mej ārakṣit karanā) cāhatā hū̃* हेलो जी! मैं कल शाम सात बजे के लिए चार लोगों के लिए मेज आरक्षित करना चाहता हूँ।
6. Where would you like to sit? *(āp kahā̃ baiṭhanā cāhẽge?)* आप कहाँ बैठना चाहेंगे? Over there, in non-smoking section *(vahā̃, dhūmrapān niṣedha bhāga mẽ)* वहाँ, धूम्रपान निषेध भाग में।
7. May I take your order please? *(kyā maĩ āp kā order le sakatā hū̃?)* क्या मैं आपका आदेश ले सकता हूँ?
8. What would you like to drink? *(āp kyā pīnā cāhẽge?)* आप क्या पीना चाहेंगे?
9. Enjoy your meals. *(bhojan kā ānand lījiye)* भोजन का आनंद लीजिए।
10. Thank you! *(dhanyavād!)*धन्यवाद!

STAYING OUT

बाहर रहना *bāhar rahanā*

1. Which is a decent motel in Kingstone? *(Kĩgstone mẽ acchā motel kaun sā hai?)* किंगस्टन में अच्छा मोटल कौन सा कौन सा है?
2. How far is it from downtown? *(vah śahar se kitanā dūr hai?)* वह शहर से कितना दूर है?
3. How much is the rent for one night for a room? *(ek rāt ke liye kamare kā kirāyā kitanā hai?)* एक रात के लिए कमरे का किराया कितना है?
4. Do you have a cheaper room? *(kyā āp ke pās aur sastā kamarā hai?)* क्या आपके पास और सस्ता कमरा है?
5. Will there be a TV, fan and phone in the room? *(kyā kamare mẽ TV, pãkhā aur phone hogā?)*

क्या कमरे में टीवी, पंखा और फोन होगा?

6. Can I first see the room please? *(kyā maĩ pahale kamarā dekh sakatā hū̃?)* क्या मैं पहले कमरा देख सकता हूँ? That's fine. *(ṭhīk hai)* ठीक है।

TRAVEL BY RAILWAY
रेल की यात्रा *rel kī yātrā*

1. Is there any train going to Banāras from here? *(yahā̃ se Banāras ke liye koī relagāḍī hai?)* यहाँ से बनारस के लिए कोई रेलगाड़ी है?
2. How long does it take to reach Banāras? *(Banāras pahućane mẽ kitanā samay lagatā hai?)* बनारस पहुँचने में कितना समय लगता है?
3. Can I leave my car at the station? *(kyā maĩ apanī kār station par ćhoḍ sakatā hū̃?)* क्या मैं अपनी कार-गाड़ी स्टेशन पर (रेल अड्डे पर) छोड़ सकता हूँ?
4. How much baggage can we carry? *(ham kitanā sāmān le sakate haĩ)* हम कितना सामान ले सकते हैं।
5. What is the price (how much does it cost) for a round trip? *(donõ or kī yātrā kā kirāyā kitanā hai?)* दोनों ओर की यात्रा का किराया कितना है?
6. Is there any discount for senior citizens (children, students)? *(kyā bujurg logõ, baććõ, ćhātrõ ke liye koī ćhūṭ hai?)* क्या बुजुर्ग लोगों, बच्चों, छात्रों के लिए कोई छूट है?
7. Can I get a window seat please? *(kyā mujhe khiḍakī wālī kurasī mil sakatī hai?)* क्या मुझे खिड़कीवाली कुरसी मिल सकती है?
8. Is this an express train (bus)? *(kyā yah dṛtagāmī gāḍī hai?)* क्या यह द्रुतगामी गाड़ी है?
9. What is the eating arrangement on the train? *(gāḍī mẽ khāne kī kyā vyavasthā hai?)* गाड़ी में खाने की क्या व्यवस्था है?
10. When does the last train (bus) leave? *(ākhirī gāḍī kab jātī hai?)* आखिरी गाड़ी कब जाती है?

CAR RENTAL
गाड़ी किराए से *gāḍī kirāye se*

1. Where will I get a car on rent? *(Mujhe kirāye par gāḍī kahā̃ milegī?)* मुझे किराए पर गाड़ी कहाँ मिलेगी?
2. I would like to rent a small car. *(Maĩ ek ćhoṭī gāḍī kirāye par lenā ćāhatā hū̃)* मैं एक छोटी गाड़ी किराए पर लेना चाहता हूँ।
3. Is it air conditioned? *(kyā yah vātānukūlit hai?)* क्या यह वातानुकूलित है?
4. I need it for a day. *(mujhe yah ek din ke liye ćāhiye)* मुझे यह एक दिन के लिए चाहिए।
5. What sort of fuel does it take? *(yah kaunasā ī̃dhan letī hai?)* यह कौन सा ईंधन लेती है?
6. Do I need a separate insurance? *(kyā mujhe alag se bīmā lenā hoga?)* क्या मुझे अलग से बीमा लेना होगा?
7. Can I return the car in New York? *(kyā maĩ gāḍī ko New York maĩ vāpas kar sakatā hū̃?)* क्या मैं गाड़ी को न्यूयॉर्क में वापस कर सकता हूँ?
8. Please give me the address for that place. *(Kṛpayā mujhe us jagah kā patā dījiye)* कृपया मुझे उस जगह का पता दीजिए।
9. Thank you Sir! *(dhanyavād sāhab!)* धन्यवाद साहब।
10. See you again. *(fir milẽge)* फिर मिलेंगे।

AT THE GAS STATION
पेट्रोल पंप पर *peṭrol pamp par*

1. Fill it up, please *(Kṛpayā pūrī ṭankī bhar dījiye)* कृपया पूरी टंकी भर दीजिए।
2. Please check the oil too. *(aur tel bhī dekh lījiyae)* और तेल भी देख लीजिए।
3. No, Thanks. I do not want car wash today. *(Jī nahĩ, dhanyavād! āj gāḍī nahĩ dhulawānī hai)* जी नहीं, धन्यवाद। आज गाड़ी नहीं धुलवानी है।
4. Please clean the car windows also. *(kṛpayā āp gāḍī ke śīśe bhī sāf kar dījiye)* कृपया आप गाड़ी के शीशे भी साफ कर दीजिए।
5. Also give us a case of Coca Cola also. *(Kokā Kolā kī ek peṭī bhī hamẽ dījiye)* कोका कोला की एक पेटी भी हमें दीजिए।

6. Please sigh here. *(kṛpayā yahā̃ hastākṣar dījiye)* कृपया यहाँ हस्ताक्षर दीजिए। Here is your receipt and your Visa card *(yah rahī āpakī rasīd aur yah rahā āpakā VISA card.* यह रही आपकी रसीद और यह रहा आपका वीजा कार्ड।

7. Should I keep the Coke at the back? *(kyā maĩ Coke pīche rakh dū̃?)* क्या मैं कोक पीछे रख दूँ? Yes, please. *(jī hā̃)* जी, हाँ।

8. Thank you! *dhanyavād! (śukriyā!)* धन्यवाद! (शुक्रिया!)

9. Please dirve carefully. *(kṛpayā gāḍī sāvadhānī se calāẽ)* कृपया गाड़ी सावधानी से चलाएँ।

SHORT ESSAYS लघु निबंध

THE HORSE
अश्व

अश्व को घोड़ा भी कहते हैं। यह एक विनीत पशु है। *(aśva ko ghoḍā bhī kahate haĩ. yah ek vinīta paśu hai)* Horse is also called *ghoḍā.* Horse is a disciplined animal. यह गाय की तरह एक उपयोगी जानवर है। *(yah gāy kī tarah ek upayogī jānavar hai)* He is a useful animal like a cow. गाय और घोड़े में क्या भेद होता है? *(gāy aur ghoḍe mẽ kyā bhed hotā hai?)* What is the difference between a cow and a horse. घोड़े के दो सींग नहीं होते हैं। *(ghoḍe ke do sĩg nahī̃ hote haĩ)* Horse does not have two horns. उसकी गरदन पर लंबे एवं घने बाल होते हैं। *(us kī garadan par lambe evaṁ ghane bāl hote haĩ)* His neck has a hairy mane. गाय के खुर दो हिस्सों में बँटे होते हैं, घोड़े के खुर उस तरह नहीं होते हैं। *(gāy ke khur do hissõ mẽ baṭe hote haĩ, ghoḍe ke khur us tarah nahī̃ hote haĩ)* Cow's hoof is divided into two halves, but not the horse's. इस कारण अश्व तेज भाग सकता है। *(is kāraṇ aśva tej bhāg sakatā hai)* Therefore, the horse runs faster. वह बलवान् भी होता है। *(vah balavān bhī hotā hai)* He is strong too.

अश्व चतुर पशु होता है। *(aśva catur paśu hotā hai)* The horse is a smart animal. लोग उसपर सवारी (आरोहण) करते हैं। *(log us par savārī karate haĩ)* People ride him. वे उसकी पीठ पर बैठकर यात्रा करते हैं। *(ve us kī pīṭh par baiṭh kar yātrā karate haĩ)* They travel sitting on his back. वह मनुष्य का एक अच्छा मित्र होता है। *(vah manuṣya kā ek acchā mitra hotā hai)* He is a good friend of human beings. प्राचीन काल में राजा लोग इसे युद्ध के काम में लाते थे। *(prācīn kāl mẽ rājā log ise yuddha ke kām mẽ lāte the)* In old days kings were using horse in the battles. किसी कवि ने कहा है : *(kisī kavi ne kahā hai)* A poet has said :

"अश्व जिसका विजय उसकी, जिसका अश्व धरती उसकी।
अश्व जिसका यश उसका, जिसका अश्व सोना उसका।"

'aśva jis kā vijay us kī, jis kā aśva dharatī us kī,
aśva jis kā yaśa us kā, jis kā aśva sonā us kā.

Victory is his who has horse,
who has horse on land he has hold,
Success is his who has horse,
who has horse his is gold.

EXERCISE 37 : Fill in the blanks :

(1) अश्व को ------------ भी कहते हैं।

(2) घोड़े के दो सींग ------------ होते हैं।

(3) लोग उसकी ------------ पर बैठ कर यात्रा करते हैं।

THE SUN
सूर्य

सूर्य गगन का एक अलंकार है। उसका उदय पूर्व की दिशा में होता है। उस समय उसका प्रकाश लाल एवं कोमल होता है। उभरता हुआ सूर्य अंधकार को नष्ट करता है, प्राणियों को जगाता है और फूलों को खिलाता है। धीरे-धीरे बढ़ता हुआ सूर्य जब आकाश के मध्य में आता है तब मध्याह्न होता है। मध्याह्न में धूप तीखी होती है। यहाँ से सूर्य क्रमशः पश्चिम दिशा की ओर नीचे उतरता हुआ दिखाई देता है। और अंत में सूर्य पश्चिम दिशा में डूब जाता है।

The sun is an adornment of the sky. It rises in the East. At this time its light is red and soft. The rising sun destroys the darkness, wakes the animals up and blooms the flowers. Marching up gradually when the sun reaches at the center of the sky then becomes noon. At noon the sunlight is hard. From here, the sun gradually comes down to the West, and eventually the sun sets in the West.

सूर्य स्वयं ही प्रकाशमान होता है। सूर्य का प्रकाश पूरी सृष्टि को प्रकाशित करता है। सूर्य जगत् को उष्णता देता है। सूर्य के समान अन्य कुछ भी तेजस्वी नहीं होता है।

The sun shines by itself. The sunlight shines entire universe. The sun gives warmth to the world. There is nothing as brilliant as the sun.

EXERCISE 38 :

(A) Fill in the blanks:

(1) सूर्य ---------------- का एक अलंकार है।

(2) सूर्य का उदय पूर्व की ---------------- में होता है।

(3) सूर्य ---------------- ही प्रकाशमान होता है।

(B) Translate into Hindī:

(1) This world is born from the sun. ------------ ।

(2) Sun light reaches earth in nine minutes. ------------ ।

(3) Sun is the cause of rain and wind. ------------ ।

(4) Sun is very large. ------------ ।

(5) Sun is very far from here. ------------ ।

(C) Translate into English:

(1) धरती सूर्य की बेटी है। ------------

(2) सूर्य जब दिखाई नहीं देता तब चाँद दिखाई देता है ——।

THE Hindī WORLD
हिंदी जगत्

हिंदी केवल भारत की ही भाषा नहीं है। *(Hindī kewal Bhārat kī hī bhāṣā nahĩ hai)* Hindī is not the language of India only. हिंदी विश्व में सभी देशों में कमोबेश बोली जाती है। *(Hindī viśva mẽ sabhī deśõ mẽ kamobeś bolī jātī hai)* Hindī is spoken more or less in the entire world. गुयाना, ट्रिनिडाड, सूरीनाम और फीजी में तो हिंदी का विशेष महत्त्व है। *(Guyanā, Trinidād, Sūrīnam aur Fijī mẽ to Hindī kā viśeṣ mahattva hai)* In Guyana, Trinidad, Surinam and Fiji the Hindī language has special importance. इसलिए इन चारों देशों के बारे में हमें जानकारी होनी आवश्यक है। *(is liye in ćārõ deśon ke bāre mẽ hamẽ jānakārī honī āvaśyak hai)* Therefore, it is important that we know about these countries.

कोलंबस जब अमेरिका पहुँचे तो उन्होंने समझा कि वे इंडिया पहुँचे हैं। उनके कहने पर ही वहाँ के पूर्व लोगों

को 'इंडियन' नाम मिला। *(Kolambas jab Amerikā pahuñće to unhoँ ne samajhā ki ve India pahuñće haiँ. un ke kahane par hī vahāँ ke pūrva logoँ ko 'Indian' nām milā)* When Columbus reached America, he thought that it was India, from his dicsovery the original people of America became known as 'Indians.'

कोलंबस के बाद सन् 1500 में वेस्पुची वेस्ट इंडीज पहुँचे तब उन्होंने भी समझा कि वे एशिया के पूर्वी किनारे से इंडिया की ओर जा रहे हैं। *(Kolambas ke bād san 1500 meँ vespući west inḍīj pahuñće tab unhoँ ne bhī samajhā ki ve eśiyā ke pūrvī kināre se India kī or jā rahe haiँ)* After Columbus, Vespucci travelled to West Indies in 1500 AD. He thought that he was at the east coast of Asia and he was going towards India. उन्होंने गुयाना और वेस्ट इंडीज के लोगों को हिंदुस्तानी समझा। *(unhoँ ne Guyānā aur West Inḍīj ke logoँ ko hindustānī samajhā)* They thought the people of Guyana and West Indies were Indian people.

वेस्ट इंडीज अटलांटिक महासागर में डूबी हुई कैरिबियन एंडीज पर्वत शृंखला की ऊपर उठी हुई चोटियाँ हैं। *(West Inḍīj aṭalānṭik mahāsāgar meँ dūbī huī Caribbean Andese parvat śṛankhalā kī ūpar uṭhī huī ćoṭiyāँ haiँ)* The West Indies are the peaks of semi-submerged chaiँ of Caribbean Andese mountain. एक समय वे दक्षिण और उत्तरी अमेरिका को जोड़ती थीं। *(ek samay ve dakṣiṇa aur uttarī amerikā ko joḍatī thīँ)* at one time they connected the South America to the North America. इनमें क्यूबा से लेकर बहामास, जमैका, हैटी, डोमिनिकन रिपब्लिक, परटोरिको और ट्रिनिडाड तक सभी देश आते हैं। *(in meँ Cūbā se le kar Bahāmās, Jamaicā, Haiti, Dominican Republic, Puerto Rico aur Trinidād tak sabhī deśa āte haiँ)* In it comes all countries from Cuba, Bahamas, Jamaica, Haiti, Dominican republic, Puerto Rico to Trinidad. गुयाना और सूरीनाम दक्षिण अमेरिका में आते हैं। *(Guyānā aur Sūrīnām dakṣiṇ amerikā meँ āte haiँ)* Guyana and Surinam are in the South America.

फिजी देश ऑस्ट्रेलिया के पूर्व में और न्यूजीलैंड के उत्तर में है। *(Fijī deś Australlia ke pūrva meँ aur New Zealand ke uttar meँ hai)* Fiji is on the east of Australia and North of New Zealand.

फीजी की मुख्य भाषा अंग्रेजी है और दूसरी भाषा हिंदी है। *(fījī kī mukhya bhāṣā angrezī aur dūsarī bhāṣā hindī hai)* In fiji the maiँ language is English and the second language is Hindī .

THE GOLDEN RULE

सुवर्ण सिद्धांत

(1) दूसरों के साथ वह नहीं करना चाहिए, जो यदि आपके साथ किया जाय तो आपको दु:ख हो। यही धर्म का सुवर्ण सिद्धांत है।

Do naught unto others which would cause pain if done to you. This is the Golden Rule of the righteousness.

(Mahābhārat : Hinduism)

(2) आप चाहते हैं कि लोग जो भी व्यवहार आपके साथ करें, वही लोगों के साथ आप करें।

All things, therefore, whatsoever ye would
that men should do to you.

(Bible : Christianity)

(3) दूसरों के प्रति वही बरताव अच्छा है जो हमें उस चीज से दूर रखे। जो चीज स्वयं हमारे लिए उचित न हो।

That nature alone is not good which refrains one from doing unto others whatsoever is not good for itself. *(Dadistan : Zoroastrianism)*

(4) जो व्यवहार आपके लिए दु:खदायक है, वह आप अपने साथियों के साथ न करें।

What ia hateful to you, do not to your fellowmen. *(Talmud : Judaism)*

(5) दूसरों के साथ वह काम न करें जो स्वत: के लिए दु:ख दायक लगता हो।

Act not with others in ways
that you yourself would find hurtful.

(Udana : Buddhism)

(6) दूसरों के साथ वह न करें जो आप चाहते हैं कि वे आपके साथ न करें।

Do not unto others
that you would not have them do unto you.

(Analects : Confucianiasm)

(7) पड़ोसी के लाभ में ही अपना लाभ जानिए और पड़ोसी की हानि में अपनी हानि जानिए।

Regard your neighbour's gain as your own gain
and your neighbour's loss as your own loss.

(Tai Shan Kan : Taoism)

LESSON 20

HINGLISH FOR ENGLISH SPEAKING PEOPLE

You do not have to abandon English in order to speak Hindī. Having understood the basics given in this book, you could speak the popular HINGLISH language to a certain extent, for the purpose of carrying on a converasation with the people who understand English.

Just remember the following Five Easy Rules :

(1) Make sure you clearly know the Hindī pronouns (Table 23-24). Use them, along with their case suffixes, in Hindī only. The basic ones are : I (*maĩ*), we (ham), you (*āp*), he, she and that (*vah*), it and this (*yah*), they and those (*ve*)

(2) Make sure you clearly know the Hindī case suffixes. You must use them in Hindī only. The basic ones are : 'to' (को); 'with,' 'by' and 'from' (से); 'together with' (के साथ); 'near' (के पास); 'for' (के लिये); 'of' (m॰ का, f॰ की); 'in' (में); 'on,' 'at' (पर).

(3) For popular nouns such as boy, girl, man, water, house, book, money, tea, milk, mother, father ...etc. you must use the Hindī words. For uncommon nouns you may use English words as if they were Hindī words by attaching the Hindī case suffixes to them.

e.g. On a tractor → tractor पर; in a chamber → chamber में; to a shareholder → shareholder को; from a pump → pump से; for an interview → interview के लिये; with the partner → partner के साथ; near the axle → axle के पास ...etc.

Similarly, common adjectives and adverbs must be in Hindī. The uncommon adjectives may be English. e.g. अच्छा, गरम, बहुत, popular, serious, expensive, modern etc.

(4) Make sure you clearly know the Hindī tense mode suffixes (Table 18). You must use them in Hindī only. The basic ones are : habitual mode (ता), a continuous mode (रहा); was, had, used to (था); future actions (ऊँगा, एगा, एगी, एँगे); potential (ऊँ, ए, एँ); interrogative (क्या).

(5) You must use the Hindī words for popular verbs such as eat, drink, go, come, sleep, write, read, walk, speak, see, hear ...etc. You may convert the English verbs into Hindī verbs by attaching one of the following two Hindī suffixes. e.g. Operation किया, puncture हुआ etc.

(5A) When an action is performed by someone, add the Hindī verb √कर as a suffix to convert the English verb into a Hindī verb and then attach the required tense and mode suffixes to this modified verb. e.g.

* I upgrade the PC = मैं PC upgrade करता हूँ (कर+ता+हूँ)। * She is typing a memo = वह memo type कर रही है। * I was shovelling snow = मैं snow shovel कर रहा था। * We will plug the battery = हम battery को plug करेंगे। * They stamped the forms = उन्होंने forms stamp किये।

(5B) When an action happens, occurs, becomes, befalls or takes place by itself, then add the Hindī verb √हो as a suffix to convert the English verb into a Hindī verb and then attach the required tense and mode suffixes to this modified verb. e.g.

* Earthquakes occur in Japan. जापान में earthquakes होते हैं (हो+ते+हैं)। * Meeting took place in two parties yesterday. कल दो पार्टियों में meeting हुई। * Rusting will take place with water. पानी से rusting होगी। * Here lunch breaks at 12 O' clock. यहाँ 12 बजे lunch break होती है।

EXAMPLES :

(1) राम IBM में programmer है। (2) आप Model Town में कहाँ रहते हैं?

(3) हम आज बहुत busy (व्यस्त) हैं। (4) कल वह कुतुब मीनार से Parachute से jump करेगा (कूदेगा)।

(5) मनोज highway पर speeding कर रहा था। (6) सोनिया जी दो cup चाय लाइये।

(7) अजीत का lawn mower पेट्रोल पर चलता है। (8) गोपाल को greeting card नहीं मिला।

(9) सीमा गाने tape कर रही है। (10) सोनू movies record कर चुका है।

(11) चाचा जी का दिल्ली में transfer हुआ है।

(12) मुझे इसकी एक Xerox copy दीजिये। मुझे इसकी दो Xerox कापियाँ दीजिये।

(13) इसका cover discard मत कीजिये। (14) दो potatoes (आलू) boil कीजिये (उबालिये)।

(15) रमेश Civil Engineer बन गया। (16) उसका भाई army में गया है। (17) यह wonderful चीज है।

(18) U.S. President हमारे प्रधानमंत्री (Prime Minister) से मिले।

(19) कल George की engagement हुई। (20) बाबूजी tour (दौरे) पर गये हुए हैं।

(21) बरफ melt हो रही है (पिघल रही है)। पानी freeze हो रहा है (जम रहा है)।

(22) यहाँ से Zoo जाने के लिये कौन सा highway (रास्ता) अच्छा होगा?

(23) अब दिल्ली में polution (प्रदूषण) कम हो रहा है। (24) आपका telephone number क्या है?

(25) कल sky diving करते हुए रमेश की हड्डी fracture हुई (टूटी)।

(26) उन्होंने company के नाम से दो million का cheque लिखा।

(27) हमने अमिताभ बच्चन का चित्र internet पर देखा।

(28) इस साल माधुरी दीक्षित को Film Fare Award मिला।

(29) आपने इस किताब की binding कहाँ से करवाई है? (30) परसों रीतेश को 102 degree बुखार था।

(31) मैं आपकी शर्टस् press करवाकर लाया हूँ। (32) इसकी तीन कॉपियाँ हमें CD या DVD पर दीजिये।

(33) यहाँ टैक्सियाँ खड़ी करना मना है, केवल कारें ही खड़ी होती हैं।

(34) आजकल pure हिंदी कोई भी नहीं बोलता, सभी लोग Hinglish बोलते हैं।

ACTUAL EXAMPLES :

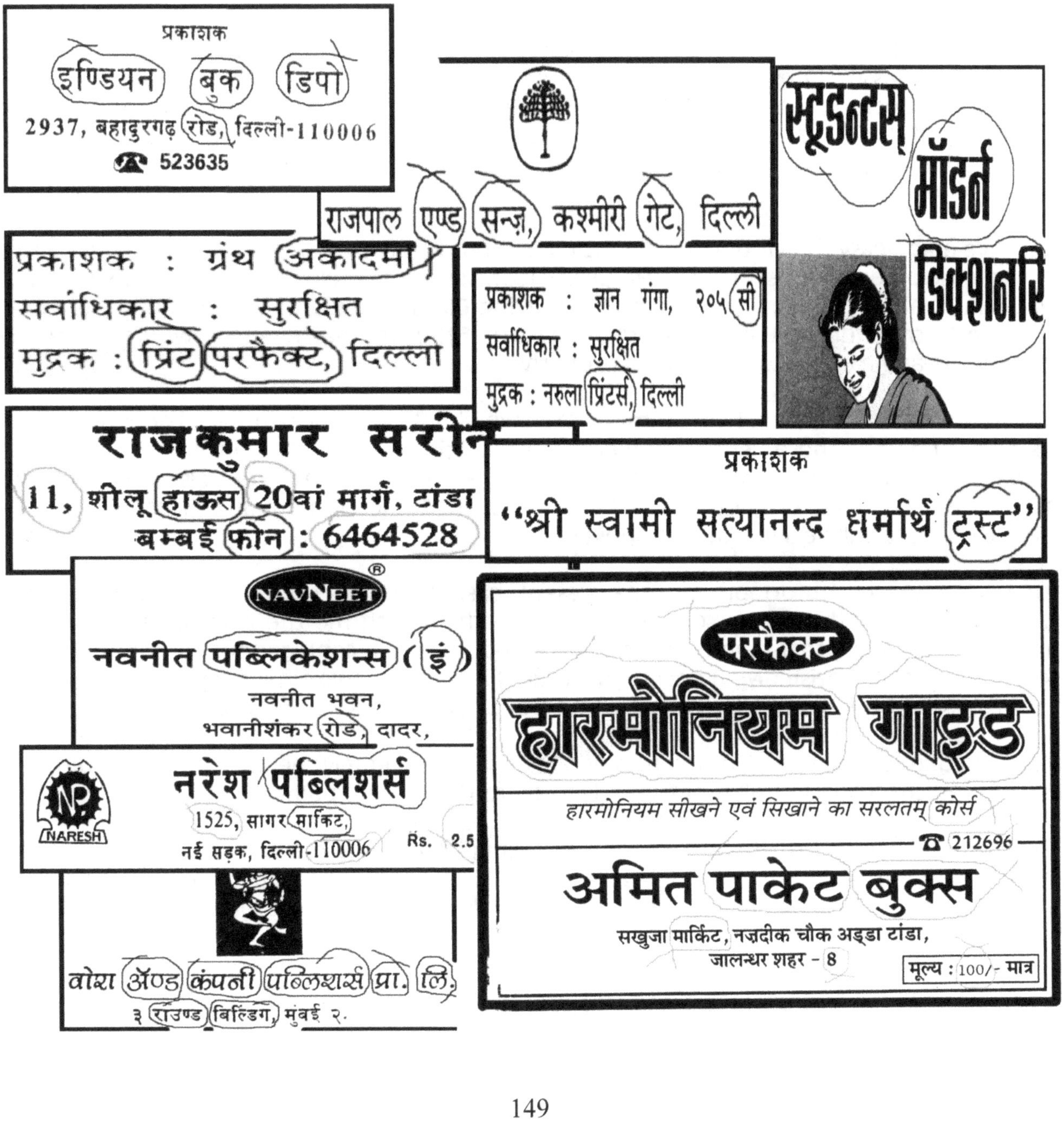

To : Dr. Ratnakar Narale, B.Sc., M.Sc., Ph.D.,
Principal, Hindu Institute of Learning,
Toronto, Ontario, Canada.

Humber River
REGIONAL HOSPITAL

Church Street Site
200 Church St.
Weston, Ontario
M9N 1N8
tel. (416) 249-8111

Sept. 6, 2006

Dear Dr. Narale,

I have been a formal student for at least 28 years, a teacher of elementary school-children, and subsequently a teacher of undergraduate and post-graduate students for 35 years. English is my only spoken language. I have studied French and Latin in college and university.

For the past few weeks I have been using your new and basic *"Learn Hindi Through English Medium"* and after having studied one half of it I would like to make a few comments about why I have enjoyed every lesson. The following approaches which you used make this book unique and ideal for me.

1.The 20 Step by Step outline of the Hindi course states clearly what material is to be covered in each step. Each lesson does, indeed, teach me patiently and superbly the details of what was outlined. My expectations were fulfilled and with each lesson, the Hindi learned was reviewed again and again. Hindi was consolidated with each section. The extensive use of transliteration and translation helped with pronunciation. I wondered whether you were the 'English-only' student.

2. You have made easy the writing, pronouncing and reading the consonants, vowels, *sandhi* and commonly used words and symbols in Hindi. I personally would feel more comfortable with the Hindi pronunciation by listening to an accompanying CD/tape made of your book by someone who speaks both Hindi and English and who is aware of the weaknesses and flaws we inherently have when we are learning to speak Hindi properly.

3. Your Hindi book shows me how to make my own simple sentences using pronouns, nouns, verbs and numerals. These sentences were often original ... my very own! Your numerous examples with answers were extremely helpful especially when you also provide the transliteration and Hindi, of questions and answers both. As I learn more and more vocabulary I am sure that there will be less 'Hinglish' spoken.

4. I am getting more comfortable with the present, past and future tenses when speaking Hindi. Your outstanding methodical lessons promise to further teach me the practical usage of the perfect tense, conditional mood, interrogate mood, adverbs, conjugations, prepositions and variety of suffixes. Surprisingly, in only a few weeks I am able to make my own simple sentences and I am able to speak Hindi! Schools and learners of all ages would really appreciate this book!

5. Your unique comprehensive Tables and Tests are extremely helpful in understanding, reviewing and consolidating what has been learned to the present point.

Thank you Dr. Narale, for providing English-speaking people like me with the opportunity to learn to read, write and speak Hindi. I look forward to conversing and communicating with others locally, in Trinidad, in Guyana and India, hopefully in Hindi, and without a loss for words.

Gratefully yours,
Carl Saiphoo.

Dr. Carl S. Saiphoo, M.D., F.R.C..P. (C)
Assoc. Prof. of Medicine (Internal Medicine and Nephrology), University of Toronto.

SUMMARY of TENSES

GROUP (A)

Transitive Action

EXAMPLE : to do √*kar* √कर (करना)

(1) Present Indefinite Tense (सामान्य वर्तमान काल)

	Singular	Plural
1P◦ Male -	I do *maĩ karatā hū̃* मैं करता हूँ।	We do *ham karate haĩ* हम करते हैं।
Female -	I do *maĩ karatī hū̃* मैं करती हूँ।	We do *ham karatī haĩ* हम करती हैं।
2P◦ Male -	You do *āp karate haĩ* आप करते हैं। (तू करता है।) *(tū karatā hai)* (तुम करते हो।) *(tum karate ho)*	You do *āp karate haĩ* आप करते हैं। (तुम करते हो।) *(tum karate ho)* (तुम करते हो।) *(tum karate ho)*
Female -	You do *āp karatī haĩ* आप करती हैं। (तू करती है।) (तुम करती हो।)	You do *āp karatī haĩ* आप करती हैं। (तुम करती हो।) (तुम करती हो।)

3P◦ Male -	He does	They do
	vah karatā hai	*ve karate haĩ*
	वह करता है।	वे करते हैं।
Female -	She does	They do
	vah karatī hai	*ve karatī haĩ*
	वह करती है।	वे करती हैं।

(2) Present Continuous Tense (अपूर्ण वर्तमान काल)

	Singular	Plural
1P◦ Male -	I am doing	We are doing
	maĩ kar rahā hũ	*ham kar rahe haĩ*
	मैं कर रहा हूँ।	हम कर रहे हैं।
Female -	I am doing	We are doing
	maĩ kar rahī hũ	*ham kar rahī haĩ*
	मैं कर रही हूँ।	हम कर रही हैं।
2P◦ Male -	You are doing	You are doing
	āp kar rahe haĩ	*āp kar rahe haĩ*
	आप कर रहे हैं।	आप कर रहे हैं।
	(तू कर रहा है।)	(तुम कर रहे हो।)
	(तुम कर रहे हो।)	(तुम कर रहे हो।)
Female -	You are doing	You are doing
	āp kar rahī haĩ	*āp kar rahī haĩ*
	आप कर रही हैं।	आप कर रही हैं।
	(तू कर रही है।)	(तुम कर रही हो।)
	(तुम कर रही हो।)	(तुम कर रही हो।)
3P◦ Male -	He is doing	They are doing

	Singular	Plural
	vah kar rahā hai	*ve kar rahe haĩ*
	वह कर रहा है।	वे कर रहे हैं।
Female -	She is doing	They are doing
	vah kar rahī hai	*ve kar rahī haĩ*
	वह कर रही है।	वे कर रही हैं।

(3) Present Perfect Tense (पूर्ण वर्तमान काल)

	Singular	Plural
1P◦ Male -	I have done	We have done
	I have already done	We have already done
	maĩ ne kiyā hai	*ham ne kiyā hai*
	maĩ kar chukā hũ	*ham kar chuke haĩ*
	मैंने किया है।	हमने किया है।
	मैं कर चुका हूँ।	हम कर चुके हैं।
Female -	I have done	We have done
	I have already done	We have already done
	maĩ ne kiyā hai	*ham ne kiyā hai*
	maĩ kar chukī hũ	*ham kar chukī haĩ*
	मैंने किया है।	हमने किया है।
	मैं कर चुकी हूँ।	हम कर चुकी हैं।
2P◦ Male -	You have done	You have done
	You have already done	You have already done
	āp ne kiyā hai	*āp ne kiyā hai*
	āp kar chuke haĩ	*āp kar chuke haĩ*
	आपने किया है।	आपने किया है।
	आप कर चुके हैं।	आप कर चुके हैं।
	(तूने किया है।)	(तुमने किया है।)
	(तू कर चुका है।)	(तुम कर चुके हो।)
	(तुमने किया है।)	(तुमने किया है।)
	(तुम कर चुके हो।)	(तुम कर चुके हो।)

Female -	You have done	You have done
	You have already done	You have already done
	āp ne kiyā hai	*āp ne kiyā hai*
	āp kar chukī hai̐	*āp kar chukī hai̐*
	आपने किया है।	आपने किया है।
	आप कर चुकी हैं।	आप कर चुकी हैं।
	(तूने किया है।)	(तुमने किया है।)
	(तू कर चुकी है।)	(तुम कर चुकी हो।)
	(तुमने किया है।)	(तुमने किया है।)
	(तुम कर चुकी हो।)	(तुम कर चुकी हो।)
3P◦ Male -	He has done	They have done
	He has already done	They have already done
	us ne kiyā hai	*unho̐ ne kiyā hai*
	vah kar chukā hai	*ve kar chuke hai̐*
	उसने किया है।	उन्होंने किया है।
	(वह कर चुका है।)	(वे कर चुके हैं।)
Female -	She has done	They have done
	She has already done	They have already done
	us ne kiyā hai	*unho̐ ne kiyā hai*
	vah kar chukī hai	*ve kar chukī hai̐*
	उसने किया है।	उन्होंने किया है।
	(वह कर चुकी है।)	(वे कर चुकी हैं।)

(4) Past Indefinite Tense (सामान्य भूत काल)

	Singular	Plural
1P◦ Male -	I did	We did
	mai̐ ne kiyā	*ham ne kiyā*
	mai̐ kar chukā	*ham kar chuke*
	मैंने किया।	हमने किया।
	मैं कर चुका।	हम कर चुके।

Female -	I did	We did
	maĩ ne kiyā	*ham ne kiyā*
	maĩ kar chukī	*ham kar chukī̃*
	मैंने किया।	हमने किया।
	मैं कर चुकी।	हम कर चुकीं।
2P◦ Male -	You did	You did
	āp ne kiyā	*āp ne kiyā*
	āp kar chuke	*āp kar chuke*
	आपने किया।	आपने किया।
	आप कर चुके।	आप कर चुके।
	(तूने किया।)	(तुमने किया।)
	(तू कर चुका।)	(तुम कर चुके।)
	(तुमने किया।)	(तुमने किया।)
	(तुम कर चुके।)	(तुम कर चुके।)
Female -	You did	You did
	āp ne kiyā	*āp ne kiyā*
	āp kar chukī	*āp kar chukī*
	आपने किया।	आपने किया।
	आप कर चुकी।	आप कर चुकी।
	(तूने किया।)	(तुमने किया।)
	(तू कर चुकी।)	(तुम कर चुकी।)
	(तुमने किया।)	(तुमने किया।)
	(तुम कर चुकी।)	(तुम कर चुकी।)
3P◦ Male -	He did	They did
	us ne kiyā	*unhõ ne kiyā*
	vah kar chukā	*ve kar chuke*
	उसने किया।	उन्होंने किया।
	वह कर चुका।	वे कर चुके।

	Singular	Plural
Female -	She did	They did
	us ne kiyā	*unhõ ne kiyā*
	vah kar chukī	*ve kar chukī̃*
	उसने किया।	उन्होंने किया।
	वह कर चुकी।	वे कर चुकीं।

(5) Past Imperfect Tense (अपूर्ण भूत काल)

	Singular	Plural
1P∘ Male -	I was doing	We were doing
	maĩ kar rahā thā	*ham kar rahe the*
	मैं कर रहा था।	हम कर रहे थे।
Female -	I was doing	We were doing
	maĩ kar rahī thī	*ham kar rahī thī̃*
	मैं कर रही थी।	हम कर रही थीं।
2P∘ Male -	You were doing	You were doing
	āp kar rahe the	*āp kar rahe the*
	आप कर रहे थे।	आप कर रहे थे।
	(तू कर रहा था।)	(तुम कर रहे थे।)
	(तुम कर रहे थे।)	(तुम कर रहे थे।)
Female -	You were doing	You were doing
	āp kar rahī thī	*āp kar rahī thī̃*
	आप कर रही थी।	आप कर रही थीं।
	(तू कर रही थी।)	(तुम कर रही थीं।)
	(तुम कर रही थी।)	(तुम कर रही थीं।)
3P∘ Male -	He was doing	They were doing
	vah kar rahā thā	*ve kar rahe the*
	वह कर रहा था।	वे कर रहे थे।
Female -	She was doing	They were doing

vah kar rahī thī
वह कर रही थी।

ve kar rahī thī̃
वे कर रही थीं।

(6) Past Perfect Tense (पूर्ण भूत काल)

	Singular	Plural
1P॰ Male -	I had done *maĩ ne kiyā thā* *maĩ kar chukā thā* मैंने किया था। मैं कर चुका था।	We had done *ham ne kiyā thā* *ham kar chuke the* हमने किया था। हम कर चुके थे।
Female -	I had done *maĩ ne kiyā thā* *maĩ kar chukī thī* मैंने किया था। मैं कर चुकी थी।	We had done *ham ne kiyā thā* *ham kar chukī thī̃* हमने किया था। हम कर चुकी थीं।
2P॰ Male -	You had done *āp ne kiyā thā* *āp kar chuke the* आपने किया था। आप कर चुके थे। (तूने किया था।) (तू कर चुका था।) (तुमने किया था।) (तुम कर चुके थे।)	You had done *āp ne kiyā thā* *āp kar chuke the* आपने किया था। आप कर चुके थे। (तुमने किया था।) (तुम कर चुके थे।) (तुमने किया था।) (तुम कर चुके थे।)
Female -	You had done *āp ne kiyā thā* *āp kar chukī thī̃* आपने किया था। आप कर चुकी थीं। (तूने किया था।)	You had done *āp ne kiyā thā* *āp kar chukī thī̃* आपने किया था। आप कर चुकी थीं। (तुमने किया था।)

	(तू कर चुकी थी।)	(तुम कर चुकी थी।)
	(तुमने किया था।)	(तुमने किया था।)
	(तुम कर चुकी थी।)	(तुम कर चुकी थी।)
3P◦ Male -	He had done	They had done
	us ne kiyā thā	*unhõ ne kiyā thā*
	vah kar chukā thā	*ve kar chuke the*
	उसने किया था।	उन्होंने किया था।
	वह कर चुका था।	वे कर चुके थे।
Female -	She had done	They had done
	us ne kiyā thā	*unhõ ne kiyā thā*
	vah kar chukī thī	*ve kar chukī thī̃*
	उसने किया था।	उन्होंने किया था।
	वह कर चुकी थी।	वे कर चुकी थीं।

(7) Future Indefinite Tense (सामान्य भविष्यत् काल)

	Singular	Plural
1P◦ Male -	I will do	We will do
	maĩ karũgā	*ham karẽge*
	मैं करूँगा।	हम करेंगे।
Female -	I will do	We will do
	maĩ karũgī	*ham karẽgī*
	मैं करूँगी।	हम करेंगी।
2P◦ Male -	You will do	You will do
	āp karẽge	*āp karẽge*
	आप करेंगे।	आप करेंगे।
	(तू करेगा।)	(तुम करोगे।)
	(तुम करोगे।)	(तुम करोगे।)
Female -	You will do	You will do

	āp kare̐gī आप करेंगी। (तू करेगी।) (तुम करोगी।)	*āp kare̐gī* आप करेंगी। (तुम करोगी।) (तुम करोगी।)
3P◦ Male -	He will do *vah karegā* वह करेगा।	They will do *ve kare̐ge* वे करेंगे।
Female -	She will do *vah karegī* वह करेगी।	They will do *ve kare̐gī* वे करेंगी।

(8) <u>Future Imperfect Continuous Tense</u> (अपूर्ण भविष्यत् काल)

	<u>Singular</u>	<u>Plural</u>
1P◦ Male -	I will be doing *mai̐ kar rahā hoū̐gā* मैं कर रहा होऊँगा।	We will be doing *ham kar rahe ho̐ge* हम कर रहे होंगे।
Female -	I will be doing *mai̐ kar rahī hoū̐gī* मैं कर रही होऊँगी।	We will be doing *ham kar rahī ho̐gī* हम कर रह होंगी।
2P◦ Male -	You will be doing *āp kar rahe ho̐ge* आप कर रहे होंगे। (तू कर रहा होगा।) (तुम कर रहे होगे।)	You will be doing *āp kar rahe ho̐ge* आप कर रहे होंगे। (तुम कर रहे होगे।) (तुम कर रहे होगे।)
Female -	You will be doing *āp kar rahī ho̐gī* आप कर रही होंगी। (तू कर रही होगी।)	You will be doing *āp kar rahī ho̐gī* आप कर रही होंगी। (तुम कर रही होगी।)

(तुम कर रही होगी।) (तुम कर रही होगी।)

3P∘ Male - He will be doing — They will be doing

vah kar rahā hogā — *ve kar rahe hoँge*

वह कर रहा होगा। — वे कर रहे होंगे।

Female - She will be doing — They will be doing

vah kar rahī hogī — *ve kar rahī hoँgī*

वह कर रही होगी। — वे कर रही होंगी।

(9) Future Perfect Tense (पूर्ण भविष्यत् काल)

	Singular	Plural
1P∘ Male -	I will have done	We will have done
	maiँ kar chuka houँgā	*ham kar chuke hoँge*
	मैं कर चुका होऊँगा।	हम कर चुके होंगे।
Female -	I will have done	We will have done
	maiँ kar chukī houँgī	*ham kar chukī hoँgī*
	मैं कर चुकी होऊँगी।	हम कर चुकी होंगी।
2P∘ Male -	You will have done	You will have done
	āp kar chuke hoँge	*āp kar chuke hoँge*
	आप कर चुके होंगे।	आप कर चुके होंगे।
	(तू कर चुका होगा।)	(तुम कर चुके होगे।)
	(तुम कर चुके होगे।)	(तुम कर चुके होगे।)
Female -	You will have done	You will have done
	āp kar chukī hoँgī	*āp kar chukī hoँgī*
	आप कर चुकी होंगी।	आप कर चुकी होंगी।
	(तू कर चुकी होगी।)	(तुम कर चुकी होगी।)
	(तुम कर चुकी होगी।)	(तुम कर चुकी होगी।)
3P∘ Male -	He will have done	They will have done

	Singular	Plural
	vah kar chukā hogā	*ve kar chuke hoṅge*
	वह कर चुका होगा।	वे कर चुके होंगे।
Female -	She will have done	They will have done
	vah kar chukī hogī	*ve kar chukī hoṅgī*
	वह कर चुकी होगी।	वे कर चुकी होंगी।

(10) Interrogative (प्रश्नार्थक)

	Singular	Plural
1P◦ Male -	May I do?	May we do?
	kyā maĩ karū̃?	*kyā ham karẽ?*
	क्या मैं करूँ?	क्या हम करें?
Female -	May I do?	May we do?
	kyā maĩ karū̃?	*kyā ham karẽ?*
	क्या मैं करूँ?	क्या हम करें?
3P◦ Male -	May he do?	May they do?
	kyā vah kare?	*kyā ve karẽ?*
	क्या वह करे?	क्या वे करें?
Female -	May she do?	May they do?
	kyā vah kare?	*kyā ve karẽ?*
	क्या वह करे?	क्या वे करें?

(11) Potential mood (विधिसूचक)

	Singular	Plural
1P∘ Male -	I may do *maĩ karū̃* मैं करूँ।	We may do *ham karẽ* हम करें।
Female -	I may do *maĩ karū̃* मैं करूँ।	We may do *ham karẽ* हम करें।
3P∘ Male -	He may do *vah kare* वह करे।	They may do *ve karẽ* वे करें।
Female -	She may do *vah kare* वह करे।	They may do *ve karẽ* वे करें।

GROUP (B)

SUMMARY of TENSES

Intransitive Action

EXAMPLE : to sleep √*so* √सो (सोना)

(12) Present Indifinite Tense (सामान्य वर्तमान काल)

	Singular	Plural
1P∘ Male -	I sleep *maĩ sotā hū̃* मैं सोता हूँ।	We sleep *ham sote haĩ* हम सोते हैं।

	Singular	Plural
Female -	I sleep *maĩ sotī hũ* मैं सोती हूँ।	We sleep *ham sotī haĩ* हम सोती हैं।
2P◦ Male -	You sleep *āp sote haĩ* आप सोते हैं। (तू सोता है।) (तुम सोते हो।)	You sleep *āp sote haĩ* आप सोते हैं। (तुम सोते हो।) (तुम सोते हो।)
Female -	You sleep *āp sotī haĩ* आप सोती हैं। (तू सोती है।) (तुम सोती है।)	You sleep *āp sotī haĩ* आप सोती हैं। (तुम सोती हो।) (तुम सोती हो।)
3P◦ Male -	He sleeps *vah sotā hai* वह सोता है।	They sleep *ve sote haĩ* वे सोते हैं।
Female -	She sleeps *vah sotī hai* वह सोती है।	They sleep *ve sotī haĩ* वे सोती हैं।

(13) Present Continuous Tense (अपूर्ण वर्तमान काल)

	Singular	Plural
1P◦ Male -	I am sleeping *maĩ so rahā hũ* मैं सो रहा हूँ।	We are sleeping *ham so rahe haĩ* हम सो रहे हैं।
Female -	I am sleeping *maĩ so rahī hũ* मैं सो रही हूँ।	We are sleeping *ham so rahī haĩ* हम सो रही हैं।

	Singular	Plural
2P∘ Male -	You are sleeping *āp so rahe haĩ* आप सो रहे हैं। (तू सो रहा है।) (तुम सो रहे हो।)	You are sleeping *āp so rahe haĩ* आप सो रहे हैं। (तुम सो रहे हो।) (तुम सो रहे हो।)
Female -	You are sleeping *āp so rahī haĩ* आप सो रही हैं।	You are sleeping *āp so rahī haĩ* आप सो रही हैं।
3P∘ Male -	He is sleeping *vah so rahā hai* वह सो रहा है।	They are sleeping *ve so rahe haĩ* वे सो रहे हैं।
Female -	She is sleeping *vah so rahī hai* वह सो रही है।	They are sleeping *ve so rahī haĩ* वे सो रही हैं।

(14) Present Perfect Tense (पूर्ण वर्तमान काल)

	Singular	Plural
1P∘ Male -	I have slept *maĩ soyā hũ* *maĩ so ćukā hũ* मैं सोया हूँ। मैं सो चुका हूँ।	We have slept *ham soye haĩ* *ham so ćuke haĩ* हम सोए हैं। हम सो चुके हैं।
Female -	I have slept *maĩ soyī hũ* *maĩ so ćukī hũ* मैं सोई हूँ। मैं सो चुकी हूँ।	We have slept *ham soyī haĩ* *ham so ćukī haĩ* हम सोई हैं। हम सो चुकी हैं।

2P◦ Male -	You have slept *āp soye hai͠* *āp so ćuke hai͠* आप सोए हैं। आप सो चुके हैं।	You have slept *āp soye hai͠* *āp so ćuke hai͠* आप सोए हैं। आप सो चुके हैं।
Female -	You have slept *āp soyī hai͠* *āp so ćukī hai͠* आप सोई हैं। आप सो चुकी हैं।	You have slept *āp soyī hai͠* *āp so ćukī hai͠* आप सोई हैं। आप सो चुकी हैं।
3P◦ Male -	He has slept *vah soyā hai* *vah so ćukā hai* वह सोया है। वह सो चुका है।	They have slept *ve soye hai͠* *ve so ćuke hai͠* वे सोए हैं। वे सो चुके हैं।
Female -	She has slept *vah soyī hai* *vah so ćukī hai* वह सोई है। वह सो चुकी है।	They have slept *ve soyī hai͠* *ve so ćukī hai͠* वे सोई हैं। वे सो चुकी हैं।

(15) Past Indefinite Tense (सामान्य भूत काल)

	Singular	Plural
1P◦ Male -	I slept *mai͠ soyā* मैं सोया।	We slept *ham soye* हम सोए।
Female -	I slept	We slept

		maĩ soyī मैं सोई।	*ham soyī̃* हम सोईं।
2P.	Male -	You slept *āp soye* आप सोए। (तू सोया।) (तुम सोए।)	You slept *āp soye* आप सोए। (तुम सोए।) (तुम सोए।)
	Female -	You slept *āp soyī* आप सोई। (तू सोई।) (तुम सोई।)	You slept *āp soyī̃* आप सोईं। (तुम सोई।) (तुम सोई।)
3P.	Male -	He slept *vah soyā* वह सोया।	They slept *ve soye* वे सोए।
	Female -	She slept *vah soyī* वह सोई।	They slept *ve soyī̃* वे सोईं।

(16) Past Imperfect Tense (अपूर्ण भूत काल)

		Singular	Plural
1P.	Male -	I was sleeping *maĩ so rahā thā* मैं सो रहा था।	We were sleeping *ham so rahe the* हम सो रहे थे।
	Female -	I was sleeping *maĩ so rahī thī* मैं सो रही थी।	We were sleeping *ham so rahī thī̃* हम सो रही थीं।

	Singular	Plural
2P◦ Male -	You were sleeping *āp so rahe the* आप सो रहे थे। (तू सो रहा था।) (तुम सो रहे थे।)	You were sleeping *āp so rahe the* आप सो रहे थे। (तुम सो रहे थे।) (तुम सो रहे थे।)
Female -	You were sleeping *āp so rahī thī̐* आप सो रही थी। (तू सो रही थी।) (तुम सो रही थी।)	You were sleeping *āp so rahī thī̐* आप सो रही थीं। (तुम सो रही थी।) (तुम सो रही थी।)
3P◦ Male -	He was sleeping *vah so rahā thā* वह सो रहा था।	They were sleeping *ve so rahe the* वे सो रहे थे।
Female -	She was sleeping *vah so rahī thī* वह सो रही थी।	They were sleeping *ve so rahī thī̐* वे सो रही थीं।

(17) Past Perfect Tense (पूर्ण भूत काल)

	Singular	Plural
1P◦ Male -	I had slept *maĩ soyā thā* मैं सोया था।	We had slept *ham soye the* हम सोए थे।
Female -	I had slept *maĩ soyī thī* मैं सोई थी।	We had slept *ham soyī thī̐* हम सोई थीं।
2P◦ Male -	You had slept *āp soye the* आप सोए थे।	You had slept *āp soye the* आप सोए थे।

	(तू सोया था।)	(तुम सोए थे।)
	(तुम सोए थे।)	(तुम सोए थे।)
Female -	You had slept	You had slept
	āp soyī thī	*āp soyī thī̃*
	आप सोई थी।	आप सोई थीं।
	(तू सोई थी।)	(तुम सोई थी।)
	(तुम सोई थी।)	(तुम सोई थी।)
3P◦ Male -	He had slept	They had slept
	vah soyā thā	*ve soye the*
	वह सोया था।	वे सोए थे।
Female -	She had slept	They had slept
	vah soyī thī	*ve soyī thī̃*
	वह सोई थी।	वे सोई थीं।

(18) Future Indefinite Tense (सामान्य भविष्यत् काल)

	Singular	Plural
1P◦ Male -	I will sleep	We will sleep
	maĩ soū̃gā	*ham soẽge*
	मैं सोऊँगा।	हम सोएँगे।
Female -	I will sleep	We will sleep
	maĩ soū̃gī	*ham soẽgī*
	मैं सोऊँगी।	हम सोएँगी।
2P◦ Male -	You will sleep	You will sleep
	āp soẽge	*āp soẽge*
	आप सोएँगे।	आप सोएँगे।
	(तू सोएगा।)	(तुम सोओगे।)
	(तुम सोओगे।)	(तुम सोओगे।)

| | | Female - | You will sleep
āp soẽgī
आप सोएँगी।
(तू सोएगी।)
(तुम सोओगी।) | You will sleep
āp soẽgī
आप सोएँगी।
(तू साओगी।)
(तुम सोओगी।) |

3P॰ Male -   He will sleep
vah soegā
वह सोएगा।

They will sleep
ve soẽge
वे सोएँगे।

Female -   She will sleep
vah soegī
वह सोएगी।

They will sleep
ve soẽgī
वे सोएँगी।

(19) Future Imperfect Continuous Tense
(अपूर्ण भविष्यत् काल)

	Singular	Plural
1P॰ Male -	I will be sleeping *maĩ so rahā hoũgā* मैं सो रहा होऊँगा।	We will be sleeping *ham so rahe hõge* हम सो रहे होंगे।
Female -	I will be sleeping *maĩ so rahī hoũgī* मैं सो रही होऊँगी।	We will be sleeping *ham so rahī hõgī* हम सो रही होंगी।
2P॰ Male -	You will be sleeping *āp so rahe hõge* आप सो रहे होंगे। (तू सो रहा होगा।) (तुम सो रहे होओगे।)	You will be sleeping *āp so rahe hõge* आप सो रहे होंगे। (तुम सो रहे होगे।) (तुम सो रहे होगे।)
Female -	You will be sleeping	You will be sleeping

	āp so rahī hoṅgī	*āp so rahī hoṅgī*
	आप सो रही होंगी।	आप सो रही होंगी।
	(तू सोएगी।)	(तुम सोओगी।)
	(तुम सोओगी।)	(तुम सोओगी।)
3P◦ Male -	He will be sleeping	They will be sleeping
	vah so rahā hogā	*ve so rahe hoṅge*
	वह सो रहा होगा।	वे सो रहे होंगे।
Female -	She will be sleeping	They will be sleeping
	vah so rahī hogī	*ve so rahī hoṅgī*
	वह सो रही होगी।	वे सो रही होंगी।

(20) Future Perfect Tense (पूर्ण भविष्यत् काल)

	Singular	Plural
1P◦ Male -	I will have slept	We will have slept
	maiṅ so ćukā hoūṅgā	*ham so ćuke hoṅge*
	मैं सो चुका होऊँगा।	हम सो चुके होंगे।
Female -	I will have slept	We will have slept
	maiṅ so ćukī hoūṅgī	*ham so ćukī hoṅgī*
	मैं सो चुकी होऊँगी।	हम सो चुकी होंगी।
2P◦ Male -	You will have slept	You will have slept
	āp so ćuke hoṅge	*āp so ćuke hoṅge*
	आप सो चुके होंगे।	आप सो चुके होंगे।
	(तू सो चुका होगा।)	(तुम सो चुके होंगे।)
	(तुम सो चुके होगे।)	(तुम सो चुके होंगे।)
Female -	You will have slept	You will have slept
	āp so ćukī hoṅgī	*āp so ćukī hoṅgī*
	आप सो चुकी होंगी।	आप सो चुकी होंगी।
	(तू सो चुकी होगी।)	(तुम सो चुकी होगी।)

(तुम सो चुकी होगी।) | (तुम सो चुकी होगी।)

3P∘ Male - He will have slept | They will have slept

vah so ćukā hogā | *ve so ćuke ho̐ge*

वह सो चुका होगा। | वे सो चुके होंगे।

Female - She will have slept | They will have slept

vah so ćukī hogī | *ve so ćukī ho̐gī*

वह सो चुकी होगी। | वे सो चुकी होंगी।

(21) Interrogative (प्रश्नार्थक)

	Singular	Plural
1P∘ Male -	May I sleep?	May we sleep?
	kyā mai̐ soū̐	*kyā ham soe̐*
	क्या मैं सोऊँ?	क्या हम सोएँ?
Female -	May I sleep?	May we sleep?
	kyā mai̐ soū̐?	*kyā ham soe̐?*
	क्या मैं सोऊँ?	क्या हम सोएँ?
2P∘ Male -	May you sleep?	May you sleep?
	kyā āp soe̐ge?	*kyā āp soe̐ge?*
	क्या आप सोएँगे?	क्या आप सोएँगे?
	(क्या तू सोएगा?)	(क्या तुम सोओगे?)
	(क्या तुम सोओगे?)	(क्या तुम सोओगे?)
Female -	May you sleep?	May you sleep?
	kyā āp soe̐gī?	*kyā āp soe̐geī?*
	क्या आप सोएँगी?	क्या आप सोएँगी।
	(क्या तू सोएगी?)	(क्या तुम सोओगी?)
	(क्या तुम सोओगी?)	(क्या तुम सोओगी?)

3P◦ Male -	May he sleep? *kyā vah soe?* क्या वह सोए?	May they sleep? *kyā ve soẽ?* क्या वे सोएँ?
Female -	May she sleep? *kyā vah soe?* क्या वह सोए?	May they sleep? *kyā ve soẽ?* क्या वे सोएँ?

(22) Potential mood (विधिसूचक)

	Singular	Plural
1P◦ Male -	I may sleep *maĩ soũ* मैं सोऊँ।	We may sleep *ham soẽ* हम सोएँ।
Female -	I may sleep *maĩ soũ* मैं सोऊँ।	We may sleep *ham soẽ* हम सोएँ।
3P◦ Male -	He may sleep *vah soe* वह सोए।	They may sleep *ve soẽ* वे सोएँ।
Female -	She may sleep *vah soe* वह सोए।	They may sleep *ve soẽ* वे सोएँ।

www.ingramcontent.com/pod-product-compliance
Lightning Source LLC
Chambersburg PA
CBHW081109080526
44587CB00021B/3517